Ethics and Qualities of Life

Ethics and Qualities of Life

Joel J. Kupperman

2007

OXFORD
UNIVERSITY PRESS

Oxford University Press, Inc., publishes works that further
Oxford University's objective of excellence
in research, scholarship, and education.

Oxford   New York
Auckland   Cape Town   Dar es Salaam   Hong Kong   Karachi
Kuala Lumpur   Madrid   Melbourne   Mexico City   Nairobi
New Delhi   Shanghai   Taipei   Toronto

With offices in
Argentina   Austria   Brazil   Chile   Czech Republic   France   Greece
Guatemala   Hungary   Italy   Japan   Poland   Portugal   Singapore
South Korea   Switzerland   Thailand   Turkey   Ukraine   Vietnam

Published by Oxford University Press, Inc.
198 Madison Avenue, New York, New York 10016

www.oup.com

Oxford is a registered trademark of Oxford University Press

Library of Congress Cataloging-in-Publication Data
Kupperman, Joel.
Ethics and qualities of life / Joel J. Kupperman.
p. cm.
Includes bibliographical references and index.
ISBN 978-0-19-530819-8
1. Ethics.   2. Life.   I. Title.
BJ37.K87 2007   2006050354

1 3 5 7 9 8 6 4 2

Printed in the United States of America
on acid-free paper

Preface

L et me express my gratitude for research support without which this book would have taken much longer to complete. The University of Connecticut Humanities Institute gave me a fellowship for 2003–2004, which released me from most of my teaching load; I especially want to thank Richard D. Brown and Françoise Dussart for creating an agreeable and stimulating collegial environment. I am grateful also to the National Endowment for the Humanities for a fellowship for 2004–2005, which allowed me to finish this and another book (*Six Myths about the Good Life*) and also some papers, including one on the logic of the "Is-Ought" relation. Let me also thank two anonymous reviewers for the press, who made useful suggestions of material that could be added to my manuscript.

Finally, I owe a great deal to an argument of about an hour with Jim Griffin over tea several years ago. The topic was why he was no longer a consequentialist and I still was. The argument ended with my views unchanged; but later reflection made a real difference in my thinking, one that helped shape the tenth and twelfth chapters of this book.

Contents

Ethics and Qualities of Life

Introduction

At the outset, two things should be explained. One is the phrase "qualities of life." The other is the contrast, which divides this book into two halves, between the practice of ethical thought and ethical theory.

By the practice of ethical thought, I mean the ways in which people ordinarily think (or do not think) about questions of right, wrong, and what can be rewarding in life. These can be shared by a wide range of people, including those who have never studied philosophy and sometimes also professors of philosophy when off duty. Part I unfolds a complicated account of the structures of ethical thought, including a variety of elements. Some of these (e.g., the way a case is interpreted or is related to a rule or principle, and also the value judgment of possible outcomes) often are explicit in our thought processes. But sometimes they are merely implicit. This is especially common when there is considerable consensus, so that the interpretation or the judgment of value seems not to need to be thought about. A portion of the argument of part I is that interpretations of cases and judgments of values of outcomes, even when they seem obvious and automatic, are generally elements of ethical thought.

The final chapter of part I argues that the fallibility of all of the ordinary elements of ethical thought naturally leads to ethical theory. Part II examines leading examples: Kantian ethics, contractualism, and consequentialism (which includes utilitarianism as one of its varieties). Here are two of the things that will be argued for in part II. One is that such theories evolve and diversify through time, so that it is a mistake to think of a theory as having a simple fixed nature. The other is that it is also a mistake to think of major theories as entries in a competition in which there can be at most one winner (with the other entries counting as false). The reality is far more complicated that this.

Much of part II will examine the place of qualities of life in ethical theory. One theory, the simplest form of consequentialism (which goes back to Jeremy Bentham), holds that judgments of quality of life in the narrow sense of what is rewarding in life are basically the whole story in ethical judgment (assuming that one knows the consequences of any choice). part II will present more than one reason for regarding this as a bad mistake. The picture that develops will not be totally favorable to any familiar form of consequentialism. Nor will it be sharply unfavorable to the thought that consequences often matter a great deal in fundamental ways in ethics.

What is quality of life? I will speak of it in two different ways. (Hence this book is about *qualities* of life.) The phrase often refers to how good a life is for the person living it. The idea is that merely being alive may count for much less than the satisfaction, or purity, or fulfillment of potential in a life. Someone who appreciates this can be expected to prefer greatly a life of high quality to one of low quality.

Quality of life can also refer to an evaluation of a person's behavior, especially in making moral choices. In this sense, we can disdain the quality of the life of someone who is cruel and rapacious. We have a much higher estimation of the quality of life (in this sense) of saints or heroes, even if a saint or hero makes such drastic sacrifices that it looks as if the quality of life (in the first sense) becomes less than it might have been. We may think, to take an extreme example, that someone who has lost sight, hearing, and limbs in order to save many innocent lives has not a very high quality of life (in the first sense) as a result, but does have a high quality of life in the second sense. We could admire but not envy such a person.

In the traditional philosophical literature, quality of life in the first sense is spoken of as well-being or as value; and much of what falls under the heading of quality of life in the second sense is related to morality. There is also, it should be said, a use of "quality of life" among economists, in which it refers not to actual well-being or value, but rather to capacities or opportunities to have a life of well-being (or to conditions favorable to such a life). This makes sense if the focus is on the potential role of governments or other organizations in bettering people's lives. It parallels the language of the American Declaration of Independence, which includes among our rights one to the pursuit of happiness, rather than one to actual happiness. An organization can try to make sure that people have reasonable means to have good lives and that conditions are favorable. But it cannot guarantee everyone a good life or happiness. In any event, the concern of this book is broadly with choices to be made by individuals and groups of individuals and is not (not primarily, that is) with those of governments and other organizations (or economic and social planners). So the use of "quality of life" that connects mainly with means, capacities, or opportunities will not occur in this book.

An interesting question that remains is what relation, if any, there is between quality of life in the two senses (which might be spoken of as the truly enviable and the admirable) used in this book. Many ancient philosophers, including Plato, Aristotle, and Confucius, thought that there was a close one. A persistent claim was that only someone of genuine, reliable virtue could have a high quality of life in the first sense; and, furthermore, that this would remain reasonably high for such a person even in extreme adversity. Aristotle, for example, maintained that although the well-being of King Priam of Troy (who was presumed to be highly virtuous) would have been lowered when his city was destroyed and his family killed, it still would be at a moderate rather than low level. Similar claims can be found in the *Dialogues* of Plato and the *Analects* of Confucius.

There is a strong opposite tendency in the Western non-Greek tradition, going back to the Book of Job. Extreme misfortune, it is assumed, could bring down even an extremely virtuous person's well-being to a very low level. It is possible that an admirable but risky moral choice could lead to this. Because of this, the relation between morality and self-interest has been treated as problematic in a good deal of Western ethical philosophy of the last few hundred years. One worry is that if morality is not (at least generally) in an agent's self-interest, it may lose some of its authority.

One way of seeing the complication of the issues is this. Most of us think that judgments of how rewarding or truly enviable and how admirable a specific life is can diverge. This, however, is *not* to imply that what is admirable cannot be rewarding. Job's admirable qualities, which certainly will be part of the texture of his life, could be judged (e.g., by Job himself) to enhance how rewarding the life is— even though other factors in the life can diminish how rewarding it is.

This book will be about quality of life in both senses. My goals, in examining the role of qualities of life in ethics, will include clarity. They will not, however, include simplicity. Indeed, a theme of the book will be that most recent ethical philosophy has been too simple in relation to quality of life (especially in the first sense, but also in the second) and its roles in our choices.

More broadly, a good deal of recent ethical philosophy has offered a one-sided picture both of morality and of the discipline of ethics. The side that tends to get left out includes factors that weigh heavily in personal well-being, either of an agent or of others. It also includes choices that cannot be appreciated except in the context of commitments, personal connections, and prior choices.

Hence this book concerns not only quality of life (in both senses), but also contains a meditation on the structure of ethics. The goal will be a more balanced picture, one that is complex and not simple. Only such a representation of the structure of ethics can put us in a position to understand the place in ethics of qualities of life.

A Writing Strategy

Complexity and readability generally do not go very well together. I will endeavor to lessen the tension between them in two principal ways. One is by providing the lexicon below. The other is in the management of references.

Most references will be parenthetical within the text. Where possible, they will be bunched together, to keep disruption of the flow of argument to a minimum. Discussion of recent philosophical literature will play a more prominent role in some parts of the book than in others.

This is in part because of a difference in the polemical characters of the two parts of the book. Most of part I concerns elements of ethical thought that are noticeable in some cases but can seem invisible in others, and that often are left out of the picture. There is no suggestion that philosophers who dwell on cases in which these elements seem invisible have argued for something false. They have not argued that the elements are not present; they have simply left them out. Hence the argument in much of part I consists of, to borrow language from Wittgenstein, "reminders assembled for a purpose." An exception is the treatment of the role of character in ethical thought. There is a lively recent literature on character traits in relation to virtue, and a part of this literature will be discussed in the appendix.

Part II concerns the contest (as it may seem) among ethical theories. This has recently given rise to some important developments of various theories. As part of the strategy of bunching up, much of the discussion of this will be concentrated in chapter 11. Polemic here, and elsewhere in Part II, will largely take the form of argument for or against specific claims.

The aim of all of this is clarity and a degree of ease in reading, but a very high degree cannot be promised. Those experienced in reading philosophy know that the process rarely is entirely straightforward. One needs to be mindful of the structure of arguments. Also, key terms in the philosopher's account will seem to carry meaning that may be subtly different from their meanings for other philosophers. "What does the philosopher mean by such-and-such?" becomes an important question.

By and large I have tried to stay close to ordinary usage of the terms of my account. But this does not guarantee entire success. Here is an explanation of the meanings of eight terms that are central to portions of this book.

Lexicon

Ethics has two senses that will loom large in what will follow, and a third that will not play much of a part but should be noted. First, ethics studies what the factors are that significantly contribute to, or detract from, the quality of lives (in either or both of the senses of "quality of life" already outlined). Classic Western examples of such examinations are Aristotle's *Nicomachean Ethics* and the ethical writings of Immanuel Kant and John Stuart Mill. Second, *an* ethics is a set of recommendations as to what the factors should be that significantly contribute to the quality of lives (in one or both senses of "quality of life"). In this second sense of "ethics," Kant's and Mill's ethics differ, and both are very different from Aristotle's. Third, "an ethics" can refer to a code of recommended or required conduct specific to a role or a position, especially one within a profession. Thus legal ethics requires client confidentiality, and morticians' ethics requires that corpses be treated with respect. There are interesting questions of whether what is required by a professional ethics always correlates well with what is admirable in a person's conduct (i.e., with quality of life in the second sense), and arguably it sometimes could be more admirable to violate a professional code than to follow it.

Morality consists of injunctions of what should be done or not done that are (or should be) treated with especial urgency, such that significant blame typically attaches itself to someone who knowingly goes counter to one of the injunctions. A classic example of a morality is that of the Ten Commandments. It conveys an attitude toward transgressions that is deeper and more hostile than the one most of us adopt to lapses of taste or manners.

This is a major difference between morality and other sets of injunctions, such as those of etiquette or of good carpentry. In noting this, I am accepting John Stuart Mill's contrast (in par. 14 of bk. 5 of *Utilitarianism*, and in *On Liberty* passim) between things we deplore that we think should be punished (by social condemnation and/or the agent's feelings of guilt, as well as perhaps by legal means) and things we deplore that inspire reactions of disdain or avoidance but not an urge that the agent be punished.

It should be clear that a morality, in the sense just outlined, will be part (but typically not all) of an ethics. Aristotle could be assumed to endorse a morality that includes injunctions against thieving or killing innocent people, and he specifically condemns adultery. But Aristotle's ethics is mainly concerned with what contributes to an enviable life of high quality. There is nothing to suggest that he thought that those who could cultivate their intellectual virtues and contemplative tendencies, but who fail to do so, should feel guilty or otherwise be punished.

Morality looms much larger in the ethics of two other philosophers already mentioned, Kant and Mill. This marks a historical development in the preoccupations characteristic of ethical philosophy. (Later in the book, I will discuss morality as social control.) But even the ethics of Kant and Mill arguably contains nonmoral elements. Mill certainly offers a "proof," in chapter 4 of *Utilitarianism*, that pleasure (and the absence of pain) is the primary value in life; he also argues that "higher" pleasures have special importance and, in the essay on Bentham, contends that happiness is more than mere pleasure. Kant can be read as holding that, other things being equal, someone who acts out of duty and also attains happiness is better off than someone who acts out of duty and is unhappy. Neither philosopher would condemn, in the way he would condemn an immoral action, someone who through ignorance or ineptitude misses out on happiness.

If morality is typically part, but not all, of an ethics, then one would expect that a philosopher could have an ethics while rejecting—or being willing to do without— morality. Morality might be rejected because so much of it could be seen as merely keyed to local custom and practice, or because the pressure (the urge to punish those who transgress) implicit in moral judgments represents a kind of tyranny of the majority over remarkable individuals. In my view, both of these reasons play a part in Nietzsche's rejection of morality. Alternatively, morality might be scorned, as in Bernard Williams's *Ethics and the Limits of Philosophy*, because of the construal of obligation held to be implicit in moral judgment.

The rejection of morality should itself be distinguished from a refusal to draw a line between morality and the rest of ethics or from the omission of such a dividing line. Some commentators have argued, in the case of Aristotle and in that of Confucius, that there is no dividing line. It does seem to me true that separating and highlighting a zone of morality (as in chap. 5, par. 14, of *Utilitarianism*, or in Kant's distinction between categorical and hypothetical imperatives), is peculiarly a modern Western preoccupation. Nevertheless, it also is highly arguable that Aristotle and Confucius do make judgments (e.g., Confucius's of filial neglect of parents, Aristotle's of adultery) that are treated much as most people nowadays treat moral judgments: morality is present, but not as a separate highlighted category.

Morality is widely held to govern only matters of choice. By *choice*, I mean something that an agent does (an action, or having a thought or an emotional response) that the agent in some sense might not have done. One might choose to get angry at something, to think of previous misdeeds of the person one is with, or to run away. It sometimes is not easy to draw a line between what is choice and what is not. Some thoughts just pop into your head: you do not choose to have them. But then you usually could, so to speak, put them out of your mind. If you continue with them, this looks like choice.

By *decision*, I mean a choice in which there is a conscious weighing of alternatives.

By *principle*, I mean a general formulation that tells us what we are obliged to do or not to do, or what is permissible or impermissible. Such a formulation may have implicit exceptions to the most literal reading of the requirement. In saying this, I am accepting points made by the Kantian ethicist Alan Donagan in his *The Theory of Morality*. We could regard "One ought to keep promises" as a valid principle while also accepting it as understood that the principle does not really say that you ought to keep a promise if lives then predictably will be lost or if keeping the promise would impose extraordinary hardships in what otherwise is a very minor matter.

A facile contrast sometimes is drawn between moralities that rest on principles and those (such as classical utilitarianism, and more broadly any form of consequentialism) that rest on estimation of consequences. However, as we have seen, one could hold a principle that promises ought to be kept, within which it was implicit that a promise need not be kept if the promise itself was fairly trivial and if a predictable result of keeping it would be serious harm for someone. Further, the form of consequentialism ("act consequentialism") that most directly rests moral judgments on estimation of consequences is, as we will see later in the book, by far the least plausible. It is, in any case, hard to imagine anyone attempting to apply consequentialism, of any kind, to actual questions of moral judgment without often relying heavily on principle-like generalizations about what generally should be done or avoided. We simply do not know the future well enough to avoid relying on such generalizations. Even chess masters sometimes make use of them.

By the *consequences* of an action or a choice, I mean everything that becomes the case if the action is performed, or the choice made, that otherwise would not have been the case. This is a broad sense of "consequences," in which consequences need not be regarded simply as in the future. The consequences of an action, in my sense, include features of the action as it is performed. They also can include features of the past: to do X is to make some things in the past preludes to X, giving them new significance and thus changing their character.

By a *moral order*, I mean a consensus or near consensus (i.e., wide but not necessarily entire agreement) in a society as to (a) moral rules that should be taken seriously, in such a way that violations are subject to pronounced social condemnation, and (b) what the general considerations are that mark actions and practices as morally unacceptable. A moral order may be merely notional (i.e., posited as an ideal or as a test of moral views) or may actually obtain. In our society, for example, a moral order obtains that includes (a) general prohibitions of murder, rape, torture, and theft, and (b) condemnations of what is interpreted as cruel, unfair, racist, or sexist. At various times in the past, such a moral order would have been merely notional.

An acceptable moral order would be one that everyone reasonably (under the circumstances) indeed should accept. It is possible that our present moral order is entirely acceptable. But it may be likely instead that it can be significantly improved in ways that we cannot now agree on.

By *value*, I mean a contribution that something (in the context in which it occurs) makes by its nature, apart from causal consequences, to enhancing a life or a world. A negative value then would be the contribution that something (in the context in which it occurs) makes by its nature, apart from its causal consequences, to lessening the desirability of a life or a world. Philosophers since Plato have contrasted goodness as an end with goodness as a means. Following this distinction, I will use "value" in this book to refer to non-instrumental goodness (in the context in which something occurs) as opposed to goodness as a means. This is the sense in which it is widely believed that happiness has value (even apart from its consequences) and that a long period of excruciating pain has negative value.

This represents a narrow use of "value." There is a broader common use in which someone's "value judgments" concern not merely what is rewarding or unrewarding in life, but also what is obligatory or impermissible. When (in this book) I take up judgments of what is obligatory or impermissible, though, I will eschew the broader use and not refer to these as judgments of "value." My narrow use of "value" includes the first of the three senses (characterized earlier) of "quality of life," although we have to leave open the possibility that some things have non-instrumental value that is not part of any lives.

PART I

FACTORS IN ETHICAL JUDGMENT

*From Atomistic Moral Decision to Goods,
Construals, Character, and the Social
Implications of Moral Judgments*

Existential Choices
and Dislocations

A running theme of this book is that ethics contains an interrelated variety of inquiries and reflections. Because of this, any inquiry, whatever its merits, risks being unrepresentative, and any example risks being misleading. We might take what is on the periphery as somehow central and as representative of the essence of ethics. The most dramatic cases naturally capture our attention, and for that very reason have the greatest likelihood of misleading us.

I will begin by discussing a class of such cases. The aim is to explore their interest and how various they are. It also is to explain the ways in which the context of choice can be relevant both to how it takes place and to how well it is made. This will lead to an argument that attention to the context of choice is crucial to a balanced view of ethics.

Existential Choice

An existential choice is one in which there is a real chance that an agent will break the pattern of a lifetime in a significant way, and that the choice will resonate in the agent's subsequent life. Perhaps there is a temptation to do what one normally would not do, or there may be pressure to behave differently. The agent may be in a new situation that is disorienting or that does not offer options which flow smoothly from previous patterns of behavior. Choices of this sort are, in most people's lives, not entirely common. They can make an agent stop and think rather than following the most comfortable intuitions or responding in a habitual way, but they also can be made blindly and thoughtlessly.

One kind of existential choice takes place when someone is self-consciously open to the thought of changing the pattern of a lifetime for the foreseeable future instead of merely for a moment. Someone has become disenchanted with life as a hardworking, very predictable kind of person, and thinks, "I could have a life that is more interesting and is free." What looks like a sudden change of life often is not so sudden, emerging rather as the result of accumulating pressures and dissatisfactions.

This is true also of the case in which someone who has chronically misbehaved decides to repent and reform. In both of the versions just mentioned of the choice to change one's life, it is always possible that what looks like a permanent break with the past can turn out to be temporary. The previously hardworking and predictable person may, after a while, go back to her or his former life, as may the reformed malefactor.

There is another kind of existential choice that typically does not present itself in terms of a change of life but that can amount to one. The occasion may involve a real possibility of going against one's moral standards, practical policies, or habits. Sometimes the thought is "Just this once." Sometimes the present situation is so different from what the agent is used to that she or he becomes disoriented and does not fully take in that a contemplated action will violate moral standards or practical policies. The new kind of situation can seem almost unreal and will be experienced as disconnected from normal life. In many of these cases, the choice will be felt to be unique, and yet nothing will be the same after it is made. The previously honest person who steals or the previously harmless person who causes someone's death may well need to reorient herself or himself in a world in which everything now seems different.

One of the features of existential choices is that usually they *look* discontinuous from the agent's previous life and values. This appearance may be highly misleading. Closer examination may reveal pressures and dissatisfactions that come to a head in the existential choice. Or there may have been little odd departures from the norm, not striking in themselves, that with hindsight can be seen to presage the way the existential choice was made. Nevertheless, an existential choice can seem so dramatically different—both in the way in which the choice presents itself, and in what then is done—from everything that happened before it that it will be tempting to describe it (and perhaps also to judge it) in a way that emphasizes its discontinuity from everything else.

Furthermore, the existential choice calls, in an especially pronounced way, for thought, whether or not it gets it. Much of life normally can seem to be a matter largely of staying on course. We need to be careful to avoid mistakes and to keep up commitments of various sorts; but at most moments there will not seem to be a serious issue about the direction of our lives. The existential choice changes that, and (whether the agent realizes it or not) opens the door to a new kind of life.

The opportunity or pressure or temptation that brings about the choice can arise so suddenly, however, that there is hardly any time for thought: something that changes a person's life can be done in an instant. All the same, an intelligent and generally thoughtful agent will be likely to see existential choices as especially important, and hence as best made if there is a good deal of thought about the alternatives. One of the arguments of this book is that such thought should best include real consideration of what the ensuing changes in the agent's character and way of life are likely to be. But for many people, and in many philosophical accounts, the thought will focus more narrowly on the case at hand. Respect for the possibilities of change can take the form of treating the present case as largely disconnected from anything in life before.

Existential Choices in Their Contexts

Let us look more closely at features of the contexts in which existential choices occur. Typically there is a dislocation that makes the existential choice possible, likely, or unavoidable. There will be an element of construal of the situation at hand, of what the possible responses to it are, or of both. There also will be a valencing of elements of possible outcomes. All of these things can affect what the agent chooses and the ways the agent experiences the choice.

By *dislocation*, I mean that something will have disrupted the pattern of life or will have evoked a disruptive possibility.

By *construal*, I mean the element of "seeing as" by virtue of which some elements of a situation emerge as salient, and some kinds of response to it pop into the mind as possibilities. Construal can have a double aspect. It can be a feature of experience, in terms of what one notices or what sticks out. It also can be a feature of the words one says or thinks: how one formulates the case, and how the possible responses are formulated.

By *valencing*, I mean a sense of certain things, that might be got or avoided, as goods or as evils. This sense may be merely prima facie and may not survive reflection. It also can be partial and particular. Utilitarianism and most other forms of consequentialism rely on comparisons of the goodness of totalities (e.g., of the total outcome if you do X or if you instead do Y). But to do justice to the actual phenomena of decision-making, we have to recognize that such comparative evaluation of totalities sometimes is more sophisticated and theory-driven than the explicit evaluations that determine people's choices. Frequently, some aspects or elements of various possible outcomes simply gain prominence in an agent's mind and determine the agent's sense of which choice will lead to the best outcome.

The remainder of this chapter will be devoted to dislocations. Construals and valencing will be the subjects of the next chapter.

Dislocations

Dislocations can be quiet and undramatic. Conversion experiences of various kinds may seem almost uneventful: someone simply decides that a certain kind of life would be better than the one that she or he has had, and begins to lead (or tries to lead) a different kind of life. I will say more about such cases later.

Dislocations in which there is a pronounced element of disorientation also can be quiet and undramatic. Someone can find herself or himself behaving differently as a result of coming to live in a country where things are done differently or of experiencing a major life transition, such as divorce or retirement. In such cases, the agent's sense of self often becomes less firm and assured than it had been. One begins to think oneself capable of a wider range of behavior than previously had seemed the case, or many decisions in life come to seem indeterminate. This can be dramatic, as people behave in new and highly surprising ways. But often the changes, both in behavior and in sense of self, are not highly conspicuous.

From Plato to the present, much more attention has gone to dramatic dislocations. In these, it may seem to onlookers, someone is pulled, pushed, or stumbles out of the previous path of life. New or unusual circumstances will figure prominently in the agent's view of what happened.

This topic is connected with one that many people find troubling: whether there is such a thing as genuine moral virtue and, if so, whether it is at all common. Most ordinary people, at least in stable and prosperous societies, think that genuine moral virtue is fairly common. Many psychologists and some philosophers are much more skeptical.

The difference here between the non-skeptics and skeptics may have a great deal to do with experience or awareness of dislocations. Someone whose pattern of life is stable and for the most part untroubled can find it difficult to believe that most of the people around her or him, who are leading similar lives, would or could deliberately do something extremely harmful. This is connected with a very assured sense of self. What you are seems firm, and you assume that much the same is true of friends and neighbors.

Someone who, say, had experienced life under a nasty dictatorship, in which ordinary citizens were under considerable pressure to arrest or betray (or directly to harm) innocent people, will be likely to have a less sanguine view. In the early twenty-first century, this will be true of those who remember what it was like during the Nazi occupation of Europe during World War II, or the Cultural Revolution in China, or the genocide in Rwanda. Plato must have remembered the dictators in Athens who ordered a group of citizens (including Socrates) to arrest Leon of Salamis, presumably an innocent man who was to be executed. The others did this; Socrates simply went home. As it happened, the government fell before Socrates would have suffered reprisals (Plato 1997, *Apology*, 32c, 29–30).

In the *Republic*, Plato presents two dislocations of a more fantastic nature. In Book II we read of the ring of invisibility that according to legend had been discovered by a Lydian shepherd. Perhaps the shepherd's life had been impeccable up to that point—who knows?—but when he realized the possibilities of the ring, he went to the capital, seduced the queen, murdered the king, and became a tyrant (1997, 359d–360, 1000–1001). Book X presents the story of Er's near-death experience, in which Er saw the souls of the dead in the underworld choosing new lives. One of them, after a life of virtuous behavior, chooses a life as a great tyrant (614b–621, 1218–1223). How could virtuous behavior lead to this? Socrates' comment is that the fool who chose to be a tyrant (and who soon regretted his choice) had lived in a well-regulated society in which virtuous behavior was simply the path of least resistance. His prior "virtue" (like the prior virtue, perhaps, of those who brought Leon of Salamis to his execution) was a matter merely of habit without philosophy (619c, 1221–1222).

Plato's view, then, is that those whose behavior is virtuous may well not be genuinely virtuous people. This is a large part of the point of his fantastic thought experiments of the ring of invisibility and the choice of new lives. A record of having done the right thing counts for very little until someone is tested. By this standard, there may be very few genuinely virtuous people indeed: genuine virtue emerges in Plato's account as a kind of knowledge, which confers moral reliability in part because of the link between knowledge and the unchanging.

Later we can consider whether there is anything to Plato's claim that philosophical knowledge is required for genuine moral virtue. Perhaps there can be other stabilizing features? Our immediate concern, however, is with dislocations that lead to existential choices. What appears to be a widespread current opinion — namely, that large numbers of people qualify as genuinely virtuous — may be connected with a difficulty either in focusing on such dislocations and their likely effects, or in taking in the malleability of selves under pressure.

We tend to think of a dislocation as happening all at once, but sometimes there can be a buildup of pressure. Presumably, there were many who, during the Nazi occupation of Europe, at first saw the new Nazi order as abnormal and regarded the standards of the old normal world as obviously the right ones. But after a year or two, the Nazi rule, and whatever that seemed to entail, may have come to seem normal to some of these people.

Similarly, we can imagine a previously virtuous person who gets the ring of invisibility, immediately takes in the fact that all of its most interesting uses would go against her or his moral code, and decides not to use the ring. Over a period of time, though, such a person could get used to repeated thoughts of what could be done with the ring. Corruption then can set in, especially if friends express surprise that nothing really advantageous had yet been done with the ring.

Part of the genius of the psychologist Stanley Milgram was that he was able to corrupt numbers of people, for experimental purposes, in a very short period of time. Perhaps, though, the word "corrupt" is wrong here, in that it might suggest an ongoing (negative) change of nature. Milgram did not think that he changed the nature of his experimental subjects for the worse. Indeed, he thought, or at least wanted to think, that he had changed the nature of some of the subjects for the better (cf. Milgram 1974). In this, he tapped into a tradition in the culture that regards virtue as often a learning process; one learns from mistakes. Milgram led most of his subjects into what amounted to moral lapses in circumstances that were discontinuous from the rest of their lives and were most unlikely to recur for them. Even if this sharp but brief dip in the moral quality of most of their lives is not termed corruption, it remains impressive that Milgram was able to induce it so quickly.

Milgram's well-known experiments used volunteers who were told that they were participating in an experiment on learning under pressure. Each of them could see, on the other side of a glass wall, someone he or she took to be another volunteer (but was actually an actor), who would be asked questions. The real volunteers were told to give this "volunteer" an electric shock every time he failed to give a correct answer. The severity of these shocks (they were told) would gradually rise as the man on the other side of the glass wall continued to make mistakes. In the end, about two thirds of the volunteers proved willing to administer electric shocks to what they thought were dangerous levels.

Earlier it was suggested that a great many dislocations could be lumped together under the headings of temptations or pressures. Plato's imagined case of the ring of invisibility clearly involves temptation, as does the imagined case of the man who chooses the life of a tyrant. When Socrates was told to go with others to arrest Leon of Salamis, there was implied pressure. He could have been killed when he did not comply. There certainly was pressure in the cases of those who in the end did not defy the Nazis or who went along with the brutal excesses of the cultural revolution in China or with the massacres in Rwanda.

The Milgram experiments are different from all of these cases. It is hard to report them as a story of people who yielded to temptation. Had all of those volunteers been fantasizing all along about giving electric shocks to strangers? The heading of pressure might at first look more promising. Many volunteers expressed reluctance to give electric shocks, especially after a certain point. They would say to the psychologist next to them such things as "He seems to be in pain; couldn't we stop?" The psychologist then would say, "The experiment must go on," and usually the volunteer would go on (despite the clear initial reluctance) to give further shocks.

Milgram presented his experiments as a study of obedience to authority. In his retrospective account he linked the experiments to the theme of Hannah Arendt's then-recent book *Eichmann in Jerusalem*. The colorless Nazi bureaucrat Eichmann professed to have been simply following orders in his organization of the extermination of Jews. "Look," Milgram seemed to say, "ordinary Americans (and, as the experiments were replicated, ordinary people of a variety of nationalities) also will do something harmful to presumably innocent strangers if told to."

But the comparison with Eichmann of those of Milgram's volunteers who complied is flawed in a number of ways, even if we put to the side the greater and more prolonged seriousness of what Eichmann did. Even in Eichmann's rather banal setting in a bureaucracy, it surely would have been dangerous for him to disobey orders. The authority in question was authority with considerable power.

In the Milgram experiments, there was no such power and no implicit threat. No doubt most volunteers regarded the guiding psychologist as having authority of sorts. Nevertheless, we speak of obedience to authority usually in contexts in which there are penalties for disobedience: arrest, fines, imprisonment, being assigned detention in a school, being fired from a job, and so on. The relation of the Milgram volunteers to authority looks more like deference than obedience. When the psychologist in charge said, "The experiment must go on," many of the volunteers must have thought, "Well, he must know what he's doing."

This thought, that the experiment could not possibly be as harmful as it looked, surely produced in many of the subjects a kind of double vision. At some stage, they must have half-believed in the seriousness of what was going on but, at the same time, half-disbelieved. This feature has been noted by some commentators. Lee Hamilton saw the actions of Milgram's subjects as more like those of corporate employees who produce unsafe products but believe that the company could not really be endangering consumers just to make a profit, than like the actions of a military subordinate ordered to shoot civilians (Blass 2000, 46–47; Hamilton 1992). Ann L. Saltzman (2000, 125–143) has pointed to the role of euphemism in dulling perception of what really is going on. An example, she says, is the "experimental cover story": "This is an experiment on learning and memory" (136). The subject, of course, is highly likely to have wanted not to believe that the experiment was harmful. As Rochat, Maggioni, and Modigliani point out, "One way participants sought to cope with their rising distress was by trying to ignore or rationalize the suffering of their fellow participant" (2000, 170).

Clearly, though, an attempt at situational etiquette was a major factor in the behavior of the subjects. Most of us at one time or another will have had an experience of trying to do the socially right thing (or, at least, not conspicuously to do the socially wrong thing). This may occur in a foreign country, or within a totally unfamiliar ceremony, or in interaction with a group of people very different from the sort we are used to.

The Milgram volunteers were like people in these situations in one respect and very unlike most of them in another. The likeness is that the volunteer—who was not a professional psychologist or a researcher of any kind—might well have had a sense of having stepped temporarily into a different world, which for all one knew had its own rules. And the quiet, confident man in charge seemed to know these rules. The obvious major dissimilarity is that Milgram created a case in which (as far as one could tell) someone was going to get hurt. This dissimilarity caused many volunteers who continued to give shocks to exhibit reluctance and inner conflict. But it does remain amazing that they nevertheless went on.

A crucial element was the gradual progression of the shocks. As Milgram (1974, 149) put it, the "subject is implicated into the destructive behavior in a piecemeal fashion." The "learner" does not say "ugh" until after the fifth press of the shock lever; only after the tenth (150 volts) does he demand to be released.

Does anyone think that if the experiment had simply consisted of the volunteer's being told to administer a single shock of very high voltage that the results would have been the same? In the experiment as performed, the initial shocks could reasonably be regarded as not serious; and many volunteers would not have fully taken in where the experiment might be leading. By the time the purported strength of the shock became high, the volunteer would have been involved in a pattern of behavior within which administering the shock of high voltage would be a natural continuation.

As a dislocation, the Milgram experiment was a very temporary one. The volunteers then returned to ordinary life. But, one wonders, was their life at all different afterward? We have Milgram's recorded optimism that there had been positive effects for some, but it would have been good to have had systematic study of how the experiment resonated in the subjects' subsequent lives.

Another kind of temporary dislocation might be provided by a highly unusual moral quandary, one that had to be addressed and could not be resolved by easy and obvious application of the moral code learned. A good example in the recent philosophical literature is the case of the runaway trolley. You are to imagine that, if no one does anything, it will kill five people. But you can quickly switch its track, in which case it will kill only one person, one who otherwise (if you had done nothing) would not have been killed.

This is a clever example in a number of ways. It probes the distinction, in most people's commonsense view of the world, between the moral seriousness of what we do and the moral seriousness of what we fail to do. Most people, for example, regard omitting to send money to Oxfam to save the life of a famine victim thousands of miles away as morally less serious than it would be to travel to where the famine victim is and to shoot him or her. The stakes in the two cases are the same (one life); but we take the choice in which the one life is lost through someone's action as morally very wrong, and most people would not make such a judgment of the choice in which the life is lost because nothing was done. In the trolley case, if you switch tracks you will have caused the death of the person who will be killed, and perhaps there is a sense in which this is murder or manslaughter. The case for regarding it as murder or manslaughter if you do nothing, and five die, may seem to many people to be much less strong.

The problem of the runaway trolley calls for the exercise of *casuistry*. Ethics of rules have tended to take a central role in most Western ethical traditions. In these there inevitably will be cases that cannot be easily and straightforwardly be dealt with by application of established moral rules. Rules need to be interpreted, elaborated upon, qualified (or stretched) to cover the case at hand. This activity is called "casuistry." It can be done well or badly. Classic discussions include the Hebrew *Talmud* and part II of Kant's *Metaphysics of Morals*. The trolley case calls for casuistry because it looks as if there ought to be an answer in terms of overarching rules of morality, but it is not entirely clear how this would work.

There has been some interesting, and sometimes brilliant, treatment of the runaway trolley case. I will not enter this arena at all, but will simply pursue the topic of this chapter (dislocation) by examining the kind of dislocation that something like the trolley case would represent. This should shed light on, among other things, the popularity of such cases in the recent literature of ethical philosophy.

The extreme and very temporary dislocation that such a case would represent occurs very rarely if at all in the lives of most of us, at least during untroubled times. Wars and social disruptions could change this. I knew very slightly an American academic who reportedly was in the Battle of the Bulge in World War II and who, under orders, shot prisoners. The Allied forces in the area were under enormous pressure and were giving ground; there was nothing that could be done with the prisoners, he reportedly was told. Perhaps in a messy war, or during a period of extreme social upheaval, someone could be forced repeatedly to make decisions like the one he had to make. One feels lucky not to have had those experiences.

The runaway trolley case would not only be a temporary dislocation, but also whatever one did would hardly look like the start of a habit, or a precedent that then could be applied to roughly similar cases likely to come up. The man who shot prisoners might have thought it likely that similar decisions probably would not recur. But he hardly could have reason to be confident of this.

In these respects, the runaway trolley lends itself, to an unusual degree, to treatment in isolation from the rest of the life of whoever has to make the decision. Let me anticipate some of the next chapter and point out other respects in which it is unusually suited to treatment in isolation from contextual elements. One contextual element we will examine is the ways in which an agent construes problematic situations. It is well known that people rooted in different cultural or moral traditions are likely to treat different things as salient in morally problematic situations, or to come up with a different view of what the alternatives are. But if there is anything near universal in this, it is the salience of life and death: its salience to a wide variety of agents can be presumed. The trolley case has this element. It also is presented quite cleverly in a way in which the alternatives are limited (no room for nuance or qualifications here), and again can be presumed to be obvious to a wide variety of agents.

Finally, the next chapter will elaborate on an argument (implicit both in Plato's *Republic* and in the *Analects* of Confucius, among other classic texts) that what an agent considers most valuable or most awful in life can be crucial to how she or he decides a difficult and unusual case. Values (in the narrow axiological sense of what is worth seeking or avoiding), in other words, are crucial to moral reliability. Values in this sense differ widely, again, among cultures, subcultures, and even individuals within a subculture. Nevertheless, virtually everyone will assign a significant positive value to staying alive and a significant negative value to being killed. Therefore, the agent responding to the runaway trolley could be presumed (uncontroversially) to have a positive value for life and a negative value for death. The contextual feature of the agent's valencing, which the next chapter will argue is crucial to what will seem an appropriate choice, again can be presumed and hence taken for granted and left out of the story.

In other words, the runaway trolley case will emerge as the exception that proves the rule. A diet of such examples in the recent philosophical literature may mislead many philosophers into thinking that such cases are normal. My concern is to look at the variety of ethical decisions that can be observed or imagined, and to avoid basing too much on any one kind of case.

Nevertheless, let me suggest a feature of agents making a decision in a runaway trolley case that might be overlooked. One variable that has not been mentioned is in how normal it seems to take responsibility for features of the world that you can significantly affect or control. In some tribes or close-knit traditional cultures, there can be a general sense of strong responsibility for much of what happens to members of the group. One helps where one can, and when people behave poorly, perhaps one sets them straight. In a liberal society, in which an enjoyable sense of freedom is made possible by widespread policies of not interfering with others' lives ("live and let live"), there may be a stronger tendency to regard the moral default position as that of doing nothing. By the default position, I mean the position from which one's departure requires supporting reasons and carries with it the weight of responsibility for whatever happens.

There is considerable variation among individuals in these matters, both within traditional and liberal societies. Certainly some people in our culture appear ready (perhaps far too ready) to take actions that have major effects on other's lives, and no doubt in the most traditional cultures, some people adopt roles of social monitors, and others do not. The important point here is that there can be variation in degrees of readiness to take positive unsolicited steps designed to have major effects on others. Imagine a number of people, each of whom could pull the switch that changes the trolley's track, who are roughly equidistant from the switch. In some groups, there might be many people racing for the switch. In others, everyone may think it would not be a bad idea if someone pulled the switch, but no one is inclined to take on the responsibility.

In the end, perhaps most people (both in our liberal society and in close-knit societies) would think it best that someone switch the track of the trolley. An important variation, then, might be not between those who vote "Yes" and those who vote "No," but rather between those who think that the answer of "Yes" is easy and obvious and those whose "Yes" is extremely reluctant and qualified. In this respect, as well as in some others, the runaway trolley case is like one imagined by Bernard Williams, in which a man traveling in Latin America happens upon an army unit about to execute twenty Indians and is offered by the army commander the choice between letting the execution of all twenty go forward or, alternatively, shooting one of the Indians himself (in which case the other nineteen will have their lives spared; see Williams 1973, 98 ff.).

One difference between the two cases is that the Williams example is presented in a way that makes it seem that the choice grows out of the wickedness and cruelty of the army commander. Because of this, one ground for reluctance in shooting the single Indian would be that it takes on complicity with something unacceptable and in effect yields to blackmail. This feature, though, makes the Williams case seem slightly less unreal and artificial than the runaway trolley case. It also makes it seem less highly unlikely to recur.

Conclusion

Perhaps all choices made by human beings can be fully appreciated only in the context of the agent's pattern of choice and the contextual factors that play a part in this. This is more obvious in some cases than in others. Those in which it is least obvious are the ones in which the choice to be made can present itself as sharply discontinuous from the rest of life up to that point. These are existential choices. They can occur as the result of dislocations of a variety of sorts. In some of these cases—especially the ones more likely to occur in philosophers' imaginations than in real life—the role of such contextual factors as the construal of the situation and of possible responses to it, and of valencing of elements of possible outcomes, plausibly can be heavily discounted, and the case can be examined as something unique at a moment in time, isolated from what had gone before. We need to understand how some of these cases lend themselves to atomization of ethical thought in order to appreciate, all the same, how artificial this is. This can lead us better to understand the ethical importance of the role that contextual factors, including those involved in the agent's previous pattern of behavior, typically play in choice.

Construals, Valencing

Two central ethical questions are "What is the right thing to do?" and "How can someone come to do the right thing?" In the end, I will argue that construal and valencing typically play a large part, one that in most cases cannot be taken for granted, in answers to both questions. For the time being, though, let us concentrate on how someone can come to behave well (which includes doing the right thing in cases in which there is a right thing). We will look first at the construal, and then at valencing.

A balanced view of the role that these factors typically play contrasts with a widely held view that is much simpler. This can be called the "codebook story." It assumes that doing the right thing is largely a matter of following the dictates of an acceptable moral code, and that it is generally very clear how this code applies to the situations we confront. It also assumes that our society has arrived at an acceptable moral code, so that except for minor or peripheral matters, there is no room for further progress in moral thought. The trick, then, is to get everyone to know, pledge allegiance to, and remember the moral code. To this end it can be instilled in young children, and there should be constant reminders of the code.

Not all of this is valueless. We certainly would not want to live in a society in which children were not firmly told that it is generally wrong to kill, rape, maim, torture, or steal from people. Clearly it is desirable that people be mindful of rules to this effect. What makes the codebook story drastically oversimple is that it ignores at least four problems that cannot be ignored, especially not by any approach that centers on broad general rules. One is that although general rules may serve well to give us all of the guidance we need in many everyday cases, there can be hard cases: ones that, because of unusual features, appear to be plausible exceptions to the familiar rules or to be situations in which more than one familiar rule applies, in such a way that the rules point in opposite directions. Someone whose judgment is guided in a simple way by traditional rules can emerge as rigid and intolerant in such cases.

A second problem is that there is a gap between affirming the recommendations of society's codebook and acting on them. One can in some sense "know" that the thing is wrong and still do it. It would be naive to prescribe more memorization, or perhaps writing the rules on the blackboard many times, as a cure for this. There can be a variety of reasons why someone who has said, with some degree of sincerity, that something is wrong yet can do it. Sometimes contrariety is a factor. You know that X is wrong; but you have been told that so many times that there comes an urge to do it, perhaps just this once. In such occasions, the inculcation methods of the codebook approach can be not merely ineffective but indeed counterproductive.

Third, something may not be taken in as an instance of a familiar general rule even though from any reasonable point of view it is. Bloggs can take property that does not belong to him but not think of it as theft, and there have been reported cases in which someone who was guilty of rape did not think of what he was doing as rape. More broadly, if the codebook includes a rule that forbids inflicting needless suffering on innocent people, it often appears not to register on a malefactor that she or he is causing such suffering. Perhaps the effects are too remote. There can be an element of thoughtlessness or insensitivity. The agent's own narrative of what is going on also can be self-serving, couched in terms that preclude recognition of what from any reasonable point of view is the nature of what is being done. How one sees it becomes crucial.

Fourth, it is unrealistic to suppose that everyone who has memorized the codebook will follow it when something that seems enormously attractive can be gained only by violating one of the familiar rules, especially if the risks of losing something else of value seem extremely minimal. If the agent thinks "No one will know" and "I can have the life of my dreams if I do this, and otherwise will never experience what seems to me most wonderful in life," compliance seems far from guaranteed. Admittedly the codebook approach does have room for some safeguards. The respect for a set of rules that could be universally accepted (something much emphasized in the Kantian tradition) can prevent many people from doing what they really would like to do, although it may not protect them from feeling sour about it afterward. (The combination of virtuous and sour is a familiar one in our culture.) Instilling the code also can be accompanied by a process that is considerably less simple than memorization: namely, instilling inhibitions corresponding to the prohibitions of the code. This can be highly effective in promoting compliance with the code (although again there is the problem of the sour feeling). This effectiveness will be limited by the fact that many people can overcome their inhibitions, especially when in the company of those who appear not to share them.

Construals

Construal of what may (or may not) be a morally problematic situation can be a far more complicated business than one initially might think. It can proceed by stages. A first stage is to be alerted to the possibility that what one confronts might raise moral problems. We can appreciate the need for this if we try to imagine someone whose every action embodies a moral decision. Cato the Much Younger, let us suppose, never does anything unless he believes that it is morally permissible. Does he have time to think about everything he does? There is an obvious problem of deciding just how many actions someone is performing in a certain period of time. If Cato takes two minutes to brush his teeth, is that one action, or does each placement and movement of the brush represent a separate decision?

Putting this difficulty to the side, we can see (even if we try to keep the count of actions from getting too very high) that the life of someone who thought about the moral permissibility of every decision would be extraordinary. It would be truly a considered life, some readers may think; but the reply is that it would be a drastically overconsidered life. Very many little bits of time would be spent on judging the obvious.

There could not be, for example, normal conversation. Most of us, after all, usually do not fully formulate what we are going to say before we say it. But Cato would have to do this in order to be sure that each utterance was morally permissible (e.g., did not involve a lie, breaking a promise, or inflicting needless suffering). Games and sports also would take on an abnormal character. The utilitarian philosopher J. J. C. Smart, an enthusiastic field hockey player, remarked that he did not, before making a move, ask whether it would promote the greatest good of the greatest number (1977, 128). But Cato would have to question the moral permissibility of any move beforehand. This certainly would put him at a disadvantage (unless, of course, his opponents were doing the same thing); but, above all, this mind-set would rob his activity of all spontaneity or possible joy.

No one actually lives like that. A plausible reconstruction of how most of us leave room in our lives for moral considerations, without allowing them to be crippling, is as follows. There is a trigger mechanism. Occasionally something in a situation provokes the thought "There may be moral issues here" or "At least one of the courses of action open to me might be immoral." Then the morality circuits, so to speak, light up. Otherwise they do not.

This triggering process cannot itself be entirely the result of conscious reflection. Otherwise we all would be back in the pinched life of Cato the Much Younger. But there can be an element of conscious reflection in the process. Someone can think, "Wait a minute; if I do that, it will make so-and-so suffer for the rest of his or her life." The "wait a minute" part is the essential prelude to conscious reflection. Even if the words are never thought, the point remains that something—some process of attentiveness—makes us think about possible suffering (and its moral implications) or possible violations of a moral code.

The second stage of construal, once a zone of the morally problematic is identified, involves relating whatever normative ideas we have (involving such things as moral codes, or the reluctance to make people or other animals suffer) to the present situation. This second stage is not as straightforward as it might sound, in part because the normative ideas typically are present in the form of language (formulations of what we think should matter); but what we are confronted with is a reality rather than a text. It is as if we are armed with morality software, which can recognize and deal with something only if that something is first put in the language able to be recognized by the software.

Before we examine what this involves, let me make two final comments about Phase 1 (the trigger mechanism of picking something out as warranting moral consideration). The first is that morality traditionally appears designed to engross our attention only at special moments rather than to be a constant preoccupation. It makes strong demands, but usually only once in a while—and most people like it that way. In particular, most members of a peaceful and stable society who are not desperately poor are not likely very frequently to have moments at which the triggering mechanism signals a moral alert.

It is an interesting question, all the same, whether they should have these moments far more often. Some revisionist moralists have argued that there are almost constant morally significant decisions that people make without its registering on them that they are making moral decisions. Examples would be decisions to spend money on luxuries or on lavish meals rather than sending more to famine relief organizations, or decisions to burn fossil fuels when it is not, strictly speaking, necessary. Because this part of the book is about the structures of ethics, and not about what the content of ethics should be, I will not directly address these issues, important though they are. However, the examination later of the implicitly social nature of moralities will bear on the issues. In any case, we should be mindful of the controversy, which includes being mindful of the possibility that (because of globalization) the nature of ethics has to change from what it was when someone living in a peaceful town would only rarely have the possibility of saving someone's life or of being aware of contributing to drastic changes of life on the planet.

The second comment about the triggering mechanism that puts us on moral alert is that inevitably it will not always function very well. There is the possibility, just noted, of mass malfunction: that most of us will not take in the moral significance of much that we do or fail to do. There also, always, have been individual malfunctions. People sometimes subject to moral scrutiny actions (e.g., trivial lies of politeness) that, at least on some views, scarcely deserve such scrutiny. A more common malfunction, though, has been not to be alert to what really did demand some moral reflection.

Specific kinds of mistake of this sort have been widespread within a culture. There may have been many slave owners, or men who systematically discriminated against women, to whom it never occurred that a central element in their lives was morally problematic. Then there are ordinary miscreants. Often someone can bring misery or deprivation to the lives of other people without its even occurring to him or her that there is something morally problematic in this. We normally like to assume that malefactors know that their actions are morally suspect; and that there then is some process of rationalization by which they convince themselves that really it is all right or, alternatively, that they need not care. Sometimes it is like this. But evidence suggests that often it simply does not occur to a wrongdoer that, say, depriving large numbers of people of their livelihood in order to augment further the wealth of a few individuals might have a moral dimension.

Triggering mechanisms are likely to malfunction when what should be salient—what should jump out to the eye of the viewer—is not salient. We need to consider, therefore, what it is that makes certain elements in a morally problematic situation salient. One factor, as has been pointed out by Julius Kovesi (1967) and by others, is that a secondary function of moral rules is to structure our experience so that the kinds of things that the rules recommend or forbid come to stand out. In a crowded room in which you can see many activities, including someone's quiet removal (unnoticed by the owner) of someone else's purse or wallet, you are likely to give prominent attention to the theft you are witnessing. That is because of the rule against theft with which we are all familiar.

Actions likely to lead to needless suffering are very salient to some of us and almost invisible to others. Even the perpetrators may have little sense that they are doing anything special. Two things contribute to these variations in sensitivity.

First, some people can have a lively sense, which many lack, of what it is like for others to have various experiences, including those that involve suffering. Perhaps a sympathetic nature makes the difference. People can learn to be more sensitive, though, to one another's psychological states. A habit of attentiveness, instead of merely thinking of other people as convenient (or not so convenient) objects, can make a difference, as can a habit of asking questions and then listening to the answers. Much can be accomplished also in the schools by teaching that includes novels and biographies that lend themselves to consideration of what it is like to be such-and-such a kind of person in such-and-such a setting. Knowing better what it is like to be mistreated or misunderstood in various ways can certainly make mistreatment or misunderstanding more salient.

Second, some experience of how actions and other events usually play out can make a difference. Something that seems harmless at the moment can predictably sadden or disturb people or make their lives more difficult. Much harm of this sort involves sheer thoughtlessness, but sometimes ignorance of the causal sequences (as well, perhaps, as insensitivity to what it is like to be one of the victims) can contribute to the thoughtlessness. To know the misery that doing X, which seems insignificant in itself, is likely to bring, is to be much more likely to see X as salient.

Let us move from Stage 1 (consideration of what might cause triggering mechanisms to malfunction) to Stage 2. Construals of situations recognized as morally problematic can vary. The degree and likelihood of the variation can depend on the case. Situations that involve clear-cut violations of widely accepted moral rules (e.g., against theft) are likely to be formulated by the great majority of people in much the same way as are many (although hardly all) situations that involve issues of life and death (e.g., the runaway trolley case). Having said this, I want to suggest that there can be some variation even in cases that in traditional terms emerge as easy and straightforward. Two people could agree that it is wrong for someone who is poor to pilfer food, and yet the poverty and the need might be more salient in one person's view than in the other's. This might affect the tone of condemnation or the inclination to be somewhat lenient in the degree of punishment.

Cases that do not lend themselves so well to a traditional story that would be widely accepted allow for much more diversity of construals. This is particularly true when what might be the most relevant elements are more subtle and harder to formulate than stabbings and purse snatchings tend to be. Much of what many people would consider to be racism, sexism, or mistreatment of gays has more to do with humiliation and discomfort than with easy-to-identify overt harming. If X is over time deprived of confidence or forced to disguise her or his true nature by the pressures of a surrounding group of people, this can look to some like serious harm and to others can look like nothing. Formulations of what might or might not be at stake will differ accordingly. What is a matter of mild discomfort from one point of view (and therefore claimed not to involve moral issues after all) can from another involve real psychological damage. Further, from that second point of view, because successful performance often requires a degree of personal confidence, slights and humiliations that deprive people of that confidence also diminish their chances in life.

Issues of construal arise also in the formulation of possible courses of action. Is one of the options stealing, or is it merely appropriating what genuinely does not belong to anyone? Is one of the options rape, or is it formulated as having sexual relations with someone in a highly impaired state who does not audibly say "No"? If Bloggs, who is desperately poor, steals bread, is the maxim of his action "I will steal when I really want something and cannot get it otherwise" or is it "When desperately poor and hungry, I will steal small amounts of food"? Or is it (more dishonestly) "Whenever I am very hungry, I will eat whatever food is available"?

Up to this point, construal has been examined in terms of which elements in a scene jump out to attention, or of how the attention to what is there will be shaped and formulated. All of this can be put under the heading of "seeing as," as can ways in which we decide to formulate the available options. How we see the alternative courses of action that are open in a given situation can, however, go beyond this.

There can be an exercise of moral imagination, which sees possibilities that perhaps would not occur to most people. If someone badly needs something for survival, there can be other alternatives besides the obvious ones of either stealing or walking away. When someone mistreats you, there may be interesting possibilities besides the straightforward ones of combativeness or retreat. Moral decisions that involve complex human interactions are particularly liable to have a host of possible courses of action, in part because matters of style and nuance can make a real difference. Sometimes how one agrees or refuses to do something can matter almost as much as whether the answer is "Yes" or "No" What you do next, and a year later, can matter almost as much, also, as the immediate response.

Sometimes, though, it has to be said, there really are, for all practical purposes, only two possible responses. We are meant to imagine the case of the runaway trolley this way. In real life there might turn out to be a third, or even a fourth, alternative; but we are not told anything that would suggest this, and so are led to consider the case as a choice between two clear-cut alternatives. Further, what is about to happen—the death either of five people or of one—is both dramatic and stark; and again there is nothing that would lead us to consider possible actions after the track-shifting switch either is or is not pulled. In these respects (and others), the example is highly artificial. There are cases like this in real life, but hardly a great many. Cases in which there are more alternatives than first meet the eye and in which nuances matter in the way in which an alternative is executed or carried forward are much more common.

The argument, then, for holding that how someone construes morally problematic cases is likely to be closely related to how well that person behaves includes the following points. (1) We cannot subject more than a small fraction of the choices we make to moral scrutiny. (2) A triggering mechanism that alerts us that the situation we are in, or what we are about to do, has morally problematic elements therefore plays a crucial role in effective moral judgment. Someone whose viewing of the world does not include a finely tuned triggering mechanism is unlikely to behave very well. (3) Even when we do take a situation, or what we are about to do, as morally problematic, we are much more likely to behave well if we are sensitive to a broad range of relevant factors (including subtle variations between cases) than if we operate with a relatively crude and inflexible set of categories. (4) Further, someone whose viewing of the world includes moral imagination, which in some cases suggests a wider range of alternatives than the average person might think of, and which also can alert one to the importance of nuances in the execution of a choice, is likely to behave better than the average person.

Valencing of Possible Outcomes

Valencing may not be as sharply distinct from construal as one might think. At the core of valencing is a special element: the sense of something that is happening or may happen as positive in a rewarding way, or negative in a way that is the opposite of rewarding, or perhaps as not mattering one way or the other. (What is rewarding or unrewarding may be an entire way of life.) Typically the something is *seen as* positive, negative, or indifferent. Clearly, it often makes a difference to people whether the something is seen as positive or negative for them or merely for other people. It would be simplistic, though, to suppose that this always makes a very great difference. People often do something because it is seen as, say, making the neighbors happy, or as likely to save the life of an innocent person. Usually, in any case, the sense of something as positive, negative, or indifferent (for others or for oneself) is strongly associated with other features of the way in which it is construed.

This is not merely to say that there is a strong correlation between valencing and other features of construal. We expect that there have to be reasons in support of any judgment of valencing, especially one that is positive or negative. These typically are embedded in a thick description, one that may well be rejected by those who lean toward a different evaluation. Further, we sometimes find a judgment of valence incomprehensible if it lacks a connection with a thick description that flows smoothly into it.

The very positive is highly likely to be salient, with some accentuation of its alluring or admirable features, which may include connections with other positive prospective elements of the world. The loathsomeness or menace of the very negative is equally likely to be especially prominent. Perhaps, then, valencing should be seen as a special case of construing, one in which direction markers for seeking or avoiding are explicit?

Regardless of how one judges this, valencing often affects people in making choices. Typically, someone is much more likely to choose something if it is seen as including (or part of, or likely to lead to) a strongly positive element (especially if it is for her or him), or as avoiding something very negative. This is not always the case, however. Some people will not move toward what appears to them to be highly positive because to do so conflicts with their habits, or perhaps (if the benefit is for them) because they do not think they deserve something that good, or perhaps because they are stupid or thoughtless. The leading cause of people not moving toward what they see as desirable, though, is morality. Moralities typically teach that there are some temptations (even, occasionally, temptations to help others inappropriately) that should be rejected.

The foregoing should be taken as a preliminary sketch that avoids some complications. One that should be mentioned is that ambivalence is a common feature of many people's lives, so that sometimes it is by no means clear whether someone sees a certain element as positive or as negative, and it can be tempting to say that the answer is "both." A further complication is that it makes a difference whether one looks at an instant, or over a period of time, when the agent is drawn to something that nevertheless she or he has reasons to avoid. Standing temptations can play roles different from those of transitory, one-time temptations.

A simple example of this contrast is between the momentary decision by someone who is dieting of whether to accept an appealing piece of cake, on the one hand, and, on the other hand, the pattern of decisions that determine whether such a person stays successfully on the diet. Common experience is that it is easier to make the required decision on any specific occasion than it is to make similar decisions with the necessary consistency. Many moralists seem to have been aware of this. Kant for example, in the second Critique, gives an example of a depraved man who is asked to perjure himself so that an innocent man will be condemned. Kant insists that it is *possible* that the depraved man will make the morally upright choice (Kant 1788/1898, 118–119). Perhaps on the noumenal level, for Kant, anything that is virtuous is possible for a rational being. But there is a sense of "possible" in which anything that clearly goes against the causal order in our experience is not possible. Kant's claim that it is possible that the depraved man will do the right thing certainly looks plausible in relation to this sense. But it also leaves room for the thought it might not be possible (in this sense) for the depraved man to become, in very short order, an entirely virtuous person.

Kant famously claimed that valencing of outcomes should not determine moral choice. One should do right, he said, even though the heavens fall. Philosophers have their own temptations; and sometimes even a great philosopher yields to the temptation of making a dramatic and overstated claim, when a milder form would have more than a grain of truth. The issues that surround this will concern us in chapter 12.

Let us return to the question of how someone can come to make a good moral choice. It is far from clear that Kant would object to claims that valencing was relevant to *this* question. Indeed, Kant goes to some pains to point out the positive valence that we can attach to the dignity of rational choice.

Kant also acknowledged that societies build in rewards for good conduct, at least of the psychological and social sorts. It is largely because of these that, he observes, one cannot find a clear case in which someone acted out of duty alone, with no other motive mixing with that of behaving morally (Kant 1785/1981, 19). Typically, someone who behaves virtuously can expect to feel good about herself or himself, and usually there is an expectation also that trust and respect from the surrounding society will be augmented or maintained. These are important goods, and they (along with fear of their opposites) motivate us in a self-interested way. Most people do not see them as the only important goods, though, so that Kant also can observe that moral virtue does not correlate well, at least in this life, with happiness.

Bearing all of this in mind can give us a more complex and nuanced view of a combination—morally virtuous but sour—that I earlier suggested was not uncommon in our culture. Both terms of the contrast by now may look more problematic. The sour person who is morally virtuous almost certainly is motivated, in large part, by non-moral inducements, including a desire for self-approval and perhaps also for community respect. There may be other motivations that go along with these. Even if the community does not respond as it ought to, there is the quiet, bittersweet satisfaction of knowing how it should respond, along with the gratifying thought that the world owes one something for this failure of response. Thus, despite the sourness, the morally virtuous behavior does not lack links to an array of positively valenced elements that gratify the agent. Indeed, it may be that, for some people who appear virtuous but sour, the sourness is a mode of self-presentation, linked in our culture to the belief that true virtue is not easy or gratifying.

Much of what the virtuous-but-sour person would like to result from virtuous behavior would be put under the heading of self-interest. But also, if morality works (as it is generally assumed it should) for the common good, the results should include some that primarily benefit other people and (in cases in which one does not particularly care about those people) would not normally be put under the heading of self-interest. Most ethical views that give room to altruism would agree that considerations that go beyond self-interest are often ethically more important than those that would be included in self-interest.

This ethical importance of values beyond those of self-interest will be explored throughout this book, beginning in the next chapter. This chapter is devoted to the topic of how people come to make good choices. Motivation is crucial in this process; and it is clear that for most people motivation will be heavily influenced by perceived self-interest. Hence, to simplify the discussion in this chapter, I will concentrate on valencing that lies within the sphere of perceived self-interest. More altruistic valencing will regain the spotlight in the next chapter.

This psychology of virtue that feels itself unrewarded (even though it has quietly arranged some inner rewards) suggests that virtuous-but-sour should read virtuous (perhaps!)-but-(somewhat) sour. All the same, it looks as if there can be virtue that on the whole is not conducive to one's self-interest. This could be debated. Aristotle, especially, would deny that someone genuinely can have a virtue without enjoying the experience of exercising it, and in his account the satisfactions of virtue loom large enough so that he would reject the genuineness of any virtuous-but-sour combination. Similar lines of thought are found both in the *Analects* of Confucius and in the *Dialogues* of Plato.

It is possible that Plato, Aristotle, and Confucius, all of whom rejected the possibility of sour virtue, had never encountered anyone quite like Homo Kantus, a form of life that later appeared. There had been Old Testament precursors of Homo Kantus, whom they would not have known about; and it can be argued that there were individuals in ancient China and Greece who had a few of the qualities of Homo Kantus. Plato, Aristotle, and Confucius all have the intuition that a virtue, to be genuine, must be entirely reliable, and to be entirely reliable must be internalized, and to be internalized must be connected with major (indeed dominant) sources of satisfaction. But there may be no entirely compelling reason why there cannot be an alternative route to entire reliability, which takes the form of a combination of skillful casuistry (when needed) with unswerving allegiance to moral laws even if the unswerving allegiance is not the source of much satisfaction.

There are complex issues here. One of them concerns the viability of a law-centered conception of morality. Aristotle's discussion of the mean explores reasons why such a conception will not work for a large part of morality (although he is willing to concede some ground within morality), and the Confucian "doctrine of the mean" develops a remarkably similar view. Confucius certainly knew of some people whose lives had been entirely dominated by principle, and expresses skepticism about the validity of such an approach to all of life's major decisions. Unlike these, he says, he is flexible (*Analects*, 18.8, 221–222).

There also is the issue of the comparative advantages and disadvantages of having the dominant satisfactions in one's life having to do (in the approach favored by Plato, Aristotle, and Confucius) with one's own virtues. On the negative side, Nancy Sherman (1988) has suggested that there is something too self-absorbed about the "magnanimous man" as portrayed by Aristotle. On the other hand, it is arguable that someone whose pattern of virtuous behavior is largely immune to sourness can be more reliable than a virtuous(?)-but-sour person will be, especially when questions of "What is the point of this?" come to the fore. This issue is empirical, and it (like most empirical issues in psychology) very likely does not admit of a single answer that fits all cases. In the end, perhaps we might determine that some people in the virtuous(?)-but-sour category have a truly firm allegiance to a reasonable set of moral generalizations, and therefore can be argued to be genuinely morally virtuous, and that others in the virtuous(?)-but-sour category if appropriately pressed, tempted, or disoriented will fail.

Let us start with some commonsense reminders of what is obvious. For most people (i.e., for all but the purest specimens of Homo Kantus), valencing influences choice. This does not mean necessarily that most people always will choose what looks most desirable, or looks most desirable for them. Nor does it mean necessarily that most people will reject morality if a general policy of pursuing self-interest carries with it greater attractions. It does mean that in many situations, people will be more likely to regard something as the right choice if it involves positively valenced elements than if it does not. They may be especially motivated to pursue such a choice if some of the positively valenced elements are ones that benefit them.

Some philosophers, including Philippa Foot at one stage, have thought that morality could not be viable unless it did not conflict with self-interest (see Foot 1978b, 125 ff.). There are anticipations of this line of thought in Plato and in Hume's discussion of the character he calls the "sensible knave" (Hume 1751/1975, nos. 232–233, 282–284). All of these philosophers have argued that, if one properly understands the moral life, it becomes clear that the choice to be or to become a morally virtuous person does not conflict with self-interest (and that conflicts between self-interest and what is morally right either are non-existent, or will be at most temporary, or are such that a reasonable person would bet against the likelihood of their occurring in a serious form).

This conclusion is intended to be greeted with relief, given the implicit dependency thesis: that morality's power over intelligent people would be rather weak if it conflicted with self-interest. I want to argue for something more guarded than the dependency thesis, namely the quasi-dependency thesis that morality would lose its hold over many people if the perceived conflict with self-interest were particularly sharp and steady.

This weaker formulation is influenced by skepticism about broad and sweeping generalizations in this area. People vary both in the degree to which morality has a hold on them and in the degree to which self-love and perceived self-interest influence their conduct. Even if we put the claims of morality to the side, many people simply are not well-focused on the promotion of what they think of as their self-interest. And perceptions of what is in one's interest vary enormously. This is especially important for Plato, who clearly believes that most people are rather stupid about what is good for them; although all the same he is very alive to the importance of having a society in which what is virtuous harmonizes well with what most people *think* is good for them.

The congruence, or lack of congruence, between perceived self-interest and the dictates of morality can matter in different ways at two different stages. One is the stage at which someone's character is being formed. The parent can ask, "Will it be to the ultimate benefit of little so-and-so if I try to shape her or him into a morally virtuous person?" assuming that the parent wants what is best for the child. The child is not likely to ask this question, but in theory could; and, in any event, in the process of character formation the child can have a strong sense that virtue generally pays, or alternatively that it generally does not pay.

The second stage will be the one at which character is largely formed but remains open to reconsideration. At an early point in this stage, an adolescent might self-consciously want to strengthen her or his tendencies toward virtue, perhaps by transforming good habits into real understanding of goodness. Alternatively, there can be a sense that the virtue with which one was inculcated as a child is at its root foolish, something that works for the benefit of other people but not for oneself. Such a perception can have an effect at any time in life. But it may be that most people are more open to reconsideration of who they are (or are in the process of becoming), and more capable of pursuing the gradual modification of their natures, in adolescence than later in their lives.

Early childhood is widely seen as the key to the promotion of moral virtue. Aristotle points the way toward a minimization of strains between morality and perceived self-interest. Those managing the child's development can take care to see that conduct that points in the direction of future virtue becomes associated in the child's mind with pleasure, and that conduct pointing to future lack of virtue becomes associated with pain. This presumably is not easy, both because misbehavior can be exciting at any age (and the effort required to behave properly can be tiresome) and also because much misbehavior will be motivated by goals whose attainment seems pleasant. Nevertheless, Aristotle holds that the child can be steered by the rudders of pleasure and pain (1984, bk. 10, sec. 1, 1852). This would have to involve rewards and punishments. It is not specified whether the pleasures and pains will be physical or purely psychological. Experience suggests that sometimes sheer approval or disapproval can be pleasant or painful, and then of course there can be privileges that are bestowed or withheld. What is crucial is that, rather in the manner of Pavlov's dogs who came to associate a bell ringing with food, the child will come to associate misbehavior with pain and good behavior with pleasure.

The point of this strategy of getting children to associate virtuous behavior with pleasure presupposes two highly plausible psychological assumptions. One is that the behavior of the great majority of people past childhood is largely determined by the previous pattern of their lives, along with the sequence of actions that they are in. In other words, most of us most of the time carry on. If, through the rudders of pleasure and pain we can nudge the child (who comes to associate virtuous behavior with pleasure) into patterns of virtuous action, then it is likely that such behavior will be continued, especially if the child, when grown, enters into sequences of behavior whose continuation fits the pattern. Barring a dislocation, we usually can regard that child as safely on a path of virtuous behavior.

A second psychological assumption is that—again barring a dislocation—the childhood sense that virtuous behavior is associated with pleasure and bad behavior with pain is unlikely to be severely eroded. First of all, even if the parents are not present to reinforce good behavior with pleasure, and so forth, in most stable societies the community in general will perform a similar function. People will be helped to feel good about themselves if they are cooperative, kind, and so on, and may be encouraged to feel bad about themselves if they are blatantly selfish, unkind, mean-spirited, and so forth. As Kant pointed out, self-interested motivations of this sort ("dear self") seem always to be part of the mix that leads to virtuous choices (Kant 1785/1981, 20). These mechanisms for maintaining the child's conditioning when she or he is an adult often are, it should be said, far less reliable and less strong than those in childhood that depend on parents and teachers. Nevertheless they cannot be disregarded.

All of this suggests that it would be oversimple to suppose that assessments of self-interest entirely determine an individual's attitude toward morality. Childhood conditioning, especially when reinforced in later life, can have considerable weight.

Further, not everyone constantly monitors how enjoyable life seems; and such monitoring, even when it takes place, is hardly a matter of precise measurement. Even if a life of virtuous behavior that in childhood was quite enjoyable gradually becomes less enjoyable, this may well not register in any disturbing way. Barring some sudden disturbance or revelation (either of which would amount to a dislocation), someone can carry on much as before without serious revision of the general view of life. Even if the decline in the enjoyability of virtuous behavior is noted, this can be regarded as temporary. The adult whose conditioning has not worn off can carry a hard-to-articulate sense that surely what one remembers as the norm will be restored.

Much of this discussion will seem to many readers to be unattractively cynical. It lacks, they may feel, the proper reverence for true goodness. But any such reader should reflect that part of what is at issue (in this discussion, and much of the remainder of this book) is just what true goodness is. From Confucius and Plato on, this has been argued to be highly problematic. Even the most rigorous moralists, such as Immanuel Kant, if they were serious and not sentimental, thought it important to be cynical about cases of apparent virtue. Some of this cynicism is self-directed (as it clearly was in Kant's case.) Conversely, anyone who thinks that she or he is perfect is definitely not to be trusted. Such a person can be governed by grossly self-interested motivations whose true nature is disguised from the person whom they rule.

Part of what I have been arguing is that, thanks in part to childhood conditioning (and perhaps continued support of this from the surrounding community), an adult can continue to associate virtuous behavior with pleasure. Even if the correlation between virtuousness and pleasure becomes weak, many people may carry on. Even if there are reasons to think that there is likely to be greater pleasure in a life less virtuous, some people may stay on course. This discrepancy between the virtuousness of the behavior and the pleasure in the life can grow considerably. This is why the sour person who, by most people's standards, counts as virtuous represents a traditional possibility in our culture.

All of this amounts to an argument for a loose, rather than a tight, connection between perceived self-interest and virtue. It may well be that for most people there needs to be some connection. A continued extreme conflict between personal virtue and perceived self-interest would be a severe test, and it is hard to be confident that very many would pass. On the other hand, it may be that many people would choose well in response to a sudden and unexpected conflict: this would be testimony to their virtue, but in some cases also would reflect the ways in which the habits and mind-sets of a lifetime are not quickly modified. Many people also might carry on in virtuous behavior despite a continued mild conflict between personal virtue and perceived self-interest. Aristotle is surely right that the congruence between good behavior and self-interest matters most in childhood.

Hence the claim argued for is not that valencing (even if this is restricted to valencing of self-interest) always is crucial to good behavior. It is, rather, that it often matters a great deal. Two ways in which it can matter stand out. One is that many people can weaken their allegiance to moral norms if there is a continuing conflict between, on one hand, following these norms and, on the other hand, perceived self-interest. The virtuous(?)–but-sour person is an exception to this pattern. But it has been suggested that being virtuous(?) but sour can well include some quiet satisfactions. If the conflict between the pattern of behavior and perceived self-interest intensified, it may well be that some virtuous(?)-but-sour people might weaken their allegiance to moral norms.

Another way in which valencing (especially of self-interest) can make a difference to goodness of behavior is this. Lapses from patterns of good behavior often occur because of temptations or threats. Plainly, how appealing the temptation is can make a difference, as can how unappealing what is threatened seems. In Plato's example of the ring of invisibility, the temptation to abuse the ring might well be overwhelming for someone who deeply desires money and power. The reader is meant to think that, for Socrates, who chiefly values the harmony of his mind and the clarity of his thought, the temptation would not be significant. A similar point applies to the implicit threats of death to those who disobeyed the order to arrest Leon of Salamis.

Even if the connection between perceived self-interest and loyalty to standards of good behavior is, as I have been arguing, loose, it is real enough for virtually everybody. The implications of this for moral education should be noted. Too often, moral education is geared to the model of the moral codebook, in which children memorize and swear allegiance to a list of rules. It may be that something of this sort is necessary to the development of moral virtue, but that does not mean that it is sufficient. The examination of the relation of good behavior to valencing of outcomes suggests that some attention needs to be given to the values and sense of perceived self-interest of those in the process of acquiring virtue.

3

The Relevance of Construal
and Valencing to Good Choice

To say that construal and valencing affect how people come to make their choices is hardly surprising. How important is this? Much depends on whether one sees normative ethics on the model of problem-solving software or instead as intended to provide understanding of the major features of good lives. Given the first view, one would regard the discussions of the previous chapters as marginal to ethical philosophy. The second view (which is integral to "virtue ethics") would see them as central and important.

Even if one regards normative ethics as primarily a supplier of problem-solving software, there remain questions of how one enables the software to "read" the problems it is designed to solve. Further, some people misuse their software or forget about it. The previous chapters shed some light on these phenomena. They also, though, point to respects in which any general rules, principles, or guidelines for decision to be got from normative ethics have to be supplemented, both by interpretative guidelines and by judgments of importance or value. This chapter will explore these.

Here is one way to see the relation between the previous two chapters and this one. The previous chapters explored processes that are important to virtue ethics, but that on the problem-solving-software view of ethics would be seen largely as stage setting. This chapter will argue that, even on the problem-solving-software view, they are not merely stage setting but in fact can be a crucial part of ethical decision. Why do philosophers who take the problem-solving-software view usually ignore this? One reason is that the recent philosophical literature tends to dwell on examples in which factors of construal and valencing can be taken for granted and thus ignored.

Construal in Ethical Judgment

There are familiar sorts of cases in which construal does almost all of the work of ethical judgment, but at the same time construal is easy and obvious. If Bill is short of money and wants to take Mary's purse while her back is turned, his friends might say, "That would be stealing." Typically, that is all that need be said. Plainly, moral codes work as smoothly as they sometimes do because their categories are mirrored in the ways in which most people immediately construe the situations they are in and the options open to them.

The last chapter indicated that the construal relevant to choice is a more complicated process than the case of Bill and Mary's purse might indicate. There is a stage in which responses appropriate to problematic cases may or may not be triggered. One can go along without any thought that what one is about to do, or to avoid doing, is at all problematic. Alternatively, the situation, or what one might be about to do in it, can be construed as problematic, or perhaps one element of the situation or possible course of action jumps out as calling for consideration.

The phenomenology of triggering does not look simple or uniform. Sometimes one feels uneasy or disturbed. One may feel revulsion at something that is present or that can be imagined as the result of some action. Sometimes a person will simply snap to ethical attention. Alternatively, someone can have a sense that this is a moment that seems to call out for ethical attention, but nevertheless brush any such inclination aside (perhaps leaving an uneasy feeling in the back of the mind). Construal at the stage of ethical attention also can be complicated. In the simplest cases, such as Bill's, we may simply reach for a label. The label can connect with an element of the ethical software ("Stealing is wrong") so that the software "reads" the case. The most comfortable possibility is that the label gives only the information required for this connection and gives no other information that might be distracting or lead to doubts or hesitations. In this respect, "That would be stealing" is perfect: we can fasten on a clear solution and get on with our lives. "That would be stealing a crust of bread, and the person about to steal it is suffering from malnutrition" is much more uncomfortable.

Perhaps a subfield of the history of philosophy should be the history of philosophical examples? A chapter could be devoted to Kant. In the *Grounding of the Metaphysics of Morals,* he helps the reader understand the workings of the categorical imperative by giving four examples of its operation. Each of them involves a simply formulated case (with no distracting or mitigating features in view), illustrating (respectively) making false promises, suicide, neglect of one's talents (which Kant regards as violating a duty to oneself), and refusing ever to help others. The examples lend themselves to a simple understanding of how ethics works, although in the same work Kant makes it clear that judgment is required to connect a case with the categorical imperative (1785/1981, 3).

In part II of the *Metaphysics of Morals* Kant elaborates on complications, giving special attention to the role of casuistry. He gives a more complicated example, related to what might or might not be suicide. Frederick the Great carried a fast-acting poison into battle with him, so that if he were captured he would not be forced to agree to disadvantageous conditions of ransom. The question is whether he could be charged with a "criminal (suicidal) intention" (1797/1996, Doctrine of Virtue, part I, chap. 1, art. 1, Casuistical Questions, 178). It is not entirely clear whether Kant did think that this case was difficult to characterize correctly and to decide, or whether his refusal simply to provide the right answer (as he did for his cases in the *Grounding*) was a result of deference to (or caution about) Prussian state censorship.

Let us return to the category of stealing, whose moral valence in the general run of cases is less open to controversy than is that of suicide. Undoubtedly on a great many occasions, "That would be stealing" is (a) clearly true, and (b) all that need be said. If someone said, instead, "That would be stealing by a short bald man with credit card debts from a tall thin woman with some money in the bank and no credit card debts," almost everyone would readily agree that this gives us more than we need to know. Everything beyond the first four words is pretty much irrelevant.

What would count as a relevant addition to "That would be stealing"? That what was stolen was a crust of bread looks relevant, in part because of smallness of what is taken and in part because it corresponds so closely to a basic need, a thought that is reinforced if we are told that the thief was suffering from malnutrition. But then we might want to know whether the person stolen from was also suffering from malnutrition. Some people would consider how the thief arrived at his parlous condition: if the thief endured an economic depression or discrimination in hiring against members of his group, this will be received differently from news that he spent all his money on drugs.

Suppose Bill simply denies that what he is about to do is stealing. The purse is, he says, one lost a short while ago by his wife or sister. Or it may be that Mary owes him a considerable sum that she has failed to pay. A slightly more complicated case might have Bill as a now unemployed worker, and Mary as the factory owner who refused to give him the back pay that he had been promised. Bill may not claim that the purse is his, but he could claim that the money inside it is. Or perhaps Bill and Mary are shipwrecked on an island, and Mary finds all of the food on the island and stuffs it into two containers she controls. When Bill attempts to take one of them, and she says, "That would be stealing," there is room for argument.

If something is a relevant addition to "That would be stealing," in what ways might it be relevant? In the simplest case, it changes the moral valence. Perhaps we would decide that the addition makes what is at stake not really stealing, and not really wrong. Some would argue that there also are cases that count as stealing but are not really wrong. Probably many people would view the case of the man with malnutrition stealing the crust of bread in this way. There is Lawrence Kohlberg's well-known example of Heinz, who steals medicine (which he cannot obtain except by stealing it from an unreasonable pharmacist) that will save his dying wife. Kohlberg thought that anyone at an advanced stage of moral development would see that Heinz should take the medicine, although he does not suggest that this would not count as stealing: all of this seems to amount to the option "Stealing but right" for this case (Kohlberg 1981).

Additional information can change our response in more complicated ways. It can be a mistake to regard our alternatives as only two: "Morally acceptable/allow" and "Morally wrong/condemn." More nuanced responses may be far more appropriate.

In the case of the man with malnutrition and the crust of bread, many might think that there have to be better options open to the man than stealing the crust. But then we want to know what these might be. It is possible in the end that, especially in a constricted society or in one that severely limits options for some of its members, the choice for the man with malnutrition really is the stark one of stealing or not stealing. Often, though, there are more complicated strategies that will get him food. In these cases, we then may have to consider difficult questions of a different sort, concerned with how capable of pursuing these strategies we reasonably can expect him to be. These different questions will have to do with the issues of blame and responsibility. Blame itself can admit of degrees, which in ordinary speech can be indicated by tones of voice. Some factors can excuse an action of a sort that we would normally blame; other factors may not excuse, but they will mitigate.

All of this constitutes a complex subject, one that deserves a whole book on its own. For the purposes of this book, two points should be stressed. One is that cases like those in which "That would be stealing" says all that we need to know, though frequent, do not exhaust the subject matter of normative ethics. Test cases for genuine virtue can be very different from these; and it is likely that most people on some occasions will encounter situations that call out for ethical consideration and will matter greatly to their lives, in which what is important cannot be stated briefly.

The second point is that the nature of the courses of action open to someone, as well as of the problematic situation, can defy simple summarization. Even when "Just say 'no'" is useful advice, there might be significant differences in the quality of this response depending on how one says "no" or on just what (having said "no") one goes on to do. Style and nuance can matter a great deal, especially in matters in which a personal relationship (or rapport, or lack of rapport) is a significant factor. In the end, much of what matters may be hardly possible to formulate adequately in words. Often in life, "Just say 'no'" (or "Just say 'yes'") turns out to be a beguiling oversimplification.

Then there are cases in which there are interesting and plausible alternatives, which may take some degree of moral imagination to think of, intermediate between "Yes" and "No." When an unreasonable political authority makes demands, for example, there can be possibilities more attractive than those of simple acquiescence, on one hand, or flat refusal or combativeness, on the other. Negotiation or temporizing or dialogue can turn out to be useful, and there can be modes of semi-compliance. There are ways of saying "Yes" that are not entirely "Yes," or "No" that are not entirely "No."

An Editorial Observer report by Tina Rosenberg in the *New York Times* (August 11, 2000, A18) nicely illustrates this possibility. There is purportedly documentation, which may well have been faked, to the effect that Lech Walesa, leader of the Solidarity movement, which was the primary force in undermining and overthrowing the tyrannical Polish communist government, during the process had signed an agreement to cooperate with that government. The writer of the report observes that "Walesa was perfectly capable of signing anything and then behaving as he pleased," and speaks of his "calculated duplicity," which was so effective that "at the height of the Solidarity movement, top Communist leaders were convinced that he could be won over." If Walesa did sign an agreement with the authorities, it was part of a winning strategy that made millions of people's lives better.

The argument up to this point is that even when what seems crucial in a morally problematic situation is an element (e.g., stealing) that the great majority of people would see in much the same way (using the same key terms), simple cases in which this is all we need to know are not entirely the norm. Other features are often morally relevant and complicate the picture. And the menu of possible responses is often more complicated than it seems at first to be.

Hence, though in some simple cases the element of construal can be taken for granted, this is often not true even when the central moral category of the case is uncontroversial and easy to apply. What of cases that have more room for controversy about whatever appears to be the central moral category? What of those in which it very often is not easy to apply?

Some psychological research on construal should be mentioned. This includes the well-known work of Tversky and Kahneman (1984) on "framing." They have pointed out ways in which how we see and judge a case can have very much to do with how it is presented. This is especially true if risk aversion is a factor, or if a choice can be framed either in terms of possible gains or of possible losses. Some framing strategies appear to tap into a deep vein of human irrationality.

To the extent that this connects with our topic, it reinforces the point that construal matters to the quality of ethical judgment. Other support comes from Timothy Wilson's contrast between conscious reflective construal of a decision and unconscious framing, provided by "the automatic pilot of the mind" (see Wilson 2002, 14). In difficult cases, it may be desirable to proceed from the rigidity of the adaptive unconscious (55 ff.) to a conscious construal that looks ahead and entertains a range of possibilities.

Construal: Two Cases

Let me suggest that conscious reflection on construal is especially appropriate when relevant categories clearly are contestable. Take, as one example, cases that can elicit the judgment "That would be sexist." This can be contentious because (a) the consensus that sexism is wrong is not as great as that stealing is wrong, and (b) there may be more frequent arguments about whether a case at hand involves sexism than there are for stealing. Another initial example is "That would violate the requirement of respect for persons." This is not a remark frequently heard on the street, but it does have importance in the way many philosophers would like to approach normative problems by means of generalizations. A requirement of respect for persons has been favored as an especially appealing version of Kant's second formulation of the categorical imperative. Even non-Kantians like me can find extremely plausible its claim to be something akin to a valid fundamental ethical principle. But it, too, leaves a great deal of room for contention.

Let us begin with "That would be sexist." The core meaning is that whatever it is would violate the principle or ideal of equality between women and men. There are live current issues here. My position is roughly that of most feminists. But that position will not be argued for in this book, and nothing will hang on whether the reader happens to accept it or not. Our concern is with the extent to which judgments of construal are required in arriving at a reasonable position on issues of sexism. People with opposed views can agree that construal plays an important required role in any apt determination of the issues.

During a long-running struggle over equality of the sexes, points of contention have kept changing. At an early stage, the intuition at the root of feminism was that if X is a woman and Y is a man, and X and Y are in situations that do not differ significantly except for the gender of the person in them, then X and Y should be treated in the same way. Gender in itself should not matter in how someone is treated.

Issues of equal treatment have been various. An early battleground, some time ago, concerned very basic economic and civic rights, such as property rights and the right to vote. These now look exceptionally uncontentious. In the early stages of the struggle for women's rights, a standard line of argument for someone on the conservative side was to say, of the case in which X and Y are in situations that are similar except for their genders, that there will be significant further differences between X and Y as a result of the difference in gender. These further differences, the anti-feminist then argued, justify different treatment. But an argument of this sort, in relation to basic property rights, looks very flimsy. It may be that some people thought, given deep inequalities in economic power, that if women voted, their votes would be overly influenced by their male relatives. But this, too, looks flimsy. No one today would take it seriously for a minute.

It is worth bearing in mind, all the same, that elements of a dysfunctional social order (or one that is crippling for some of its members) can mutually reinforce one another. It is unlikely that they will all be changed at once. Hence, that other elements of the social order are such-and-such often can be used as an argument against changing the one that people currently are trying to modify.

In this way, the limited economic opportunities available to women and the social norm that presumed that a woman would marry and then concentrate her attention for at least several years on her children could be used to deny higher education to women. Once this barrier was removed, a fallback position was to deny to women (or severely to restrict) graduate and professional training. One argument was that, even if a woman did have some kind of career as a doctor, lawyer, or academic, the odds were that it would be truncated because of the years spent at home with children. It seemed a more efficient use of social resources to devote these to the training of men, who almost certainly would not take time off.

One way to meet such arguments is to take the long view that insists "Other things will need to be changed." But the further change may not be inevitable, and it is likely that some people will question whether it will be advantageous. Arguments about further changes in social norms will be complicated by the unpredictability, and also the mixed nature, of the results that will attend any significant social change.

It also may turn out to be virtually impossible to find a single major change in moral norms and social policy, ever, that (however good it was) did not have some consequences that were not good. Throughout history, clouds have had silver linings, and bright advances have had cloudy elements. Some African-American scholars have argued, for example, that increased housing opportunities for African Americans as a result of the civil rights movement had drained inner-city ghettos of some positive role models (cf. Brooks 1996, 231 ff.). It also has been suggested that increased professional opportunities for women in the last half of the twentieth century have led to a decrease in the number of brilliant and charismatic women pursuing careers as secondary school or elementary school teachers, with a consequent negative effect on the quality of schools.

These examples are chosen, it should be said, precisely because they involve improvements in opportunity required to satisfy very minimal standards of justice. Hardly anyone now would question their desirability. They are a reminder that the fact that a change involves *some* unfortunate consequences need not be a telling argument against it. One needs to look at larger pictures.

In any event, some of the live issues now of gender equality are very different from those in earlier phases. Not all of the old issues have gone away, by any means. But two very different sorts of issue have assumed importance.

One concerns comparability. There used to be clear-cut cases in which a woman and a man, doing the same job, would be paid different salaries. (An argument sometimes used to defend this appealed to a secondary difference: men were presumed to need money to support families.) Undoubtedly, there still are cases of this sort of thing, but a more common ground of contention is the case in which a woman and a man do different kinds of jobs, but their jobs appear to be equally demanding (in terms of skills, energy, and time). Should they not be paid the same?

Another sort of issue arises from the argument that the old order, built around inequality of the sexes, has not entirely changed and perhaps never will. In the foreseeable future, for example, many women will spend a great deal of time and energy on the care of small children, and relatively few men will. Many more women than men will interrupt their careers because of this. The socialization of girls and boys also will continue usually to be (in all likelihood) different in ways that will enable more men than women to be comfortable with the idea of conspicuous success in career competition and to be assertive toward this end. (For related issues, see Meyers 1987.)

Differences here, it should be stressed, will hardly be uniform. There can be increasing numbers of assertive and extremely confident women who devote themselves entirely to their careers, and of men who are not extremely assertive or competitive and spend considerable time with small children. Nevertheless, it is quite possible that, if we look at entire populations instead of at individuals, there will continue to be differences that favor the success of men over that of women.

If so, then providing women and men with equal opportunities will require various allowances for handicaps imposed by remaining elements of the old order, and perhaps strategies to compensate for the effects of these. The core intuition in the position that many feminists would take does not concern an X and a Y who are presumed the same except for gender. Rather it concerns an X and a Y likely to be unequal in their prior advantages or in the handicaps that they can expect. The argument is that what by the older standards might have counted as equal treatment would in fact amount to (in the real world of differential advantages and handicaps) ratifying inequality.

If two groups are to have equal opportunities, the argument goes, then they need more than merely equal permission to do this or that. Confidence and the ability to rebound from reverses without being too discouraged can count toward success quite as much as innate ability. Hence truly equal chances of success may require extra efforts at confidence building in some places. It also may require making allowances for family-related interruptions in careers or for periods of diminished productivity caused by the demands of caring for small children.

All of this is open to debate. Indeed, for the purposes of this book that is the main point. Anyone whose view of morality begins and ends with examples like "That would be stealing" or "That would be murder" and so on will think of morality as cut and dried, an area in which familiar rules or principles straightforwardly solve all of the problems and all normal adults can be presumed to know right from wrong. But there are important moral problems, which are not cut and dried, connected with such judgments as "That would be sexist." Considerable judgment and reflection are required, and a conscientious person not wedded to a position may reasonably think sometimes that she or he does not *know* what is right and what is wrong.

The mere judgment "That is sexist" can be contentious in at least two ways. First, there can be room for argument about what counts as sexist. If a woman and a man, both about thirty-five years old, apply for a position, and the professional accomplishments of the man are slightly (but only very slightly) more impressive, but the woman has devoted several years to the primary care of small children, is it sexist to favor the candidate with the slightly stronger record? A lot depends on how one "sees" the case.

Second, we need to remember that categories that play a major role in moral judgment typically involve a bias or a stance in relation to what is acceptable or unacceptable. "That would be stealing" gets its power from a presumed tendency to condemn "stealing." Probably no one would call this a "bias," because there is such a strong consensus that stealing is generally unacceptable. The main issues have been settled very long ago. A staunch anti-feminist, though, would certainly deny that the main issues regarding sexism have been settled and would insist that the very use of the category incorporates a bias.

Someone who takes this position could respond to uses of the category "sexism" in one or both of two ways. One is to contract severely the zone of what he or she thinks genuinely constitutes sexism, denying that many cases really fit the category. The other is to block the attempted association of normative thrust with the descriptive label. This can be done by putting the key word in quotation marks. "Perhaps that is 'sexism,'" the staunch anti-feminist might say, "but what is so bad about 'sexism'?"

There is a natural transition here, from the contentiousness of construal related to sexism to the other promised example, the judgment "That would run counter to the principle of respect for persons." Much in feminism—the part that most people find easiest to understand—is concerned with the rewards of success (chiefly money and prestige) or with the costs of lack of competitive success (such as poverty and low social status). The feminist argument here can focus on (a) fairness in allocating rewards and costs, or (b) what is required to equalize chances for success and risks of lack of success. But many forms of feminism go beyond issues of success, money, and prestige and focus at a deeper level on ways in which social roles connect with forms of human fulfillment. Discrimination and poverty are evils, but additional objects of concern in some forms of feminism are the phenomena of condescension, lack of respect, and lack of encouragement for anything directed toward personal fulfillment.

The root intuition is that there are important things in life besides money and being well-fed, well-housed, and comfortable. Fulfillment of important capacities in personal relationships and in aesthetic or intellectual pursuits matters a great deal. If women are educated and treated in ways that discourage this, that is a great loss for them. We may recall that one of the four examples that Kant deploys in the *Grounding* concerns the moral requirement to develop one's talents. Neglect of one's talents then counts, for Kant, as morally wrong. Presumably, then, anything that tends to discourage or prevent a fellow rational being from developing her talents will be morally questionable, to say the least. (The pro-feminist implications of this are a separate matter from Kant's personal views, whatever they were. His theory had legs.)

In general, it can be argued that to treat someone who has rational capacities as not possibly having talents to be developed (which is how many women traditionally were treated) should be construed in the Kantian mode as failure of respect for persons. Plainly a wide variety of moral lapses could be placed under this heading. Respect for persons most clearly includes not behaving toward someone else in a way that one would not will to be a universal law (which includes your not behaving toward someone in a way in which you would not want someone to behave toward you). In this light, murder, theft, rape, and torture all are failures of respect for persons. Indeed, in Kant's scheme the requirement of respect for persons includes all of morality. This is linked to Kant's insistence that the three versions he provides of the categorical imperative are equivalent: the first (which insists on the ability to will what one does as universal law) lays out the formal requirements of morality, while the second (respect for persons, which includes not treating others merely as means and not as ends) identifies the objects of respect that ground morality, and the third (which requires that we act as if we are in a realm of ends in which virtue can be presumed of everyone) tells us the ideal toward which morality points.

For anyone who has studied Kant, this is elementary. What is less elementary is that the three formulations, equivalent though they may be, provide pictures of moral life in which different elements—and different kinds of case—are emphasized. We might concede that murder is always, in some sense, a failure of respect for persons. But that is not a way in which we would normally talk about it. We do not speak of serial killers in terms of heinous and repeated acts of disrespect for persons. Conversely, if someone is raped and humiliated, our first complaint is not likely to be that this cannot be willed to be a universal law (although we would agree that it cannot). We will be struck most by the contempt and brutal disregard in what was done.

One moral concept that seems extremely important when we look through the lens of respect for persons is that of personal dignity. Kant did a great deal to advance the idea, radical in the hierarchical society of his time, that any rational being, regardless of abilities or accomplishments, had to be treated with a certain minimum regard, had to be regarded indeed as morally consider-able. The idea that a rational being should never be treated as a mere means is meant, among other things, to rule out harming (physically or financially) an innocent rational being for one's own purposes or convenience. But it also would seem to rule out arranging that person's life without consideration of what it is that she or he wants. Even benevolent management of the lives of other adults might be argued to count, in the Kantian scheme, as a failure of respect for persons. It could be seen as treating rational beings who have autonomy as if they were dogs, cats, or small children.

All of this is arguable in broad outline, it should be said; but then there will be many issues open to judgment. What counts as due consideration of someone's wishes? In what kinds of case is it justifiable, in the end, simply to override what a person being helped prefers?

Let us return to the broad apparent implications of a principle of respect for persons. One could argue that a good deal in common courtesy has, viewed from this angle, a quasi-moral element, as does taking the trouble to listen to what other people have to say. This suggests a topic to which we will return: the way in which respect for persons can be thought of not so much as an abstract principle encoded in our moral software, but rather as a set of attitudes and habits that play a part generally in human interactions. This is a wider role that goes well beyond what we would normally think of as moral choice.

As appealing as the Kantian invocation of respect for persons is, its imprecision by now should be evident. Is it a failure of respect for persons if someone abruptly hangs up a telephone when hearing a telemarketer's voice? If Heinz, in Kohlberg's case of the man who steals medicine to save his dying wife, simply takes it without an extended attempt to get the extortionate pharmacist to see reason, is that a failure of respect for persons? If a government requires seat-belt use, is that a failure of respect for the persons of adults whose choice is not to wear them?

An example of a different sort is provided by Kant's insistence that were human society to dissolve, the last murderer should first be executed (Kant 1797/1996, The Doctrine of Right No. 49, 106). Is failure to execute the murderer a failure of respect for persons? It seems likely that Kant thought that the answer was "yes": not to execute the murderer marks a failure to treat him or her as a responsible adult.

Part of the point here is connected with W. B. Gallie's insight that there are important concepts (such as freedom or democracy) that are "essentially contestable" (1964). The concepts have great normative weight, and at the same time their extensions are not tightly fixed, so that there is the constant possibility that people will refer to rather different things as freedom or as democracy without flatly going counter to a widely understood and agreed upon meaning. This is an important insight, although I would quarrel with the word "essentially." Any concept can become contestable, especially if it happens to have great normative weight. Conversely, a consensus can form around what is meant by a term that had been contestable. "Sexism" at present is, as we have seen, a contestable concept; but it is imaginable that in a few hundred years it will not be.

"Respect for persons" is contestable in much the way in which "democracy" is. This is not to say that either term is entirely indefinite and diffuse in its meaning. A political system in which one person rules (and there are no claims of popular support for the ruler and no elections) would fall outside any intelligible use of the word "democracy"; and there are comparable cases of arrogant and contemptuous behavior that could not be construed as respect for persons. Cases in which there are elections and expressions of popular support, but also considerable room for doubt as to how genuine these are, become debatable instances of democracy. Ones in which there is some consideration for other people's needs and wants, but not much, become debatable instances of respect for persons.

Concepts such as sexism and respect for persons can have important uses in ethical reflection, focusing our attention on aspects that matter, even if the concepts are contestable and not at all precise. Their use points toward a model of ethical judgment very different from the one that might be suggested by cases in which Bill takes Mary's purse (simply because he needs money) and Bill's friends say, "That is stealing." The concept of stealing, in ordinary cases of this sort, completes a very contained reflective circuit and should end discussion. The concepts of sexism and of respect for persons open up a much larger area of consideration, and often should not end discussion.

This is connected with another contrast. In the case in which Bill needs money and takes Mary's purse, almost all of us see things in the same way, so that the element of construal becomes unnoticeable. Further, no one has to explain herself or himself to the others, or engage in the kind of interpretative negotiations that are required when interested parties see a situation in different ways. Cases of alleged sexism or failure of respect for persons can be very different from this. Construal, so transparent in the textbook cases like that of Bill and Mary, begins to shimmer before our eyes.

Much of moral life, including most of the more interesting and troubling parts, has this quality. Construal is a prominent factor in judgment. We cannot convince anyone that the choice we favor is the right one until we can convince them that our way of seeing the problematic situation, and what the possible responses to it are, is better than the alternatives. Part of making good decisions then is seeing things the right way.

Skepticism about Construal

The phrase "seeing things the right way" may strike some readers as jarring. Someone who has followed the argument and who agrees that there are important moral questions in relation to which construal is crucial (and is not at all transparent) may want to go a step further and deny that there is any "right way" of construing what is relevant to such questions. The denial can take two forms. The radical version is the relativistic claim that we are never in a position to say that any way of construing a problematic situation (or the possible responses to it) is better than any other. A less radical alternative is to agree that there are good and not so good construals, but to deny that there is ever an optimal construal that can simply be labeled "the right" one.

A full argument against relativism of construals will come later in the book. Considerable investigation of ethical theory is required for it to be assembled. In the meantime, there are considerations that might suggest the implausibility of a relativism of construals.

One reason why such a relativism might be initially appealing is this. It might seem that the only time there clearly are standards for good and bad interpretations is when there is a text to be interpreted and an author or authors whose intentions might be relevant. Morally problematic situations lack the characteristics on which interpretations can be grounded, a skeptic will contend.

An outline of an answer to this is that construal in the writing of history and social science parallels that in ethical deliberation. Judgments of importance can be made, based on how significantly lives are changed. These judgments in turn rest in part on axiological judgments of positive or negative values and on estimations of causal connections that elements of an unfolding reality may have with one another. Without appealing prematurely to investigations in the last part of this book, we can say that there are standards for apt or reasonable construals of morally problematic situations (and of the possible responses to them) that are parallel to standards for objectivity in history and the social sciences. Much as there are accounts in history and the social sciences that any reasonable and knowledgeable person would consider insufficiently objective and biased, so also there are construals that are unreasonable because they are one-sided, neglect important features, or overemphasize what is trivial.

Some examples can convey the implausibility of a relativism of construals. If a child is not allowed to go to school and is forced to live with a chain around his or her neck and to sleep in a dog house, is it an adequate construal if we describe this simply as a firm attempt to impart discipline and a sense of humility? If a powerful ethnic group sets up "rape camps," in which women of a different ethnic group are repeatedly violated and humiliated, can this be construed as a well-intentioned attempt to remind those in the camp of the realities of power and of sexuality? It seems most implausible to maintain that these construals are as valid as an alternative vision that takes the two examples to illustrate brutal failure of respect for persons.

What about the less radical denial (which does not amount to relativism) of the claim that there is a single "right" construal of morally problematic situations (or of possible responses to them)? It should be clear by now that this less radical denial need not be far from my position. We might agree that there are good construals and inadequate construals, and that the relativist is wrong in holding that any one is as good as any other. I will concede that in fairly complicated and subtle cases, there is more than one good way (and no way that is definitive and optimal) to construe what is relevant.

However, there are cases that lend themselves to stark and discrete alternatives, both in how they are to be construed and in what we should recommend as appropriate choice. The one in which Bill, because he needs money, takes Mary's purse is of that sort, as are those of the humiliated child and the women in the rape camps. No doubt there are subtle variations in judgments of how we should construe Bill's action and behave toward him, and similarly in the other cases, such that it would be difficult to adjudicate which (of the very similar judgments) is optimal and could be said to be best. But for practical purposes, we can say that any good construal of the case of Bill and Mary is that what he is about to do is stealing and he should not do it, and any good construal of the other two cases is that what they present is monstrous and should not be allowed. In ordinary speech, we can say that these seem to us to be the "right" ways of seeing the cases. To speak of the "right" construal in such cases does not imply any denial that there could be subtle variations among which it might be impossible to adjudicate. It does imply that for practical purposes no reasonable person (in such cases) would worry about them.

Valencing of Possible Outcomes

One of the criteria of a good construal is that it treats as important—as having weight in what we should do—what deserves to be treated as important. This leaves room for a distinction between, on one hand, what deserves to be treated as important because, in its moral taintedness or moral luster, it directly contributes to certain choices being wrong (or right), and, on the other hand, what deserves to be treated as important because it is part of a deplorable or desirable outcome. This distinction roughly corresponds to what are termed "deontic" and "teleological" considerations. The contrast between these has been a staple of ethical philosophy for hundreds of years.

How sharp is this distinction? It may seem very sharp: after all, the second kind appeals to means-end thinking, and the first does not. But even this separation may not be as straightforward as it might seem. In any event, it seems useful to sort out the elements of ethical life first in a pre-philosophical way, presenting them as they would present themselves to the average person. The discussion of this chapter thus can be taken as a preliminary approach to problems that will be taken up in the final part of the book.

We can start from the assumption that, for the great majority of people, absence of ethical reflection is the normal state in life and that explicit ethical judgment appears called for (if at all) only at special moments. Such moments typically involve a sense that what one is about to do, or might do, will make a real difference and that there are options from which to choose.

This sense can be very positive, that something wonderful may be in the offing. Or it can be negative, that there may be something that one really should regret. In either case, if we think of the normal unreflective state as somewhat relaxed, the triggering of reflection will be experienced as a disturbance. Even the possible highly positive state could enter awareness as a sense that you may be missing something important.

A sense that there is something morally questionable about what one is about to do, or might do, in its most primitive form would be one of discomfort, of a possibility that goes against the grain. There can be hazy pictures, of course, in this moment when things are "up for grabs," of how one would like things to be, and of how one would much prefer things not to be. Clearly, teleological considerations will figure in such pictures; but so in a way will deontic ones, as they take on teleological aspects. The possible world about which you are uncomfortable may be one in which a prominent feature is that you have done something that you cannot quite shake off. The sense of moral taintedness (or its absence) can be very important in weighing possible outcomes.

This phenomenology of ethical alertness may well seem uncontentious. But it is an important corrective to a quick assumption that many people make, that decision-theoretic models are good representations of how decisions generally are made in the real world. Such models may be useful in relation to highly complex decisions, susceptible to detailed analysis, such as many made by economic planners. But in ordinary life, the vast majority of decisions are made, even by professors of philosophy, on the basis of the appeal or disturbance qualities of various images of possible outcomes, and/or more basically on what rubs (or does not rub) one the wrong way.

Does this make ordinary ethical decision not rational? Think of chess, normally viewed as a quintessentially rational activity. Calculation is usually not the only factor in decisions made by chess masters, and sometimes it is not even the most important factor. Memories of how various kinds of position have played out in the past, along with the associated intuitions (positional sense) of the kind of position to aim at, are crucial. (The importance of this positional sense is a factor in a recent documentary film, *Game Over*, about the match between Garry Kasparov and the IBM computer Deep Blue. Kasparov and his handlers became suspicious of the team managing the computer because Deep Blue showed positional sense, thus "did not play like a computer.") This positional sense is a highly sophisticated counterpart to the ordinary person's tendency to avoid doing what rubs the wrong way, or that risks leading to a kind of outcome one is uncomfortable about.

In ordinary processes of ethical decision, it may be well nigh impossible to separate the thought that there is something not quite right about doing such-and-such from the thought that in the end, you might be the person who had done such-and-such. Analytically, we can make the separation, prying the two apart. Whether and why this might make sense will be considered later, as part of an extended account of the relevance to ethical choice of valencing of outcomes.

Our present task is simply to give an argument that valencing of outcomes can be an important factor, not merely in how we come to make certain choices rather than others, but also in how we should choose. Examples will serve this purpose. It might be contended that all we need to make good ethical choices is an acceptable set of moral principles and rules, supplemented perhaps by casuistry. Well-chosen examples, however, can make clear that (a) there are some good ethical decisions which cannot be plausibly regarded as following from moral principles and rules, and instead have to be understood as being grounded in the positive valence of certain outcomes; and (b) a sense of the positive or negative valence of certain outcomes can generate new morality.

For examples we can return to the territory of sexism. There were moments, even fairly early on, when some argued that women lacked something important: the possibility of education comparable to that of men, and chances to develop their talents as sculptors, composers, philosophers, physicists, and so on. In some cases, money and comfort in life were at issue, but often these were not at stake. What was important was a sense of living life fully (along with the reality that corresponded to it), and the Kantian afterglow of having developed one's talents.

Were these things valuable and important? What counts as a reasonable moral judgment of policies and attitudes that denied women opportunities depends very much on the answer.

Not a large number of people, female or male, have extraordinary creative potential. But a substantial percentage of the population can be argued to be able to benefit from higher education, and also from opportunities to develop skills in challenging occupations. If we look back, say, nearly two hundred years, and ask how important it was that women were largely denied such opportunities, can philosophy offer an answer?

Not all philosophy would be useless. Elements in Plato's and Kant's philosophies, for example, suggest that development of talents and knowledge should have significant weight. It is not so clear that the classical utilitarians were as well placed. Bentham viewed pleasure as the ultimate good; J. S. Mill said as much, also, but he sometimes talked about a happiness that clearly was not equivalent to pleasure. Mill's expanded sense of happiness went not only beyond pleasure but also included enough "higher" elements to go beyond what we normally would term "happiness."

Is there more pleasure typically in the life of middle-class women with a career nowadays than there was for their stay-at-home counterparts nearly two hundred years ago? One wants to answer "Yes"; but it is hard to say, not only because the information does not come in a form convenient for measuring, but also because the available language is slippery. Is there now typically more happiness (in the ordinary meaning of the word)? Again, it is hard to know what to say. It is easier to be confident that there is now typically more happiness in the expanded sense in which fulfillment of capacities plays a major role.

The strength of the argument for enlarging opportunities for women, in other words, is affected by the ways in which outcomes are judged. If it had been argued that the early-twenty-first-century array of opportunities for women would create more pleasure or make women happier (in the ordinary sense of the word), this prediction might well have seemed debatable. An argument in terms of a sense of "happiness" much enlarged from the ordinary colloquial one, so that it means something like "fulfilled, engaged, having a sense of a meaningful life," was and is far more to the point. Such an argument can be found in Mary Wollstonecraft's *A Vindication of the Rights of Women* and in John Stuart Mill's *On the Subjection of Women*. The argument goes beyond simple views of what is important in life, such as Bentham's hedonism.

If one accepts that increased opportunities for women make a significant positive contribution to their lives, then this creates cases for two judgments. First, insofar as the contribution is significant, this gives reason to hold that whether or not to provide the opportunities is a moral issue. Second, it creates a prima facie case for a feminist response to the moral question. It plausibly can be regarded as morally wrong to withhold opportunities that would make a significant positive contribution to someone's life, unless there is some overriding reason not to allow the opportunities.

That valencing plays a crucial role here can be seen by reversing the valence. Suppose for the sake of argument that, after a closer look, we were to agree that usually the ways of life women lead as a result of increased opportunities are less fulfilling and less desirable than those common nearly two centuries ago. This certainly would not flatly refute the view that the opportunities should be provided: those who view increasing liberty to the maximum as the axiomatically right policy whatever the consequences could still hold the view. But the case for providing or allowing the opportunities would certainly look less strong if the valence of the lives that usually resulted were negative rather than positive.

So valencing becomes part of the issue here. There are other issues of which this is obviously true. Suppose, for example, that there is an addictive drug that does not interfere with much of ordinary life or diminish life expectancy, but that dulls people's intellectual and aesthetic capacities significantly. Is there a case for thinking it right to do as much as one can to discourage use of the drug? Complicated issues of liberty and of the limits of our responsibility for others can be relevant to this. But the immediate point is that the case for thinking it right to discourage use of the drug is much stronger if the drug dulls people's intellectual and aesthetic capacities (and if we think that such capacities are sources of significant value in human life) than if it has no effect on people's intellectual and aesthetic capacities (or if we judge that these are unimportant).

In the abstract, valencing is part of the issue in all ethical judgments, including moral decisions about saving lives or moral judgments to be made of Bill's taking Mary's purse because he needs money. If being killed or having one's money stolen were not thought of as misfortunes, these cases would look different. However, because there is a fair degree of consensus in the valencing of death and theft, the valencing becomes transparent, and it becomes easy to overlook it as a factor.

The point may become clearer if we revisit the trolley problem. Here are two variants. In one, we will suppose that the trolley is about to run over five terminally ill patients, whose lives have become very painful to them. If the track is switched it will run over only one such patient. The second variant is set in a world in which numerous miracles have given everyone a firm sense that there is life after death, along with some ability to estimate how likely it is that someone after death will enter paradise rather than hell. The five people about to be run over are prime candidates for paradise. If that is stipulated, the moral issue looks very different indeed.

To avoid misunderstanding, I should emphasize that I make no claim that the value of consequences—or what is reasonably thought to be the value of consequences—determines what should be done. The implausibility of act consequentialism, which does make claims of this sort, will become clear later in the book. My point here is instead that the strength of the case for doing or avoiding something is usually strengthened if it is reasonable to believe that what is recommended will have good consequences, and is weakened if the consequences are bad. Just how important consequences are, and what the limits might be on treating them as relevant, are topics that will be addressed later.

4

The Importance of Character

Few would dispute that character plays a role in the way we make ethical decisions. The philosopher Gilbert Harman is one of these few (see Harman 1999).
In the appendix, I will argue that his case for skepticism rests on a combination of
unwarranted assumptions and leaps beyond the psychological evidence. Most philosophers, even if they hold the moral software view of what normative ethics is,
would regard character as a causal factor in moral choice. This chapter will offer an
argument parallel to that of the previous chapter: that character is not merely a part
of the stage setting for ethical judgment, but in fact often plays a crucial role in the
quality of judgment.

Virtues and Character

First, we need to determine what character is and how it is related to virtues. A great
many philosophers, from Aristotle onward, have discussed ethics in relation to an
array of virtues. Some of the traditional virtues are keyed to specific kinds of choice.
Courage, for example, is excellence in choices that involve risk; generosity is excellence in choices related to giving to others. Temperance is moderation in matters
that lend themselves to self-indulgence. Aristotle had a separate category of intellectual virtues that are not keyed to choices but instead correspond to abilities in
various fields of knowledge. David Hume included among the virtues that of
cheerfulness—which, he pointed out, is like other virtues in making life better (1751/
1975, sec. 7, 203).

All of these virtues are specialized, involving some areas of our behavior or
responses and not others. When Heinz is considering whether to steal medicine for
his dying wife from the extortionate pharmacist, there is an issue of justice. Neither
cheerfulness, generosity, nor temperance is a factor. Courage may enter in, but this
is clearest if we first agree that the choice to steal is the right one. Philippa Foot has
contended that even great daring in actions that constitute misbehavior does not
qualify as the virtue of courage (Foot 1978c, 14–16). Even if courage is a factor in

Heinz's action, there are many ethical decisions to which it is irrelevant; for example, it normally does not take courage for Bill to decide not to take Mary's purse.

Part of the idea in talking of virtues, it seems to me, was a primitive, pre-Newtonian narrowing of what had to be considered in choice. By and large matters of generosity require consideration of how much possible help is needed and how much good it will do, as well as the limits of one's own resources and the seriousness of other demands on them. Decisions of courage are in large part assessments of whether something amounts to reasonable risk-taking. In both cases, to view a choice through the lens of the virtue is to downplay or to banish more global considerations.

Sometimes, however, the best thing to do is not to be generous (or, conversely, to give in a way that does not meet normal standards for reasonable allocation of resources). There also can be times when one appropriately can refuse to take reasonable risks, for good reasons unrelated to assessment of risks in the enterprises in hand. An agent can reasonably decide (in the light of projects, commitments, loyalties, etc.) that, at this moment, there are more important things in her or his life than doing the courageous thing or the generous thing, especially if what is at stake in the matter of generosity or courage is not large.

Thus the narrowing of what has to be considered, that virtue talk promotes, is not always useful. But it often is quite workable. Examples are most decisions of whether to give money to a specific panhandler, or whether to enter a building to try to save a stranger from a raging fire. The narrowing of focus is less workable (as has been suggested) when goods that are not relevant to a particular virtue impinge on cases that normally would be judged in relation to that virtue, and also when two or more distinct virtues become relevant to a single decision.

There also can be complications related to combinations of virtues or of virtues and faults. The traditional view was that different virtues involve different areas of judgment; but some ancient philosophers subscribed to the thesis of the unity of the virtues, which is that to have one virtue is to have them all. Presumably the idea of this was that the crucial factors, which include knowledge of what is appropriate and also the ability of reason to control appetites, are uniform across the spectrum of a life. Twentieth-century psychological research revealed what common sense should have known all along, that this thesis is preposterous (cf. Hartshorne, May, and Shuttleworth, 1930).

Indeed, it is notoriously true that often people who are extremely honest are not especially kind, and that generosity can coexist with some lack of courage. If we want to look at the pattern and texture of a person's life and choices, approaching this through examination of particular virtues (and particular vices or faults) may be a clumsy way of appreciating the interconnections and the wholeness of the life. It has been suggested, both by Confucius in the *Analects* and by La Rochefoucauld in his *Maxims*, that the virtues and faults that a person has can be intimately interconnected (Confucius, 1938, bk. 4.7, 103; La Rochefoucauld 1665/1959, Maxim 182, 57).

To reject the traditional thesis of the unity of the virtues need not, however, lead us to posit its extreme opposite. Even if it is granted that most of us are more rational in some parts of our life than in others, and that we control some appetites more readily and consistently than we control others, it may be that some forms of training or education have a "ripple effect" that extends broadly through a life. This could be true of anything that involves, say, control of impulsiveness, or a willingness to take into account other people's views. Such a general effect could be consistent with, say, Bill's having better control over impulses related to money or sex than over those related to food and drink. This could remain true of Bill even if (as a result of training or education) he became, in general, less impulsive.

Let us define a character trait as a pronounced tendency to behave in a certain way or ways in certain kinds of situation. To say that someone has a "pronounced tendency" does not mean that he or she always behaves the same way. If we take seriously the difficulty of making psychology-based predictions of a person's choices with 100 percent confidence, we also can be more receptive to the idea that many traits involve *typically* or *usually* behaving in certain ways, or being more *prone* than most people to behave in certain ways. That someone occasionally flies into a rage can be an important character trait.

Here is a short version of the relation between character traits and virtues. Good character, like virtues, requires pronounced tendencies to behave well in matters of importance. However, virtues often have been interpreted as governing broad areas of behavior. Courage, for example, is often construed as requiring generally good behavior in the full range of choices that involve risk-taking (and the ability when it is appropriate to rise above fear and anxiety). Character traits, however, can be quite narrow. Someone can be very brave in situations of a certain sort (say, when there are risks of being shot) but much more timid when threatened by dogs or when asked to challenge the unreasonable decisions made by someone in a position of authority.

The foregoing develops a view of character traits that is part of the argument of this book. A specialist reader, however, may want more discussion of the interesting recent polemics about character traits, especially in relation to virtue ethics. This is provided in the appendix.

Character, Causality, and What You Are

The causal role of character traits in behavior can be understood as follows. Sometimes, when we are trying to explain why Bloggs did such and such, we refer to the situation he was in. (A tiger suddenly appeared, and of course Bloggs ran.) The idea is that there are situations in which everyone, or virtually everyone, would behave in much the same way; and to know what the situation was is to know what conduct to have expected. We can pick out the situation as the principal cause of Bloggs's running, although we might add, "And Bloggs is not the kind of man to stand and face a tiger in the wild."

In many situations, though, there is no entirely dominant "normal" response. Suppose that Bill responds to criticism by making some extremely cruel remarks about the critic. Well, some people respond to criticism in that way, but most of us do not. Why did Bill say those awful things? Part of the causal story will be the situation—that Bill was criticized—but a prominent part will be that Bill tends to get nasty when criticized. Character here is clearly a cause, although the causation cannot be presumed to involve anything like a universal and entirely predictable relation between two variables. The next time Bill is criticized, he may manage to stay calm and behave decently.

This brings us back to the topic of what character is. The discussion thus far amounts to a portrait of character traits as descriptive features of what people are like, in relation to how we can expect them to behave. However some character traits (especially those related to virtue) also can be regarded as a person's mechanisms of controlling what she or he does. Mary may have a sort of kindness that curbs her impulses to be harsh with people she thinks little of but that she senses are vulnerable. Her self-control in such matters is integral to her kindness. All of this remains consistent with the thought that character traits typically are narrow rather than broad: the self-control that avoids hurting others can operate in a different way in different situations and may not operate at all in some contexts. Mary may think twice about what she is saying when her words could be hurtful, but she may also drive recklessly or forget to send a letter of recommendation that a coworker or student badly needs.

It also could be held that character is a person's inner nature. The poet John Keats, in a letter to his brother and sister-in-law in Kentucky, speaks of this world "as a vale of soul-making" (Keats 1970, 249–250). In this, Keats seems to have used the word "soul" in a way that approximates "character." You were not born with a soul, in the sense in which Keats used the word; but in the process of growth and development, you become—with some degree of definiteness and stability—one sort of person. This is an "inner" becoming in that, on any particular occasion, much of what you are like need not be manifest in your behavior. Thus it is that you construct what Keats would call a soul, and what most people would call a character.

The Formation and Dominance of Character

The line of thought central to this chapter starts from a banal claim: people, by the time they reach late adolescence or early adulthood, usually act in character. They usually, that is, behave in a way that falls within the range of behavior that (if we know them well) we would expect of them in the present situation. This is first and foremost a claim about the causal role of character in how people come to make choices. But, I will go on to argue, understanding the roles of character often has implications for how we *should* make choices.

There are two parts to this argument. The first appeals to the role of character as providing connective elements among an individual's choices. The second appeals to the role of character as inner nature. Cultivation of inner nature can be an important factor in choice. Also, to the extent that outcomes matter in determining what should be chosen, effects on the character of the agent (or the characters of others affected by what is done) can loom large.

The connective role of character best can be appreciated if we look closely at how most choices present themselves. In most lives, existential choices (discussed in the first chapter) are very much the exception rather than the rule. Typically, a choice occurs while you are in the midst of life, and the nature of the choice involves continuing (or not continuing) the sort of thing you have been doing, or have done in the past. Sometimes there will be time to think and to articulate reasons for or against various alternatives. Often you just find yourself doing such-and-such. You have made a choice without, at the time, thinking of it as such.

We might think that true rationality would require taking each choice—or at least each major choice—out of the context of the path of life in which it is embedded, and would then require analysis (detached from this context) of the pro's and con's of all available alternatives. In some cases, especially those discussed in the first chapter, this can be done and can work well. Most of what we do, though, is so embedded in the surrounding path of life that any campaign to abstract these choices and examine them one at a time would be like deciding anew every five minutes what kind of person we want to be. The abstraction and analysis, on the face of it super-rational, in fact would be highly irrational. It would waste time and energy, and would destroy the coherence of a life.

This is most clearly true of choices related to ongoing projects or to personal commitments and relationships. It should be emphasized that my view is *not* that it never makes sense reflectively to examine such choices. Projects, commitments, and relationships can go bad; and there can be moments at which an agent gets a disturbing signal that should trigger reflection. The resulting reflection then typically will focus, however, not just on a single choice, but more broadly on the pattern of life that led up to it.

These moments, when something gives us serious reason to break a pattern, are uncommon for most of us; a satisfying life might be spent without one such moment. Should most of us very frequently reflect on individual choices embedded in the pattern of a life? There can be good reasons for *some* frequent reflection, even if everything that I have said is accepted.

There can be many options, subtly different from each other, that all are broadly consistent with established character (and with established projects and commitments). A little reflection might improve on what one does. Further, a life that is on autopilot can be dull, and there can be much to be said for exercises of mindfulness (in varying behavior a bit) as opposed to enveloping mindlessness (see Langer 1989). As part of this, it is possible to enter into even fairly trivial things in a way that will enrich both the actions and the felt quality of life.

All of this suggests advantages of frequent consciousness of choice. The conscious choice, though, can be made very much in the context of previous patterns of character and established projects and commitments. Frequent choices that are viewed atomistically (that is, entirely apart from this context) would have fewer advantages and also would carry serious risks. Such a life might well have a felt quality like that of disintegration of self. At the extreme it would be like reconsidering walking: "First I move the right foot; then should I move the left foot?"

We should be mindful of the value of having a life that is, and can be appreciated as being, reasonably integrated. How significant this value is can depend, of course, on what it is that is being integrated. All the same, the negative features of a life that lacks the unifying themes of ongoing character and that looks and feels highly episodic and disjointed can be considerable. There is much to be said for avoiding this, and such a consideration reasonably can be a factor in choice.

Hence for most of us most of the time, the best advice is to act in a way that remains in character: to be ourselves instead of somebody else. This is consistent, though, with paying attention to possible variations on what we are doing, and with incorporating a degree of improvisation and perhaps even playfulness. We can reject rigidity and extreme repetitiveness. Nor should a judgment that remaining in character is usually advantageous preclude moments when we reasonably think that our character would benefit from reshaping. Remaining in character could be thought of as a kind of default policy.

One complication is that the exceptions to this general recommendation especially include some moral judgments. When something of major importance to other people is at stake, we might say to someone, "Whatever you have been up to now, and whatever your commitments and projects are, decide this case on the merits," where "deciding on the merits" indicates a strongly decontextualized appraisal of the case. This must be conceded: it does make sense to make some major moral decisions atomistically, abstracting as much as possible from surrounding context (including our character up to now).

However, this is not true of all moral decisions, even of all major moral decisions. It is one thing if what we are about to do chiefly will affect strangers, and the choice is not one in a series of related choices. The trolley case is a good example. It is another thing if our choice chiefly concerns people with whom we have had extensive prior relations, and if it is one in a series of choices that concern these people. Much in the conduct of personal relationships, or in living within a community, fits this pattern, as do some of the choices that politicians must make that will affect their working relations with other politicians and their ability to implement future plans.

There is a general pre-philosophical awareness of much of this, although it is hard to articulate using existing concepts. The concept of responsibility is sometimes borrowed to voice the point just made about moral choices that resist decontextualization. The word "responsibility" is at home in cases in which there are obligations that we have explicitly taken on, or that normally are part of roles we have taken on. We have a responsibility to do what we have promised. A job carries with it certain responsibilities, and parenthood involves some to the children. If something one does disturbs the lives of neighbors, or of people with whom there have been friendly relationships, this can seem important. We might say, "Think of responsibilities to friends and to neighbors."

But unless there have been specific promises, what is involved will not exactly fit the model of responsibilities. The intuition (all the same) is that the agent is not, after all, some abstract being, but rather is situated in a specific place and in a network of prior relationships and forms of behavior and that these things should count. Suppose that we are in a Kantian mode and are armed with a rather short list of things that we allow to count in an ethical decision. These will include very general moral obligations and rights and responsibilities. It then is tempting to borrow or extend the word "responsibility" to enable some prior or ongoing relationships to fit on the list. There is no harm in this, but it tends to mask how complex and diverse our normal moral thinking is.

A second complication is this. To act in character has a clear and simple meaning when what is in question is which of two or more sharply different alternatives should be pursued. It has a more subtle meaning when the alternatives are not so sharply distinct, and when matters of style and attitude begin to look important. The expression of character can then reflect an agent's involvement in what she or he is doing and can have a quasi-artistic quality. I will return to this later in the chapter. Arguably, it concerns a major role of character in good lives.

Here is the second part of the argument that understanding the roles of character often has implications for how we should make choices. A crucial point is that the causality between character and choice runs in both directions. How and what we choose on a specific occasion can influence future choices; and to the degree to which a pattern of choice is modified, character is modified. Accordingly, if we want not to do damage, one factor we will need to consider is damage to our own character. Conversely, if we wish to make things better, reinforcing a character that is already reasonably good (or shaping it in an improving way) can play a part in this.

There is already considerable commonsense recognition of this. People sometimes say, when they are considering behaving in a way that seems to them to be doubtful, "What kind of person would that make me?" Part of the meaning is that certain deeds or misdeeds can seem emblematic of a person. But there also is a sense that you can become, after doing certain things, a different person from what you had been.

It is widely thought that it can be awful—a very serious loss in life—to become a much less admirable person. The quality of lived experience would not be the same. In particular, research in the psychology of happiness shows that self-esteem has a major role in a person's degree of happiness (see Argyle 1987, 124). Some ways of becoming a different person would put happiness at risk.

Style and Attitude as Factors in Choice

There is a further case for thinking that character, or something very like character, should be a factor in choice. It raises points that are more debatable, I think, than those made thus far. It also has more drastic implications for our view of the shape of ethics.

We can begin by saying a little about the background in philosophical literature. Much recent ethical philosophy has tended to formulate choices as between sharply discrete alternatives. Style and attitude often do not enter into these descriptions. Much Asian philosophy, in contrast, places heavy emphasis on the role of style and especially attitude in determining the quality of a choice. A number of Nietzsche's remarks point in a similar direction.

The differences here have a great deal to do with differing preoccupations, and with resultant differences in the kinds of cases that typically are focused upon. The major preoccupation of modern Western ethics, going back to the ancient root of the Ten Commandments, is on major choices that, if made wrongly, could amount to a disruptive social violation. Choices of whether to kill or steal have been prime examples. This focus leads to what (in very early work) I termed "big moment" ethics (Kupperman 1968). The image has been that ethics makes significant demands of us but, for most of us, only sporadically. For most of the time, we do not have to worry about ethics and can do what we like.

Classical Greek ethics is very different from this, but the ethics of Confucius is perhaps diametrically opposite. Certainly people in ancient China knew that murder and theft are wrong, and there is nothing to suggest that Confucius does not assume this. He takes it for granted. All of the cases he discusses in the *Analects* are of very different sorts. They all are embedded in established political, social, or personal relationships, and thus are heavily contextualized in relation to ongoing patterns of behavior.

The central theme of the *Analects* is the refinement of self. Even when there is a clear obligation, such as that of children to take care of their parents, how it is discharged is at least as important as the broad nature of what is done. In the treatment of parents, Confucius says, it is the demeanor that is difficult (bk. 2.8, 89).

Attitudes matter and can be visible to the trained eye. The Confucian ongoing emphasis on ritual, which is likely to seem indigestible to many Westerners, might be thought of merely as cultural baggage taken on by the philosophy. But in fact it is more than this. Ritual is viewed as a kind of social dance, in which one develops and refines one's personal style in concert with other members of the community. In the usages of ritual, the *Analects* suggest, it is *he* (harmony or naturalness) that matters. "Harmony" (the more common translation) here can be understood as between the outward behavior and the person's attitudes. More broadly, it is a matter of getting yourself into the social manifestations of the ritual so that they become second nature. You become comfortable with them, and there is a genuine expressive quality in what you do. Think of the expressive behavior (even in our culture) of someone who has become acculturated to the ritual of thanking someone for a favor, and in the process has added gratitude to her or his emotional repertoire.

The *Analects* center on the transformation of self involved in refinement of style and attitude. Is this a modification of character? It is hard to know what to say. Insofar as the matters of style and attitude in question center on the ways a person projects herself in interactions with others, the word "personality" might seem more apt here than "character." Nevertheless, if we take *character* broadly to be the inner self of a person that becomes manifest in patterns of behavior, the subject of the *Analects* does qualify as being character. I will treat it as such, with the understood qualification that this may be slightly stretching the ordinary meaning of the word.

Arguments can be pieced together from bits of the mosaic of pithy passages that constitutes the *Analects*. One argument is typical in moving from psychological claims drawn from experience to logical implications of these claims. It runs like this. Some people, after laying the groundwork for virtue by developing good habits and reasonable attitudes (i.e., the Chinese counterparts of the Greek youths who were ready to hear Aristotle's lectures on ethics), can (through poetry, ritual, and music) refine their sensibilities and patterns of behavior. This creates a second nature for which virtuous behavior is a form of satisfying self-expression, with stylistic features that make it semi-artistic. Someone who attains this will find it so fulfilling that it will not be outweighed even by setbacks in matters of money, prestige, recognized success, and the like.

Given these psychological points, we can see that the people who attain this second nature can be expected to have an attitude toward the ups and downs of life that is different from that of most people. The average person values most money, prestige, and the like. These are very much subject to luck, and hence someone who cares greatly about them will feel vulnerable and constantly will be looking for good luck. The ideal Confucians, though, will have what they value most (the satisfactions of harmonious self-expression) securely within themselves; hence they will be (and will feel) much less vulnerable, and will be calmer and happier (see *Analects*, bk. 7.36, 131, and bk. 4.2, 102). All of this multiplies the rewards of refined virtue. It also ensures reliability of behavior in difficult or disorienting circumstances, in that the Confucian worthy will have a stronger and more entrenched sense of self than the average person is likely to have.

This view of true goodness as a kind of acquired second nature is not exactly the same as Aristotle's, although it is not totally different. In some ways, the Confucian view is more worked out, with more psychological insight into the importance of style and also the process of self-modification that leads to true goodness. One objection that is sometimes made to ethical views of this sort, however, is that they are elitist. This may seem to some people to be a devastating point, whereas it may look very weak indeed to others: an example of argument-through-labeling. Let me suggest that it is neither devastating nor very weak.

We can see that the charge of elitism need not be devastating if we consider that ethical judgments sometimes require real thought, experience, and ability to make fine discriminations. Can it turn out that some people, especially ones who have devoted much of their education and attention to such matters, are better at this than most of us are? No one quails at the suggestion that some people are much better judges than others of the design of physics experiments or of historical inferences. Why cannot something like this be true of some kinds of ethical judgments?

A partial reply, though, is that there is an important part of ethics—the core moral codes that all of us learn as children—that can function well only if virtually everyone is presumed to have roughly equal knowledge of them. We have to hope and assume that the stranger on the street knows the wrongness of certain kinds of actions as well as we do. This social function points in the direction of a kind of ethical egalitarianism.

Do the previous two paragraphs point in flatly contradictory directions? Or is more accurate to say that ethics includes elements of more than one sort, whose requirements can be very different? Might there accordingly be pulls in different directions?

Such questions arise in an especially sharp form in relation to the one modern philosopher, Nietzsche, who most matches Confucius's emphasis on the ethical importance of style. In at least two respects, of course, Nietzsche is very different from Confucius. One of the pervasive themes in the *Analects* is the importance of social responsibility, which links the ethical reflections with a vision of a good society. This concern is largely missing from Nietzsche's philosophy, a fact that many who otherwise admire him find distressing.

The other obvious difference is in Nietzsche's extreme individualism and pluralism of value. Independence and personal creativity are important values for Nietzsche, and in his view they can take a wide variety of forms. Because of this, there is no single prescriptive ideal (*ubermensch* is an umbrella term for a variety of possibilities); and thus, given these many paths, there cannot be anything quite as specific as Confucius's account of how one proceeds to the recommended refinement of self.

Nevertheless, it is clear that Nietzsche, like Confucius, considers the style and attitude with which something is done to be of ethical importance. This comes through most clearly in the "On the Three Evils" section of *Thus Spake Zarathustra*. Selfishness, sex, and the will to power, it is claimed, cannot be judged in some broad generalized way. Each takes many different forms, some despicable and some admirable. It all depends on how it is pursued.

Let me suggest that this emphasis on style and attitude, which Confucius and Nietzsche broadly share, works well for some cases (and gets at something important), but does not work at all well for some others. There is a point of method that is highly relevant to the comments that now follow. Even physics does not yet have a unified field theory, and there surely is no reason to assume that an entirely unified account of ethics is possible. We need to be open to the possibility that some areas or problems of ethics are best approached in ways that would be inappropriate and unfruitful for other areas and problems.

Does what I am suggesting here lead to a kind of double-mindedness or schizophrenia? Any double-mindedness here is only of the healthiest and most sophisticated kind. We can appreciate this if we look at the main alternative: a philosopher sees something important (say, a significant feature of many of the choices that give a life its character and satisfactions) and then assumes that this feature is to be found very generally in such choices or ignores the features of sharply different kinds of case.

Take Nietzsche, for example. He had a brilliant awareness that in much of life there are nuances of style and attitude that cannot readily be captured by the available broad labels, that are as important as the broad nature of what is done, and that make a huge difference not only to the agent's quality of life but also to our estimation of the agent's conduct. (Think of the "selfishness" of a Beethoven who is single-mindedly devoted to his work versus the "selfishness" of a petty and conniving wartime profiteer.) Original insights sometimes are blinding, and Nietzsche may have been blinded to the ways in which—in the general run of cases of murder, rape, torture, and theft—style and attitude are far less important than the broad nature of what is done.

Confucius talks very little about matters such as murder and theft. There are passages that suggest that an increase in the rate of such crimes should be, in his view, blamed on poor moral examples provided by the leaders of society. But I think it is clear also that Confucius would have agreed that, in the cases of murder, rape, torture, and theft, what is heinous is the broad nature of what is done. This is consonant with his brief negative comment about "petty acts of clemency" (*Analects*, bk. 15.16, 196–197).

In short, a philosopher can perfectly well think that there are important ethical choices in which matters of style and attitude make a significant difference to the quality of what is done, and also that there are important ethical choices in which this is not the case. Later on, we will explore some of the sources of this contrast. The immediate point, though, is that (whatever is true of murder, rape, torture, and theft) there are a number of important choices in life in which style and attitude make a major difference. These include the great majority of choices involved in maintaining, or not maintaining, a friendship, a love relation, a marriage, strong bonds between parents and children, political alliances, a collegial atmosphere in a workplace, relations with neighbors and a community, and so on.

Let us suppose that someone achieves patterns of behavior, in the areas of choice just mentioned, that exhibit attitudes and elements of style that enhance the relationships and projects in question and make many of us admire the agent more, and that also enhance her or his quality of life. We can relate this to the emphasis in Aristotle's *Nicomachean Ethics* on the contribution to *eudaemonia* of exercise of the virtues, and add that *how* they are exercised surely can matter. This satisfaction with (enjoyment of) the way one plays the game of life is a major element in the security and serenity that Confucius believes a sage will achieve. It also can play a major role in enabling someone to pass Nietzsche's litmus test for quality of life: would one be happy to have the same life repeated again, just as it has been?

If all of this is right, then an agent can reasonably treat as a factor, in many choices, the desirability of developing and maintaining a style of behavior that will both be satisfying and promote good relationships with others. The application of this will be not so much in the most often discussed sorts of major moral decisions (which typically take on the character of existential choices) as in those that involve ongoing personal relationships and patterns of behavior. Some of these latter cases can qualify as matters of moral choice, especially when much is at stake that can affect people's happiness. Some of the most interesting cases, which deserve a book of their own, involve political decisions that are not "one-off," but rather are embedded in a political figure's relations (alliances, accommodations, etc.) with others of different political and moral views.

Conclusion

Chapter 1 began with an image of ethical choice that has been dominant in recent Western (especially Anglo-American) philosophy. A rational being (we don't need to know anything more about him, her, or it than that) is at a moment when there are two or more available courses of action open. The alternatives are specified in terms of the broad nature of what would be done. Some description of consequences may be included. The rational being then is in a position to determine what is the right choice.

This is a very comfortable image for a tradition of "big moment" ethics. The view is that most of the time we simply live, but on occasion we step outside our lives. We have an ethical choice. This is taken on its own terms, merely those contained in a description of the situation and the alternatives.

The argument of the first three chapters was that this simple view of ethical choice is always at least somewhat inadequate. As sophisticated moralists such as Kant have recognized, every choice has as a crucial factor an element of construal: how the situation and the various alternatives are seen and formulated. In addition, there is always an element of valencing: how various aspects of what is done or other parts of its outcome are valued or disvalued.

In some cases, though, these elements can be taken for granted and thus easily disregarded. The trolley problem is a favorable example of this. Virtually everyone would formulate the case and the possible courses of action in the same way, and there is virtual consensus also on assigning considerable negative value to the death of a (presumably innocent) person. Often, however, construals and/or valencing judgments are contestable in ways that are vitally relevant to ethical appraisal of the case.

In this chapter, we have seen that the role of character in unifying a person's life and conduct always is and should be a factor in choice. Forming, maintaining, and improving a good character all have values that should count in ethical choice. In some cases, however—especially the most familiar kinds of major moral decisions—character does not emerge as a prominent factor. This is in part because such decisions typically present themselves as discontinuous from the rest of a person's life, and in part because typically what is centrally at stake (the harm that might be done) is so very important. But often, especially in choices embedded in personal relations or ongoing projects, considerations of one's character should have a major role.

In sum, we have moved in four chapters from the simple, attractive image of ethical choice as atomistic problem-solving, in which a variety of contextual elements can be ignored, to a much more complicated image. The initial simple picture is not totally condemned: it may be moderately serviceable for some cases. But many cases demand not only more attention to contextual factors, but also greater awareness of how construals and values may differ.

We are well along in the project of providing a complex and balanced view of ethical choice. One element of the initial, beguiling image remains: the lone problem solver who must choose on the basis of factors that make sense to her or him. Not all of this should disappear. In particular, ethical choices are made by individuals, even when they are acting in concert with other members of a group; and a healthy regard for individual responsibility should incline us to stick to this story. But there certainly are occasions on which it makes sense for the individual to make some degree of accommodation to the group, and (as Sartre pointed out in "Existentialism Is a Humanism") decisions that may look individual and personal can in their purport be decisions for everyone.

Further, elements of ethical theory can creep into the decision making of even the most resolutely unphilosophical. We will need to look at the variety of ways in which choices are made, and at the roles that ethical theory can take in this.

Personal Morality and
Its Social Implications

When we think of morality, often we think of an individual who knows that she or he has a choice and tries to decide whether one of the alternatives is immoral or is obligatory. This is a common experience. Consciously to make a moral choice is to go through a process that has its own felt qualities and, for many people, may have characteristic features. It also is to engage with a conceptual structure, linked to the categories of moral discourse, that has implications that are not always grasped. To use words is to take on meanings, whether or not one had those meanings in mind.

In this chapter, I will connect the two poles of conscious moral choice: the personal felt quality and conceptual implications. This should continue the work of the previous chapters. It will further undermine the seductive image of ethics as centering on lone individuals making decisions for decontextualized cases that can be considered in isolation from those they would make in any other cases.

Part of the argument will parallel that of the previous chapters. The position is that there are cases for which the seductive and oversimple image is largely adequate. In these, the complicating factors implicit in my account are so obvious and able to be taken for granted that we will see right through them (and not see them). Often, though, it is not so simple. If we attend to *these* cases, the image of ethical thought and discourse must become much more complicated and diverse.

Intuitive Morality

In most societies that have some degree of stability, there is at least a core of a shared morality, which is taught to children and to which normal adults are presumed to subscribe. This will center on broad categories of what is forbidden (e.g., killing an innocent person on the street, taking your neighbor's property without permission) and what is obligatory (e.g., keeping promises of various kinds, especially when made in circumstances in which it was clear that the promise was taken seriously by all parties). These categories not only guide action but also structure perception.

Even in complicated situations, we are quick to pick out and notice acts of murder, theft, and breaking of serious promises.

All of this is so ingrained in most of us that it is common sense. It enables us to make quick, straightforward judgments of cases in which one of the alternatives involves what would appear to virtually everyone to be a clear case of doing what is forbidden. Although a philosopher (e.g., Kant) can offer a reconstruction of what is allegedly implicit in such judgments, they typically are experienced as intuitive, as almost a matter of seeing or sizing up a prominent feature of the situation at hand.

This intuitive feeling also can characterize judgments that seem harder to make and more contestable. In a case, for example, that involves what appears to be a betrayal of trust—one, however, that would have some positive consequences—someone might say, "It just feels wrong." It is as if this person looks at the case, looks at it again (with various considerations in mind, such as the needy people who would be helped), and cannot shake the sense that there is something wrong with the proposed action.

In one way, it may seem that what is being tested is a linguistic intuition. The word "wrong" is hovering over the image of the proposed action, and the repeated question is whether it is an apt word for that option. There also, though, is the factor of personal inhibition. Morality works on most of us in part through motivational constraints we acquire in childhood that make it hard for us to behave in certain ways and cause these forms of behavior to feel uncomfortable. Sometimes a crucial element in moral judgment is a sense of whether we would be able to bring ourselves to do something. There can be times when we find ourselves unable to say what it is that would be wrong with a certain action, but we think we know that we could not perform it. Sometimes we could do it, but would not feel comfortable about it, and this sense of discomfort can have moral force.

All of this looks personal. A lone individual is deciding what she or he will do, in the light perhaps of whether labels such as "right" or "wrong" feel as if they apply to various alternatives, and in the light also of personal inclinations and inhibitions. Much explicit choice has the character mainly of looking at the situation, and the obvious alternatives, from various angles. Reflection may take the form of bringing out aspects of the case that had not at first come to one's attention, such as the effects of a possible action on various interested parties, or their probable responses. Looking at these can change the way the case feels to the person whose decision it is, the agent.

Reflection also can take the form of moving beyond one's personal response to *this* case toward consideration of how a proposed action might fit into a pattern of behavior shared with other people. Other people can stimulate this thought. "How would you feel if someone did that to you?" is a standard question. It is closely rivaled by "What would it be like if everyone behaved that way?" These questions have found their way into philosophical ethics; but we need to bear in mind that they often are asked by people who have not studied philosophy, and they have deep pre-philosophical roots.

One reason why the word "morality," rather than "ethics" (a broader term—see the lexicon in the introduction), appears in the title of this chapter is that morality is implicitly social. Some other parts of ethics are not, at least in the same way (cf.

Strawson 1961). Hence, once a judgment is presented as being moral, or about morality, conceptual baggage is taken onboard that includes implications as to what would be a morally acceptable way for people other than the agent to behave.

Bloggs may say that he is making a moral judgment that is entirely personal, not merely in how it is arrived at, but also in that he has no opinion on how other people should act. But if Bloggs claims that his doing X in situation Z is morally acceptable, then he is not in a good position to complain if someone else does X in a situation that looks rather like Z. He is not in a position to complain even if someone does X to him. Further, if he persists in holding that his doing X is morally acceptable, then consistency requires that he have doubts about the moral arrangements of a society — even one distant in time and place—that brands X as morally impermissible.

Judgments of ideals also have implications beyond the individual, but the implications are not normally viewed as having the same force and inescapability as those of moral judgments. If Bloggs thinks that the contemplative life is the best one that we can imagine, then presumably he must think that this judgment holds for his friend Smurf as well as for himself. On the other hand, Bloggs can say, "The contemplative life is ideal if you are cut out for it," or remark that some other way of life would suit Smurf better. In contrast to this, it would be distinctly odd if Bloggs opined that promise keeping is morally obligatory if you are cut out for it.

The claim that moral judgments are implicitly social, in ways in which other kinds of ethical judgments (such as those of ideals) are not, may seem initially implausible in relation to some moralities. Smurf may have a morality that is so idiosyncratic that there is no reasonable expectation, even on Smurf's part, that anyone else will agree with his moral judgments. Nevertheless, Smurf's morality must be viewed as a candidate for the position of dominant morality in (at the least) the relevant society or subculture. If Smurf says, "My moral views would not be the right ones for anyone else to hold" or "Any society in which everyone held my moral views would be a real mess," we would wonder whether Smurf had properly learned the meaning of the word "moral."

Let us, for the sake of the present line of inquiry, agree that any judgment that X is morally obligatory, permissible, or impermissible implies that it would be right for the entire society or subculture to subscribe to the judgment. (A qualification will emerge later, but it does not affect what is central to morality.) A natural question is *why* this implication holds for moral judgments. A natural answer would be that the ground for the implication is somehow one of logic. But what kind of logic is this, that works differently for moral judgments than it does for other kinds of ethical judgments? And why does it—or should it—work differently for moral judgments?

This clearly is a crucial question for ethicists in general, but especially for Kantians. Kant treated the categorical imperative—which in its first form insists that any judgment that something is acceptable for one person requires that it would be acceptable for everyone to adopt the same maxim—as a deliverance of reason. This suggests that there is a logical truth underlying the categorical imperative. But Kant never explained what it could be, or for that matter how the categorical imperative could be logically derived.

This chapter relies on some elements of the account of the logic of ethical judgment, especially of universalizability, provided by R. M. Hare (1963, pp. 10–50).

One way of putting his thesis of universalizability is as follows. Any judgment that X is Z (where Z is any property that is a matter of ethical judgment) for agent A in circumstances C logically implies that X would be Z for anyone in circumstances closely similar in every relevant respect to C. As Hare presents this, it functions as an indicator of burden of argument. If Smith claims that X would be Z for her, in her present circumstances, but would not be Z for Bloggs (in his circumstances), then Smith must be prepared to point to some difference between her circumstances and Bloggs's that justifies the differences with respect for X's being Z. Normally the fact that her hair (or skin) is a different color from his, or that her name begins with a different letter, will not do: she will not be able to make a plausible case that it should make a difference.

Hare's account is as good as it is because he is keenly aware of difficulties. One is that similarity is always a matter of degree. Two cases inevitably will have points of difference. These are compatible with a judgment that they are "similar" in relevant respects. The problem of vagueness is finessed by the recourse to burden of argument. If you think that your situation is not similar enough to mine to warrant an insistence that the same ethical judgment applies to both of us, then make a case that there is a difference that justifies different judgments for your situation and for mine.

There is also the difficulty, as we saw in the case of Bloggs's and Smurf's ideal ways of life, that one person's tastes, capacities, and inclinations can differ from those of another in such a way that what would be recommended for one would not be recommended for the other. In Hare's account, such differences can be subsumed under the heading "differences in situation." Because they are such different people, Bloggs and Smurf are not in the same situation when each decides what his ideal way of life is.

All of this seems right to me. But note that Hare's logic gives us something that falls short of the strength and sweep of Kant's categorical imperative, or of what I have been arguing is embedded in moral common sense. It certainly does not explain why it is that moral judgments (and not other kinds of ethical judgments) imply a social code that should be acceptable if followed by everyone.

One difference between the universalizability thesis and the apparatus of Kant's categorical imperative is this. Kant holds that a moral judgment in a specific case rests on a maxim, which in its nature is of the moral quality of a *sort* of thing (e.g., breaking promises when it suits you). Hence any specific moral judgment implies the acceptability, even if everyone followed it, of a broad one (concerning actions of a certain sort). Hare calls this a claim of *generalizability*, moving outward from a specific case to cases of the broad sort that includes the case at hand. It may be of course that not all cases within the broad sort will be similar in all relevant respects. Hence generalization cannot be logically implicit in ethical judgments, although *universalizability* (the move from the particular case to all other cases that are similar in relevant respects) is.

In my view, Hare's carefully contained account is right for ethical judgments in general, and Kant's implicit claim of generalizability says something important about the special domain of morality. Whatever the merit is of the Kantian insight about moral generalization, it cannot be explained along the logical lines explored by Hare (see Kupperman 2002). We are left with a mysterious rationality, in relation to morality, that needs to be accounted for.

Special Features of Morality

Let us gather together some respects in which moral judgments seem to commit us to more than do other kinds of ethical judgments. First, poor moral choices are far more likely to be taken as other people's business than are poor ethical choices of other sorts. If Bloggs does something morally wrong, others can mind this in a way they normally are not in a position to mind other kinds of poor ethical choices. Second, if ethical judgments in general offer guidance (commending choices to the person making them and to others in very similar situations), the guidance typically is more forceful—more like a shove than a friendly nudge—in the case of moral judgments.

The third special feature that moral judgments appear to have is more complicated. Let us continue to assume that Hare's thesis of universalizability is right. Whatever is right for Bloggs in circumstances C is also right for Smurf in circumstances that do not differ in relevant respects from C. As Hare recognizes, this leaves the substantive question of what can count as relevant differences between one agent's and another agent's situations.

My earlier suggestion was that in relation to choices of ideals or of major goals in life, it can be relevant that Bloggs and Smurf are different kinds of people. Smurf may not be cut out for something that would be very good for Bloggs. Could something like this be true also in relation to moral choices? Intuitively, it would seem not. The presumption is that morality, like the law, should apply "irrespective of persons."

Finally, some would argue that morality, unlike other parts of ethics, commits us to general rules. Remember that Hare's logical thesis gives us universalizability of all ethical judgments, but not generalizability. Indeed Hare remarks that some persons may in time arrive at a morality in which many judgments are specific to a case (plus imaginable cases that are not different in any relevant respect), so that a principle "defies formulation in words at all" (1963, 39–40).

Could one go so far in this as to eschew articulable general rules entirely? The views of someone who decides all moral questions on a case-by-case basis may look oddly different from anything that we would think of as a functioning morality. Because of this it might seem that something about morality leads to a need for general rules.

These are preliminary comments, made as an approach to complex issues. One other preliminary comment should be added. It may be tempting to think that if morality has special requirements, these represent implications that enter in when words like "morality," "immoral," or "morally wrong" are used. However, it looks as if the implications can enter in even when none of the key words is used. A judgment that Smurf's killing an irritating neighbor was a poor choice would normally be taken as having stronger implications, of various sorts, than the judgment that Smurf's spending his time lolling on the beach (instead of pursuing the contemplative life) was a poor choice. The presumption that one choice falls under morality, and the other does not, can do the work that would have been done by a key word.

A better way to understand the special features of morality is to investigate the purposes that it serves. These can be quite diverse. There is room to distinguish between primary and secondary functions.

For example, one function of morality, for many of us, is to offer occasions for feeling superior to other people (who are violating moral norms that we fulfill). It also allows for moral indignation, which can be an enjoyable feeling. These certainly are not primary functions, and they may not always be attractive. They have been pointed to by Chinese Daoists and by Nietzsche; and the great Confucian philosopher Mencius, who did take moral norms seriously, thought it necessary to warn against trying to "dominate people through goodness" (1970, bk. 4, B.16, 130). Whatever one thinks of this, it seems most implausible to suppose that morality was invented for these purposes. Once a thing exists, of course, it can be used in various ways.

The most obvious thing to say about morality is that it was invented to protect a society or individuals within a society. This is a story that has become familiar through the work of philosophers like Thomas Hobbes. If we try to imagine a "state of nature" that lacks law and morality, we realize that in such a world, life would be uncertain and impoverished. Morality (along with law) emerges as part of a package of social protections for individuals and their property.

This is a simple story, and we must take care not to make it too simple. First, even if it is largely correct, we need not assume that the purposes that spurred on the development of morality are exhausted by the formula of generally protecting persons and property. Despite what the thought experiments of philosophers and political theorists (e.g., Rawls 1971) might tell us, any real moral and political order is likely to represent implicit agreements among individuals, some of whom are in stronger positions from the start. It would be naive to suppose that these stronger individuals waive their advantages in the process of forming moral and political rules for a society. So we have to be open to the thought that the primary functions of a morality, beyond the generic purpose of protecting individuals and property, may often have been interpreted as involving special forms of protection for those who are in strong positions.

There may be other ambiguities or lapses in relation to who—and whose property—is protected. In many traditional societies, women and slaves did not exactly have full roles in the implicit social contract. Foreigners also can have an ambiguous or negligible status. Indeed, if we look at what many would consider moral progress, much of it consists not so much of changed moral rules as it does of extensions of existing rules to people (women, subjugated racial or religious groups, etc.) who previously had not had full protection.

Finally, even if we assign primary functions to morality, that does not mean that every morality is very successful in fulfilling these functions. Some moralities may turn out, on examination, merely to be clumsy attempts. This is especially true if the goal of protecting entrenched power is pursued in a way that impairs any general function of protecting society's members and their property. Sometimes, indeed, what protects entrenched power in the short run may undermine it—perhaps by producing lasting hatred—in the long run, so that a morality of the sort just characterized can turn out not to fulfill any of its purposes well.

What must be true of a morality if it is to protect the persons and property of a society? Clearly, whatever other features it has, it will have to forbid obvious forms of harmful behavior. It will have to do this in a way that is clear to the great majority of people rather than obscure, and forceful rather than mild.

In short, given this primary function, a morality can be expected to forbid various forms of killing (grouped together as "murder"), various forms of taking other people's property without their permission (grouped together as "theft"), along with rape, torture, and, more generally, grievous bodily harm. Prohibitions of these sorts are very widespread, and indeed we would be surprised to find a group with no prohibitions against, say, killing other members of the group with no provocation or taking their property without their permission. In short, bearing in mind the primary functions, we can discern a near-universal core of morality.

Plainly, though, moralities often cover much more territory than this core does. If morality develops as a pressure system to protect individuals and their property, it might be only natural for the pressure system to extend to other behavior that was widely found repugnant. Moralities could be concerned also with sexual behavior and with violations of taboos.

Early anthropologists, notably Ruth Benedict and Margaret Mead, emphasized variability of morality among different cultures. But much of their attention was focused on sex and on marriage rules. Although these are important, they cannot be viewed merely as protections pure and simple; they (along with established forms for the transfer or inheritance of property) might be considered more analogous to traffic rules governing social interactions.

It should be emphasized that this analogy is far from perfect; but it includes the fact that some possible sets of rules will be more conducive to human flourishing than others, and also that one desideratum is that risks of people getting hurt are to be avoided. There is a strong case for preferring monogamy to polygamy or polyandry. But this is compatible with the thought that a society that practices polyandry or polygamy is not wicked in the way that one which winks at casual murder and torture is. It remains the case that the core of morality—what most of us feel must be almost universally respected if we are to live minimally decent lives—consists of basic protections of our persons and property.

Could such core morality be formulated as a compilation of judgments of particular cases (along with imaginable cases that did not differ from them in any relevant respect), such as "Taking someone else's property in circumstances C_1, C_2, C_3, etc., is not allowed"? This would be obviously unworkable. Many of us would have trouble in keeping track of such case morality. Further, if core morality is to do its job, it must be grasped even by young children and retained even by dimwitted adults. Case morality would be totally inadequate for this. Broad general rules are what is required.

There is a difficult problem here, one that will enter this and the next chapter at various points. There are two extremes in the formulation of core morality that are unpalatable to many people. One extreme is exemplified by any morality that consists simply of broad general rules that seemingly do not allow for exceptions.

The name sometimes given to this approach is *rigorism*. There has been debate as to whether Kant was a rigorist. He often writes as if he is one, but some of his admirers during the last half century or so have suggested that the apparent rigorism cannot be taken at face value (see Paton 1953–1954). In any event, rigorism has declined in appeal since Kant's day. Thus we have Lawrence Kohlberg, a late-twentieth-century admirer of Kant, creating the case of the man who needs medicine for his dying wife which he really should steal (if there is no other way to get it) from the local, highly unreasonable pharmacist.

If core rules of morality have exceptions, then a natural response is to give up on rules. Perhaps none of them is totally exempt from imaginable exceptions. It might seem that one can be safe with the other extreme from rigorism, the minimalist policy of what I have been calling "case morality" and what elsewhere has been termed "situation morality."

There is a third alternative. Alan Donagan, in developing his version of Kantian morality, has argued that exceptions can be implicit in a rule (1977, 91–94). Promise keeping is a good example: those of us who were brought up to take promise keeping seriously know that there are cases in which hardly anyone would expect a promise to be kept. If your promise to meet someone for coffee at 3 o'clock turns out to require you to neglect a friend who desperately needs help or to miss an opportunity that would completely transform your life, then it is understood that you should not keep your promise. Understanding this is like knowing how to use words in a language: it does not require specification of every imaginable case (which would be impossible) but merely an ability to be intuitively reasonable about what is appropriate.

Given Donagan's model, we can take account of the functions of morality without having to embrace rigorism. Of course we want the people around us to have learned core morality in terms of general rules rather than case morality. For that matter, we might trust ourselves more if we had learned general moral rules, which sometimes can offer a little more protection against temptation in unusual and disorienting circumstances than case morality can. But if it becomes clear that general rules have imaginable exceptions, we can continue to accept the rules in a reading that allows for reasonable exceptions.

One possible objection to the Donagan strategy might be this. To accept a general rule while allowing for reasonable exceptions has the air of holding on to the rule and at the same time letting it go. If we are ready for exceptions, then what power or protection does the rule afford?

The answer is that there are two features of the learning of core moral rules that give them power over us even if we believe that there are imaginable exceptions. First, there is the factor (already discussed) of learned inhibitions. Second, the Donagan strategy certainly does not imply that one should be on the lookout for exceptions to moral rules. Indeed, there would be something corrupt about a person who was quick to notice possible exceptions, even apart from how this person actually behaved. We normally assume that, even if moral rules have imaginable exceptions, part of learning a morality is to become thoroughly used to the idea that situations in which the moral rules straightforwardly apply are the norm.

There then are twin dangers: excessive rigidity on one hand, and excessive openness to exceptions on the other. My sense is that the former often is more likely than the latter, and that (given the alternatives) perhaps it should be. The Donagan approach does not preclude teaching of morality that allows for this.

Let us return to the earlier remarks about apparent differences between moral judgments and some other kinds of ethical judgments, refining and developing them in the light of morality's functions. First, there is a general contrast between moral judgments (very likely to be taken as the business of others besides the agent) and other kinds of ethical judgments, such as those of ideals or of what a person's major goals should be (which may well be regarded as not the business of anyone but the agent). If morality has a function of maintaining a social order that protects individuals and their property, then there will be an understandable tendency to regard violations of moral norms as everyone's business. Certainly a morality that successfully fulfills this function will need some degree of active, felt community support. We need to bear in mind how tempting violation of moral norms can be, and how cumbersome and unworkable it would be to rely only on legal machinery in dealing with all of them. A morality that does not elicit strong social pressure, as a force against immorality (and really as a form of what Mill, in the 14th paragraph of chapter 5 of *Utilitarianism*, considers punishment), is highly unlikely to do a good job of protecting us.

This line of reasoning must be qualified in two ways. First, it does not rule out the possibility that a number of individuals, and perhaps also cohesive groups, within a society will consider violations of central norms as not their business. The argument of the preceding paragraph shows, I think, that a morality cannot be effective unless the dominant attitude in the society encourages people to take violations of central moral norms as being their business. The degree and uniformity of this encouragement can vary from morality to morality. But if either is very low—if too many people regard violation of central norms as not their business, or if the degree of concern is typically very mild—we will become hesitant to label what we are talking about as a morality. It would be as if someone were to label as a "knife" a perfectly spherical object that is useless for cutting.

Second, the contrast with which we began, between moral judgments that notionally are everyone's business and judgments of ideals or major goals of a person's life that are not, is contingent. We could imagine a society in which all ethical judgments are taken as everyone's business. In such a society, even leisure activities that harmed no one would be subject to severe criticism. Perhaps Calvin's Geneva came very close to being such a society. The Afghanistan of the Taliban provides a more recent example.

This possibility—a society that constantly, so to speak, breathes down its members' necks—does not, however, count against the claim that there is a *general* contrast between moral judgments and other kinds of ethical judgments with respect to the ways in which they will be taken as the business of people other than the agent. It is true that there can be societies that regard Smurf's lolling on the beach or playing cards in his spare time as just as much everyone's business as acts of theft or murder would be. But such social organizations of attitudes have so many disadvantages that it is no surprise that the societies that center on them have been fairly rare and do not persist for very long. It is contingent that any given society allows for the contrast under discussion between the moral and the non-moral. But it is predictable that societies *typically* do allow for the contrast, and this looks like a valid social generalization.

One problem for a society that eliminates the contrast is that what in most places are clearly non-moral judgments—for example, that an intelligent person is better off pursuing the contemplative life than in entirely eschewing contemplative activity and spending most of her or his time in mindless diversions—take on the conscious attention and high pressure to conform that justifiably characterize central moral norms. To that extent, these judgments will begin to look like moral judgments. The division to which most of us are accustomed, between the distasteful and the sloppy or tacky on one side and the immoral on the other, will seem less real. Inevitably, this extension of the reign of conformity and conscious attention will be experienced as wearying and oppressive, which is why it is more likely as a short-run reaction to perceived previous disorder than as a long-run state of a society.

A similar set of points applies to the general contrast between the strongly felt guidance of moral judgments and the less strong guidance (a nudge instead of a shove) of judgments of ideals and of what one's central goals in life should be. Some individuals or groups can have what looks like a highly relaxed attitude toward morality, seeming almost indifferent as to whether central moral norms are respected. But a morality cannot be effective unless the dominant attitude in the society to central norms is not so relaxed.

It also is possible for individuals or groups to take some non-moral judgments as offering guidance of the strength one normally associates with moral judgments. Even aesthetic judgments could be taken that way. Poor taste in music could be greeted with the hostility normally accorded to murder and torture. Ultimately, though, it is no surprise that this is somewhat rare. As Mill points out, even when we have a clear negative attitude toward what he terms foolishness or depravation of taste (1859/1978, 77), this typically takes a form that is different from our negative attitude toward such things as murder and torture. The felt urge is more akin to avoidance than to hitting out.

Could there be a morality that includes different moral requirements for different individuals? This is a complicated question for two reasons. First, it appears true that we expect more of some people than of others, even in situations that center on execution of a moral choice. This is especially true when there are moral commitments tied to a religious vocation. Second, it might seem obviously true that people in different positions in society have special obligations connected to those positions. Lawyers have obligations that non-lawyers do not have; parents have obligations that non-parents do not have; and so on.

Nevertheless let me suggest that there is a way of giving an answer—in relation to what appear to be the most difficult cases—that is a qualified "No." It is true that we expect more of some people than of others. Some of this relates to virtues that can be seen as matters of degree. We may expect more from Smith than Bloggs in matters of generosity or courage. But a traditional way of speaking of this involves praise of Smith's high degree of generosity and courage as *supererogatory*; the baseline moral requirement is the same for Smith and Bloggs.

Many of the cases in which we expect more of one person than of another can be addressed by means of hypotheticals. If someone is a lawyer, then (*if* we assume that a central requirement of professional ethics also is a moral one), she or he is morally bound by client confidentiality. If Mary is your child, then you ought to give her various forms of help and consideration that could not be reasonably expected of you for someone who is not your child. If your religious vocation included various vows, then you ought to act accordingly unless you are willing to renounce the vocation.

This creates space for holding that morality applies equally to all of us, and that much of it consists of "if" clauses. Part of morality tells you how you have to behave if you are (or become) a lawyer, or a parent, or someone's loyal friend. This strategy for saving the idea of morality that applies equally to everyone may look ad hoc, but we should reflect that on any account, morality is full of "if" clauses. Traditional morality tells you what you should do if you have made a promise, if there is something you need that at present belongs to someone else, and so on.

A further complication should be mentioned in relation to the special situations of parenthood and friendship: in both, there are things that should be done out of love, rather than a sense of duty. But this complication counts against regarding some of the obligations as being *moral* obligations. It does not count against the claim that, if there are moral obligations, these apply to anyone who is in the appropriate situation.

In light of all of this, it is tempting to conclude that morality, like the law (and unlike what would be reasonable judgments of what the goals of life should be), applies irrespective of persons. Hence what morality recommends in a given situation (taking "situation" to exclude what the person who is in that situation is like) will be the same for any rational agent. Part of the appeal of this is that it blocks facile attempts to make oneself an exception to some moral norm. It does not allow someone to say, "Such and such would be right for me, because of the person I am, but would not be morally acceptable for anyone else (or for most people)."

This conclusion must be approached cautiously. To begin with, two sets of issues need to be disentangled. There is, first of all, the issue of whether someone can claim a special exemption from a moral requirement because of the kind of person she or he is. But there also are issues of generalization (as opposed to universalization). Can someone legitimately say, "It would not be desirable if people in general did the *sort* of thing that I am doing, because there would be subtle but important differences between the nature of what most of them would do (and the likely consequences) and the nature of what I am doing"?

There may be a fine line between saying this (claiming special skill, involving subtle details, as a moral problem solver) and saying, "It would be right for me but wrong for others, because of the kind of person I am." But there are reasons, which we shortly will explore, for ruling out the claim for exemption from a general moral requirement that is based on the kind of person one is. On the other hand, the claim that ultimately is based on appreciation of subtle factors that might well elude others is not so easily ruled out. It points to a tension within morality that we later will need to examine.

The main reason for ruling out the "because of the kind of person I am" claim of exception is this. If someone can opt out of what looks like a general moral requirement because of the sort of person she or he is, then the rest of us might think "Perhaps I too could opt out of such and such an unpalatable moral requirement?" Morality's hold over us inevitably would be undermined by the associated envy and resentment. In the end, the power of morality requires that it notionally have the same power over everyone.

Reservations

Part of what we have seen thus far is that morality can fulfill the functions that we expect it to fulfill only if there is a core of general rules, many of them designed to prevent obvious forms of harm. It may be tempting to suppose that what is true of the core must be true of morality, period. We can begin to explore why this is not so.

Preliminary grounds for reservations can be found if we look at some great ethical philosophies that are very different from Kant's. Two that have some similarities to each other are those of Aristotle and Confucius. One of the similarities is in the limited role of general rules.

Aristotle makes clear this limited role in Book II of the *Nichomachean Ethics*, in his account of finding the mean. To find the mean, in his view, is to rely on judgment grounded in experience (rather than on general rules) to determine what is appropriate in each case. Confucius speaks of his flexibility, of his not having an inflexible "Thou shalt not" (1938, 18.8, 221–222). There is a Confucian *Doctrine of the Mean* that was, according to legend, written by Confucius's grandson.

A further similarity is that arguably neither Aristotle nor Confucius distinguishes a special category of ethical judgment that corresponds to our category of the "moral." Nevertheless, it is abundantly clear that both philosophers hold an ethics that includes what we would term moral judgments. Aristotle makes this clear in his remarks on adultery in Book II. Further, there is no reason not to assume that both Aristotle and Confucius would agree that what we would consider murder, rape, or theft is generally wrong, and that they would treat this wrongness in much the way in which we treat moral wrongness.

It looks though as if each of them also would treat some judgments that he thinks do *not* fall out from general rules in much the way in which we treat moral wrongness. Gross misjudgments, in cases in which a great deal is at stake, that take an agent far from the mean look eligible for this treatment. Someone who is too quick to conciliate a repressive ruler and to go along with policies of unreasonable taxation might be treated by Confucius in that way (1938, 11.16, 156–157). Aristotle might have a similar response to someone who carelessly misjudged the risks in a situation that called for courage.

Part of what this suggests is this. Even if we accept the previous argument, that the functions of morality dictate that it contain a core of general rules, this does not imply that *all* of morality consists of general rules. We should bear in mind that the need for general rules, which can be readily learned and remembered, is especially great in relation to standard cases involving actions of the sort that virtually everyone wants to be protected against: murder, rape, torture, and theft. General rules regarding these are at the core of morality.

But there typically is more to morality than its core, and there may be less urgent need in some areas to have simple general rules to rely on. Also, there can be non-standard cases even in relation to murder, theft, and so on that cannot plausibly be regarded as resolvable merely by application of a familiar general rule. The fact that we need and can rely on general rules in the most urgent moral choices that people typically have to make does not imply that we can formulate, in general rules, all that matters in every non-standard case.

This brings us back to the tension within morality earlier mentioned. Can there be "hard cases" in which standard and generally acceptable moral rules may appear to dictate one kind of decision, but which an intelligent and sensitive agent reasonably can believe constitute exceptions to the rules? There are obvious examples in relation to promise breaking and lying. Plausible examples in relation to major moral rules, governing such matters as murder, rape, and torture, are not so easy to construct; and it always is arguable that there are not any. We will address this in the final chapter, in relation to the difficulties and possible roles of consequentialist considerations.

In the meantime, there are the kinds of issues that both Aristotle and Confucius appear to have had principally in mind. These involve matters of some importance such as those in which one has to decide what constitutes reasonable risks, or who should be helped (and how much), or how one should fulfill (or perhaps, in a present case, reject) civic responsibilities.

Both Aristotle and Confucius seem to think that good solutions typically require intelligence, some relevant experience, and also a reasonable degree of flexibility. There can be good or poor moral problem solving. The first step in good problem solving (in such cases) is not to assume that mechanical application of familiar moral rules will necessarily provide the solution.

All of this can seem very plausible. Surely a frequent feature of moral life is the challenge of moral problem solving: sorting out a reasonable response to a difficult case. But we do need to be mindful of the tension within morality earlier mentioned. The social dimension of morality, as we have seen, is such that any personal moral decision can be regarded as a recommendation to others. There is the further complication, to be explored in chapter 9, that others who follow one's lead might perform actions that are of the same general sort but not entirely the same. Hence there could be reasons for wanting to disavow the implied recommendation even if one thinks that the specific action, by what one construes as the best standards of moral problem solving, is otherwise acceptable.

The tension thus is that there can be room for a positive judgment of a course of action (if one remains within the normal boundaries of reflection on moral problem solving), and at the same time a negative judgment of the implied recommendation (and its likely effects) implicit in the course of action. One sees this kind of tension in military cases in which someone intelligently arrived at a successful course of action, violating normal procedures or rules, and (because of the unacceptable precedent that this represented) was court-martialed.

This may be taken to suggest that the structure of morality, besides being more complicated than it often is represented as being, can leave room for occasional indeterminacy. "What is the best thing to do in this situation?" can, in this view, have more than one answer. The answer may depend on whether we look simply at the normal considerations of moral problem solving or whether we focus on what can be recommended as a model for general moral use. On the other hand, because all morality is implicitly social, there is something implausible about holding that an action that we could not recommend is acceptable. My view is that some intermediate verdict, such as "unacceptable but in some cases forgivable," is appropriate.

Conclusion

We have seen that any morality, no matter how idiosyncratic, is implicitly a social morality; and that this has further implications. It requires that morality apply irrespective of persons. It also requires a central role for general rules.

Philosophers like Kant, who correctly saw the central role of general rules and the importance of morality's applying irrespective of persons, may have been too quick to assume that this is the whole story of what morality is. Others (especially proponents of "situation ethics"), who realized that the general logic of ethical judgments yields neither result—and who further saw that in some cases of moral judgment, crucial elements cannot be formulated in general terms—have been too quick to brush aside Kant's insights.

In all of this, as before, we need to be mindful of the variety of judgments that fall under the heading of "ethics" or, more narrowly, under the heading of "morality." The Kantian picture grows out of preoccupation with standard moral decisions of a central kind. Difficult, non-standard cases, and choices in areas of morality away from the core, may fit it less comfortably. An extreme anti-Kantian disdain for requirements of general rules, on the other hand, can be plausible only if one focuses on difficult non-standard cases and ignores the implications of morality's social role.

6

Steps to Theory

Earlier it was suggested that many moral judgments, even among people trained in philosophy, appear grounded first and foremost in a sense of what feels right (or wrong). This has contributed to ethicists talking about intuitions, such as the strong intuition virtually everyone has that it is wrong to torture someone just to see how he or she reacts. Intuitions like this can seem extremely reliable. One might readily think that most of the people one knows have sound intuitions, at least in relation to core ethical requirements. The natural question, then, is "Do we need more than intuitions to have an adequate ethics?"

In particular, we could question the need for ethical theory. By ethical theory, I mean a broad, systematic account of a range of ethical problems, in which some claims are treated as more fundamental than (and either as providing justification for, or a way of testing) others. The most influential Western theories of ethics have been Kant's and utilitarianism. But there are many variants. The late twentieth century has seen, for example, John Rawls's theory of justice and, more recently, T. M. Scanlon's theory of what we owe to one another. Hobbes can be held to have developed a contractualist ethical theory, which in some respects is a forerunner of Scanlon's.

It is hard to say whether Plato or Aristotle had an ethical theory in the sense under discussion. In some respects, their accounts of ethics can seem like the examples above, at least in their breadth and in their presentation of integrated views of what is good in life. There is, however, less of a clear-cut sense of a fundamental level that justifies or tests less fundamental claims, than there is in the ethical philosophies of Kant, Bentham, and J. S. Mill.

Perhaps it is no accident that Kantian and utilitarian ethical theories appear after the achievements of Sir Isaac Newton? It is possible to think that ethics came to imitate physics (a discipline that was much more successful in achieving clearly visible progress), and that this has been unfortunate. This can lead back to the thought that ethical theory, especially in the full-blown form represented by Kant and Mill, is unnecessary or even a mistake and that sound intuitions are all that is needed.

Elements of this anti-theory line of thought are useful, and should not be disregarded. There are good reasons for suspicion of attempts to model ethics on physics. These include the obvious contrasts between the two, not least in degree of precision. Differences in construal, also, play an important part in ethical disagreements among ordinary people, in a way not paralleled in ordinary people's views of the physical world. As Thomas Kuhn and others have pointed out, differences in construal are key to some of the advanced debates among scientists about the adequacy of rival theories. But this is a far cry from their pervasiveness in ordinary discourse about right and wrong.

Despite such reservations, this chapter will begin an argument for ethical theory. Clearly, the kind of theory that will emerge will not be very much like a scientific theory. The second part of the book will continue the argument, shaping it largely as one for the importance of judgments of quality of life (in the sense of value) in any fully adequate theory. This chapter's beginnings will concern elements of ethical theory that have to be seen as useful, and indeed as indispensable for adequate ethical reflection. The fact that these elements are heterogeneous will lead to another theme of the second part of the book: that the best ethical theory will be multi-level and not monolithic or tightly unified.

The Problem of Refractory Intuitions

It is notorious that often something seemed obviously acceptable to people (who by the normal standards of their communities counted as decent), but that virtually all of us now judge that those people through moral blindness accepted evil. "Nice" people accepted slavery, imprisonment of debtors, religious persecutions, racial discrimination, and denial of opportunities to women. It can seem amazing that such things did not bother them. We like to think of ourselves as "nice" people. But what practices do we accept, about which our descendants will be equally incredulous?

This worry connects with one of the themes of Jonathan Bennett's "The Conscience of Huckleberry Finn" (1974). This paper takes off from the episode in the Mark Twain novel in which Huckleberry Finn (who has been sharing a raft on the Mississippi with an escaped slave, Jim) comes to feel morally obligated to return Jim to his owner. After all, as he has been brought up to believe, Jim is property; and to remove someone's property without that person's permission is, as he knows, theft. But somehow he cannot bring himself to do what his conscience tells him is right.

Bennett produces other cases, some from real life, in which a conscience has yielded instructions which virtually all of us would agree represent a moral mistake. Heinrich Himmler's conscience told him that it was wrong to enable Jews to avoid being sent to concentration camps. To please his doctor, he sometimes helped Jews, but then his conscience bothered him.

The obvious question is how anyone can check on whether what his or her conscience commands is a mistake. Bennett has a general suggestion. It is that the deliverances of sympathy for others can operate as a check on the pronouncements of conscience.

This clearly works for the cases that Bennett presents. Would it work for all problematic cases? The examples of slavery and of the general denial of advanced education to women are instructive. No doubt the great majority of slaves did not want to be slaves, just as Jim did not want to be returned to his owner. To the extent that sympathy involves sharing the motivations of the person sympathized with, sympathy would enable someone to have the correct reaction to their plight.

But could there have been an occasional slave, here or there, who did not mind being a slave, who simply took it as normal? This might seem preposterous. Slavery, as we all know, was a monstrous evil. But a judgment like ours is more easily made when a certain point in general awareness has been reached, and this in turn is made possible by a change in general social conditions. Before these changes, some people (among the mistreaters and perhaps among the mistreated) may not think to question arrangements that they are used to and that seem "just the way things are."

It is instructive that in *Uncle Tom's Cabin*, which did so much to increase opposition to slavery, Harriet Beecher Stowe focused on cruelty to slaves: both physical cruelty and the psychological cruelty involved when families were separated. We are especially ready to sympathize with victims of cruelty. This response makes it especially easy to think that there is something deeply wrong with the institutions that make this cruelty possible. However, it cannot be ruled out that there may have been a slave establishment here or there in which the these forms of cruelty were not a feature.

Slavery was monstrously wrong even in these cases. Something can be very wrong even if the victim does not consciously object or suffer in some dramatic, visible way. But in a case like this, the route to realizing what is wrong cannot be through what we normally term sympathy for the victim. Sympathy connotes sharing of feelings. If we think that someone has been cheated in life, but that person has no visible feelings about it, the normal emotion will be indignation, including a strong sense that the victim deserved more—but without any clear sense of shared feelings.

This is relevant to the denial of opportunities to women, especially in those earlier periods in which it may be that many women had not developed a sense that they were being cheated in life. Of course, one would have a strong sympathy for the woman who realized that she was a victim of systematic injustice and who struggled against it (or simply quietly resented it). A different emotional response, if the case was one of a woman who treated as normal the denials of opportunity that constricted her life, might be a mixture of indignation and pity.

All of this suggests that sometimes a general capacity for sympathy will not serve to alert us that deliverances of our consciences are faulty. Not all victims suffer. Some merely live constricted lives.

What can serve, in these cases of victims who are uncomplaining and unresentful, is a sense of the potentialities of life. The person who has been denied freedom or opportunities can be seen as having missed out on the possibility of a fuller life. Many ethical theories or proto-theories have room for the judgment that it is wrong to acquiesce in a social order that denies people such possibilities. Aristotle would think it a real loss not to have developed (and then exercised) certain virtues, especially intellectual virtues, if one had the capacity to do so. Mill might think that being cheated out of a chance to enjoy some kinds of "higher" pleasures is a grievous loss, whether or not the victim knows what she or he is missing.

Kant's theory, however, provides the sharpest view of why a conscience is deficient that acquiesces in denials of autonomy or of opportunities to develop talents. Much of what he provides is linked to the insistence on the dignity of rational beings, which he holds entails the requirement of respect of persons (the second form of the categorical imperative). Whether or not Kant himself would have seen it, this implies the wrongness of denying higher education to women who could benefit from it. It certainly implies the wrongness of slavery.

How do we arrive at a realization of the dignity of rational beings, and the importance of respect for persons? Kant is remarkably sketchy in what he says about this. It all seems connected in his mind with the claim that rational beings can arrive at the endorsement of universal moral laws, but the nature of the connection is left obscure. We can return in the last part of the book to the justification of respect for persons. For the time being, let us agree, for the sake of argument, that slavery was and is wrong and that it was wrong to deny higher education to women. Let us agree, further, that a sense of the dignity of rational beings can play a useful role in getting people to realize the wrongness of slavery or the denial of higher education to women, even when the victim does not suffer or complain.

The suggestion is that elements of theories can be crucial in liberating us from faulty intuitions or mistaken deliverances of conscience. Two such elements look especially useful. One is the sense that, other things being equal, it is better that a person (or an animal) not suffer. This is at the root of many of the strongest cases of sympathy. The other is the sense that persons are not like inanimate objects, and further that to be a rational being is to have at least the potentiality of something fine, and that to keep in mind this potentiality is to engender respect.

These elements occupy a middle ground between developed theories and intuitions. Someone who had not arrived at the idea of the categorical imperative or of the utilitarian calculus could have one or both of the "senses" or general ideas just discussed. These would provide a way of seeing moral problems and their possible solutions, without necessarily committing one to the more definite approaches involved in fully developed theories.

There are two important points here. One is that the history of moral thought, up to and very likely including the present, has been a history of feelings about right and wrong, some of which turned out to be indefensible. If we want a second source of judgment on the moral issues involved, we need to turn to something like an element of theory. Only through sympathy, or a general attitude of respect for persons, or perhaps something else that has played a comparable role, can we get beyond the stock moral responses we have absorbed.

The second point is this. Not only do the theory-like elements in the end need some kind of justification, but also they need interpretation. In practical terms, we need to know what the bounds (and practical implications) of sympathy are. Should we be sympathetic to someone who is being punished for evildoing? How much help might we owe to someone whose misery largely arises from persistent ineptitude? There are similar questions about the bounds and the practical implications of respect for persons.

All of this can be seen clearly in relation to another theory-like element that has loomed large in recent philosophy, namely the requirement of fairness. An idea of fairness, like sympathy and respect for persons, occupies a middle ground between intuitions and theory. Some things simply seem unfair to us, and this is a long step toward the conclusion that they are wrong. But a theory also can systematize an interpretation of fairness, and make it play a pivotal role in some kinds of moral judgment. The title of an important early essay by Rawls that points in this direction is "Justice as Fairness" (1958).

Let us agree that fairness is so important that a determination that something is unfair should count decisively against it. This still leaves us with the question, "What is fairness?" We need to investigate our standards for what is fair, and the ways in which they might be debated. There also is the question of whether there are many situations in which fairness should not be the main consideration. For a plausible candidate, imagine a case in which an entirely fair way of dividing food among some very hungry children would take hours to arrive at.

Fairness

Less than a century ago, it was widely thought to be fair that a woman be paid less for a highly skilled job than would a man who did essentially the same work and had the same job description. One rationalization was that many male wage earners, and not so many female ones, were the sole support of children and of a spouse who stayed at home. A man therefore could be presumed to need more money than a woman.

It should be said, right away, that the rationalization for a practice may not be the real reason it is adopted. In this case, the underlying cause very likely was simple bias in favor of men. Nevertheless, in what follows we can (for the sake of argument) take the rationalization at face value. In one respect, I think that it fits the facts. It fits, that is, what many people thought, and sincerely accepted, once they had to think and to justify themselves.

This case is a useful example of a number of points. First, there was a widespread intuition about what was fair that now a great many people would regard as preposterous; even those who continue to support unequal treatment tend now to adopt a very defensive tone. Interpretations of what constitutes fairness can be highly questionable, even if for a while they are widely taken as obviously right.

Second, the case illustrates how such intuitions can be deeply embedded in a cluster of social arrangements. Plainly, established patterns that had made it unusual for married women to have careers played a large part in the judgment that male wage earners needed more money. Conversely, the appeal of the intuition that men should be paid more than women for essentially the same work lost some of its strength and pervasiveness when increasing numbers of married women continued to work.

One odd feature of the rationalization for this intuition—that the men needed more money for their families—is this. It was widely accepted by socially conservative groups. Yet it has more than a slight resemblance to the Marxist dictum that people who produce according to their ability should be paid on the basis of their need. Why was it so widely accepted despite this potentially discordant feature?

A plausible answer is in terms of perceived social utilities. Assume that a society is going to retain a basic arrangement of married men usually working (and supporting families) and married women not so often working and supporting families. This could be seen as normal, just the way things are. Then, it might seem (especially to someone who took an optimistic view of working men's support of their families) that there is more good involved in increased money being channeled, in effect, to the wives and children of working men than in working women getting more money than they are typically thought to need.

Whether this would have been a correct judgment of the utilities is open to debate. (In one respect, it looks extremely faulty, by not factoring in the way in which the established pattern penalized some women for leading fuller and more independent lives and made it more difficult for others to try.) But it is clear that it is how the utilities could have looked to many people. It strongly suggests that intuitions of what satisfies a concept such as that of "fairness" can be influenced by judgments of how possible policies affect people's lives—given the established social arrangements, which are regarded as normal.

Judgments of what is fair, in any case, are very often determined mainly by what people have been brought up to think they can expect or demand. Was it fair that for long periods of time in Europe the bulk of a man's property would be inherited by the oldest son? No doubt there were some younger sons (and perhaps an occasional daughter) who wondered about this. But my guess is that most people took the fairness of the arrangement for granted. It was the normal, expected thing.

Further, the privileging of older sons over younger ones did connect with a persistent element in our intuitions of entitlement. The older sons had been there first. It is still widely held to be fair in many matters that those who are first ("finders, keepers") have special rights.

The cases that I have been describing are ones in which most of us will think that we have a much better judgment of what is fair than people in the past had. Certainly there has been a general change in outlook, marked by an equalizing tendency. The notion that older sons have privileges, or that one race or gender has privileges as against another, will now seem extremely backward and archaic. The temptation is to say that we now pretty much know what is fair and what is unfair.

Let me agree with this on one point, and express a strong reservation on another. My agreement is with the notion that current concepts of fairness are much improved over the ones I had been describing. There has been real progress. The progress, however, is perhaps more limited than my brief description would indicate. In many quarters, unreasonable unequal treatment persists, but it is defended by a shifting set of rationalizations, delivered in a more defensive tone.

Here is the reservation. The temptation, to which even very good philosophers may have succumbed, is to treat "fairness" (or for that matter "justice") as a fairly precise concept. It will be thought then that we can provide accounts of fairness in which, by and large, contestable interpretations do not play a large part. My view is that "fairness" is far from being a precise concept. There are some obvious cases (involving such things as racial and gender equality) in which a strong consensus, which I support, has developed about most of what it requires. But there are other large areas in which interpretation of the concept remains—and perhaps always will remain—highly contestable.

We can get at the imprecision, and at the sizable areas in which what counts as fairness is contestable, in two ways. One is by looking at areas in which what is fair seems contestable, and getting a sense of how difficult it would be to reduce the contestability. The other is to examine the logical core of the ethical requirement of fairness, taking care to distinguish the core from other elements.

Here are a few examples of issues of fairness that resist the kind of resolution that would attract a consensus of reasonable people. (1) It is well known that highly intelligent people tend to be paid a good deal more for their work than are people of average or below-average intelligence, even when it appears that the latter work harder than the former. Most people would regard this as intuitively fair: after all, the highly intelligent typically "contribute" more. Also, there are market factors to consider. The services of highly intelligent people are more in demand. But some radical philosophers, especially during the 1970s, have suggested that the pattern is unfair and unjust. Higher intelligence often is largely a matter of genetic luck, rather than special effort. Why should people be rewarded for what is merely luck? Intuitively, it has been suggested, what should be rewarded is effort, which is within an agent's control. A more extreme view is that even effort is often conditioned by luck: your capacity to make an effort is to a large extent a function of such things as childhood upbringing, which again were not much in your control. This might suggest that there is no reason, apart perhaps from need, to pay anyone more than anyone else.

To avoid misunderstanding, let me say that in this example (and the examples to follow) of a variety of possible views of what is fair, I am not suggesting that all views are equally reasonable. There are good arguments, it seems to me, for the most widely held view of what the relation between intelligence and rewards should be. They are not, however, entirely compelling arguments. It is important to see that other views can be held by people who are not fools or depraved, and that such views rest on intuitions (e.g., that people should not be rewarded for what is just luck) that have some plausibility.

(2) There are somewhat similar issues of fairness in access to post-secondary education. A much larger number of people could benefit, in a variety of ways, from some form of post-secondary education than in fact receive it. Some are prevented by lack of ability in the academic pursuits central to the most common forms of post-secondary education. Sometimes inadequate financial resources are a factor. It could be argued, though, that this is unfair: that much of what goes into academic ability is a product of the luck of genetic endowment and upbringing, and that having financial resources also is often a matter of luck. If a larger number of people could benefit from suitably tailored post-secondary education, then (it can be argued) it is unfair not to give everyone this opportunity.

(3) In the late twentieth century, there has been extended philosophical consideration, much of it centering on Rawls's A *Theory of Justice*, of what is a just distribution of resources within a society. But there also are issues of fairness that move across societal boundaries. Is it fair, it can be asked, that someone who has

considerable skills and works hard (say as an engineer or a teacher) in a Third World country should be rewarded far less than her or his counterpart in a prosperous and liberal society? Sometimes the luck of genetic endowment and of an upbringing conducive to good performance pales in comparison with the luck of having been born in a wealthy and advanced country. Again it can be argued that it is unfair that people be rewarded or deprived on the basis of luck.

The reader who expects me now to provide a set of rational arguments in relation to these (and similar) cases, establishing what the most reasonable view is, will be disappointed. There are two reasons why this task will be shirked. The first is that this is a book about the structure of ethics, and the role within it of quality-of-life judgments. Attempting to produce a new theory of fairness is not part of my brief.

The second reason is that, at this stage in the argument of the book, there are not the resources to do a proper job of arguing for a set of judgments of what is fair. It would be easy to do a semi-adequate job, giving highly plausible reasons for, say, the arrangements that most of us are used to. But this would be more like casuistry (extended from individual decisions to social decisions) than the arguments based on philosophical analysis that one would hope for.

One step in the philosophical analysis is to disentangle elements in our contestable concepts of fairness. We need to distinguish those that may involve logical validity from ones that require judgment of particular cases or relations. This will be a distinction between the core of the concept and elements that have gathered (or could gather) around the core.

At the core of fairness is the requirement to treat similar cases similarly. If the reasons for Mary to get some reward or form of treatment are substantially the same as Mabel's, then it is only fair that Mary should get what Mabel gets. Further, in a just society, Mary will simply expect that she will get what Mabel gets.

The imperative to treat in the same way cases that are substantially the same follows from R. M. Hare's (1963) thesis of universalizability, which he argues (in my view correctly) is a logical truth. The thesis applies to all normative judgments, not merely those of fairness. For example, if two paintings are substantially the same—if they have descriptive characteristics which in any aesthetically relevant respect are substantially similar—then if one is beautiful, the other is beautiful.

What makes fairness special is that it concerns treatment in situations in which how people are treated really matters, and should be guided by what they deserve or reasonably could have expected. Not all of our treatment of other people, of course, need be guided by desert. Love involves very different considerations from those of fairness. Also there are many aspects of our treatment of others whose importance falls below the level that might call for fairness. In these it can be appropriate merely to be spontaneous. If X and Y have a relationship with you that is substantially the same, and one day you telephone X to chat, it is not "unfair" that you do not telephone Y to chat. But if they are your employees and you give X a raise or extra vacation time, it is only fair that you do for Y what you did for X, unless there is some relevant factor in X's case that does not apply in Y's.

It would be hard (and I think illogical) to dissent from the requirement (in cases that matter, where desert is a factor) of equal treatment in substantially similar cases.

The key question then becomes "How do we determine whether two such cases are substantially similar?" Once we face this question, considerations of fairness that might have looked precise begin to look subject to interpretation; and contestability enters in.

Any two cases are bound to differ in some respects. Even if they look similar, there will be differences in historical background. Here is an example of how historical background might matter. Suppose X and Y are applying for a job. They are roughly the same age, and have roughly the same qualifications, except that Y's look slightly stronger. X, however, is representative of a group that is underrepresented in the more desirable professions, and this underrepresentation can be explained as the socioeconomic and psychological aftermath of some very unfortunate history. Members of X's group typically are as children given less confidence in their ultimate success in life. X, however, through intelligence and persistence, has risen to a position that is competitive with Y. Which of the two would it be fair to hire?

Many readers will recognize this immediately as the issue of affirmative action, which in many countries has been much debated in the last few decades. What is striking about these debates is that both those who want to consider historical factors and their aftermath for many members of a group, and those who do not, will frame their positions in terms of what is "fair." Plainly the intuitions of what fairness is are sharply different. Much of the difference is in which factors are considered relevant and important.

Some differences are pretty clearly trivial. That two cases involve people whose last names begin with different letters is clearly trivial. So, it would be widely agreed, is a difference in the skin color of the two protagonists (if this is considered entirely apart from any historical or psychological concomitants). There is no flat-out logical contradiction in basing a difference in treatment simply on such differences, but reasonable people would regard it as flimsy and stupid.

Some differences are not trivial, but nevertheless should be judged to be irrelevant; they do not justify differential treatment. Let us revisit the cases of a woman and a man doing essentially the same work eighty or ninety years ago, in a social setting in which men were presumed usually to have families to support and women were not. Presumed (or actual) need is not a trivial factor. To take it as relevant was not stupid, but in my judgment it was a mistake. My guess is that most readers will agree with me that it was (and is) unfair to consider presumed need in setting pay rates. The hard *philosophical* question is how one can justify one intuition of what is fair in such cases as against another.

All of this argues for a mixed assessment of the role of intuitions of fairness in ethical decision-making. Clearly such intuitions can play a progressive role. It is possible for someone to look at the kind of treatment of people that is widely held to be acceptable, and to realize that it is unfair. Such realizations have improved the condition of women, racial and religious minorities, debtors, and daughters and younger sons. On the other hand, it is not always easy to determine what is fair. There are many contestable areas, such as that of affirmative action, in which what should count as fair is highly disputable.

All the same, intuitions of fairness have had a major role in moral progress in the last two centuries. Much of this rests on the simple insistence that there needs to be a reason (and appears not to be one) to treat Moslems, Jews, and Catholics differently from Protestants, or to treat people of color differently from Caucasians, or to treat women differently from men. It may seem tempting then to say that there is a simple general solution to all social problems that involve different treatment of different groups: "Why not treat everyone in the same way?" This may seem a natural outcome of the developments of the previous centuries, in which the rights of women, minority groups, representatives of unpopular religions, and others have increasingly been respected.

There are two major difficulties though. One is that it is not easy to decide who is to be included in "everyone." Animals present especially complicated issues. The most clear-minded and sophisticated advocates of the view that animals require moral consideration, from Jeremy Bentham to Peter Singer, have held that animals are to be included in "everyone" for some purposes but not for others. In their view, animal suffering counts for as much as human suffering. But that does not mean that every kind of animal has as much right to roam the streets freely as humans generally do. Further, Singer (1993, chap. 5) makes careful distinctions among different types of animals with regard to the likely degree (and causes) of suffering that we should be worrying about.

The controversy over whether the human fetus counts among the "everyone" whose well-being deserves the same consideration is too well known to need rehearsing here. There also is room for controversy, and perhaps for uncertainty, as to the respects in which the mentally ill (or those who are suffering from Alzheimer's disease) are entitled to the same treatment as the rest of us. In many respects clearly they are, but issues of freedom of movement are especially bothersome. This is the second major difficulty: there may be cases in which there are special reasons to treat some people differently in some respects from the way one would treat others. The fact that the tendency of recent centuries has been toward equality of moral consideration (at least among human beings) does not carry any implications that would resolve all of these controversies and difficulties.

It would be nice to have a rational, systematic way of adjudicating issues of fairness. Theories such as Kant's or classical utilitarianism do offer some elements of this. But they do not eliminate all problems of interpretation; indeed they themselves need interpretation, as do their relations to specific issues.

Nevertheless, such theories have offered a clearer way of pondering, and arguing about, a wide range of ethical issues. Even if two people who accept the same theory do not agree in their judgment of a specific issue, they can agree on what kinds of considerations are relevant and which arguments cogent. This is a modest sort of usefulness. Realizing the mixed usefulness of such broad intuitions as that of fairness becomes a step toward realizing that of theory.

Respect for Persons

Another broad intuition that can help to get us beyond first judgments, and the deficiencies of our ethical habits, is that there are limits to the ways in which one can appropriately treat persons. What is a person? In most accounts, a person is a living thing that has some sense of self, of the future, and perhaps of responsibility for actions.

Recent studies suggest that gorillas and chimpanzees meet these standards, and can be considered persons. However, all or virtually all of the persons that most of us deal with are human beings. Are all human beings persons? Newborn babies do not meet the standards for personhood outlined above. But perhaps they are honorary persons, in that they can be expected in time to meet them? Most retarded humans meet the standards, but some who are severely retarded do not.

In practice we tend to conflate the category of person with that of human being. So we say such things as "That's no way to treat a human being." This is widely taken as a strong reason against the conduct in question.

It is an interesting historical question, which I will not pursue, how much thoughts of this sort have contributed to ethical progress. It is plausible to suppose that some of the people who came to oppose what had been widely accepted practices, such as slavery or the use of torture in interrogation by police or magistrates, came to say things like this. Perhaps it was a way of crystallizing a growing distaste. But it also then serves as an effective way of communicating the distaste to others.

Let me point out in passing that the usefulness of a general intuition that demands respect for persons can be expected to be much greater in the case of some refractory intuitions than in others. It could make a real difference in relation to traditional views that (by accepting slavery or the torture of prisoners) license blatant degradation, reducing humans to work machines or to their bodies. Its effect on more subtle forms of disregarding (and thus helping to stifle) human potential, such as the intuition that higher education was inappropriate for women, may be less. It is instructive that there is no evidence that Kant, the second form of whose categorical imperative enjoined respect for persons, saw a problem in that area. Its relation to some abuses of the past is even more tangential. Was it a failing of respect for persons (respect for younger sons and for daughters) that only eldest sons inherited? This could be argued only on the back of an independent argument that it was unfair and wrong.

The main thing that I want to argue about respect for persons is that the concept, like that of fairness, is much less precise and much more subject to interpretation, and the judgments of it are much more contestable, than one might have hoped. In neither case does this amount to denying that the concept is useful and important. Rather, it points toward the conclusion that more is needed.

A starting point is to survey a range of interpretations of "respect for persons." A very broad interpretation is at one extreme. Respect for persons can be taken to be the requirement that one never do anything to someone that is wrong, never do anything that the person in question has a right (or, in the case of things you do to yourself, a requirement) not to have happen. This broad interpretation is consonant with Kant's insistence that the requirement of respect for persons is equivalent to the other forms of the categorical imperative.

The trouble with the broad formulation is this. In order to have anything like a definite meaning, it requires some independent standard for what should not be done to someone else (or to oneself). As it stands, it can license very different moral positions, falling out of very different standards for what should not be done.

Here is a somewhat less broad interpretation. The words "respect" and "persons" do have connotations that narrow the focus of the requirement, and also emphasize some aspects of questionable behavior. First, the word "persons" makes clear that the requirement concerns the effects of one's actions on what Kant would term rational beings. It is hard to be sure what he would have said (had he been given modern evidence) about gorillas and chimpanzees, but it does look clear that the requirement does not govern treatment of, say, dogs and cats. Kant's view is that we should not mistreat such animals, but that respect for persons is not a factor in this.

Further, the word "respect" strongly suggests that any conduct that violates the requirement will involve a person who is a victim or whose life is diminished. The person whose life is diminished could be oneself. It is blameworthy for a woman, in Kant's account, to sell her hair (for use in wigs). To do so would be to treat parts of oneself as articles for sale (1797/1996, 177). The immorality of prostitution similarly is a failure of self-respect. By the same token, it is in a way a failure of self-respect for anyone to neglect development of his or her talents. Such neglect violates what Kant states as a major imperfect duty: the duty is "imperfect" in that there is latitude in the ways in which, and the occasions on which, it can be fulfilled.

Even great philosophers who are also very good human beings have their blind spots. Mill had a blind spot with regard to imperialism, and in *On Liberty* defended the arrogant and indefensible Opium War. Kant appears to have had a blind spot in relation to the potentialities and rights of women, about which Mill writes so eloquently and perceptively in *The Subjection of Women*. It is highly arguable that the imperfect duty to develop one's talents implies a correlative duty to make it possible for others to develop their talents, or at least not to obstruct them in any effort they might be inclined to make. In his presentation of the imperfect duty to develop one's talents, or at the place at which he condemns women's violations of self-respect (as in selling their hair), one might expect Kant to say something about a woman's positive obligations to develop her talents—and also correlative obligations that others might have. He does not.

Perhaps, though, this would be to expect too much. After all, just what is it, regarding women, that follows from the requirement of respect for persons? Most of what Kant has to say about the imperfect duty to develop one's talents, and about failures of self-respect, focuses on deficiencies rather than on advances. Could it be that the meaning, for Kant, of respect for persons is mostly concerned with failures to reach a normal standard of behavior? The normal standard at the time for women may have appeared not to require a university education.

This is to say that the requirement of respect for persons is hardly precise, and is highly subject to interpretation. It may be unfair to expect Kant's interpretation of his own words to be very much in advance of the interpretations common in his time. We, on the other hand, can see a strong case for regarding the requirement of respect for persons as demanding that women have equal opportunities to develop their talents.

Beyond this general formulation, though, what does it require? Does it include a requirement to aid people in the development of their talents by means of large and generous scholarship programs? On the negative side, can we draw a sharp line between, on one hand, acts in relation to one's own body that involve failures of self-respect and others that do not? Is there something morally questionable in earning a living as a model, or in selling a kidney to someone who needs it to live, or in bearing a child as a surrogate mother?

Despite the difficulties of interpretation presented, it should also be said that an emphasis on respect for persons normally is enormously useful. It encourages us to take other people's points of view seriously. Much of its usefulness also is outside the territory of morality. It can make everyday social interactions far more civilized.

The point is not that the concept of respect for persons is useless. In some contexts, it can be a real eye-opener. Rather, it is that the concept leaves us with a number of questions about its meaning and the kinds of case in which it is relevant. Perhaps in the end these questions cannot be answered to everyone's satisfaction. But there are ways in which we can make headway in learning to address them in a coherent and consistent way. These ways involve ethical theory.

Sympathy

Let us return to Bennett's suggestion that sympathy for others can get us beyond our intuitive moral first responses. It is undeniable that in many cases this is true. But we need to think further about how reliable and straightforward moral learning through sympathy is. Are there cases in which what the appropriate sympathetic response is becomes a matter of interpretation? May one sometimes sympathize with a puta-tively injured party without changing one's original intuitive judgment that treats as acceptable what is done to him or her?

By and large, the people we tend to be most immediately sympathetic with are those who visibly suffer. They are clearly very unhappy with what is happening (or is about to happen) to them. Our sympathy is especially forthcoming if we ourselves would be unhappy with whatever it is. Prime candidates for sympathy then are people (or animals) who are suffering physically, or are about to suffer physically or to die. Someone who has suffered a major reverse of a familiar sort also is a prime candidate for sympathy. Thus we tend to sympathize with people who have lost all of their money, or have been rejected in love.

Clearly, how a case is presented to us affects our sympathy. This is especially important in works of imaginative fiction or in films or plays. Often a character has done something (say, of a criminal nature or involving social behavior of a highly flawed sort) that leads to his or her suffering or experiencing a major reverse. If the case were presented briefly, say, in a newspaper, many people might think "serves him (or her) right." But if (as often happens in films) the criminal or flawed behavior is treated schematically, with an emphasis on the character's uncertainty and fear, virtually everyone can become very sympathetic. There may be limits. To the best of my knowledge, the possibility of sympathy with Hitler (who may well have suffered in defeat, and had an unpleasant death) has been treated only as a joke in film and theater. But the limits are pretty broad.

Of course we can sympathize, even in real life, with someone who we think deserves what happened (or is about to happen) to him or her. "What happened was just," we say, "but it is hard not to feel sorry for so-and-so." Even so, in many cases sympathy for such a person is linked (and this is relevant to Bennett's point) to a sense that things do not have to go the way they are going, that this suffering or extreme disappointment could be somehow softened.

Perhaps sometimes the sense that the transgressor's suffering could best be softened is appropriate, and sometimes it is not? How can we reasonably make a determination? Sympathy itself cannot help us much in this. As our experience of fiction, films, and plays tells us, we can be induced to sympathize with a broad range of transgressors. Even if this makes them all candidates for treatment that involves less suffering or less extreme disappointment, there need to be ways of weighing the merits of cases apart from our sympathy. It would be unreasonable to reduce justice to sentimentalism.

Further, the direction of our sympathy is very dependent on whom we focus upon. Many decisions by governments, and sometimes by ordinary responsible individuals, will affect a number of people in a mix of positive and negative ways. A familiar example is a government's decision to extend tariff protection to an industry, say steel. This will have a beneficial effect, at least in the short run, on both producers and on the workers whose jobs are then protected. On the other hand, other kinds of domestic producers, who have to pay more for the protected commodity, will experience a negative result, as will those affected by other countries' retaliatory tariffs.

Whatever the government decides to do (or not to do), there will be people to sympathize with. If the government decides not to extend tariff protection, we can feel sorry for the workers who lose their jobs. If there is tariff protection, then there will be workers and producers in other industries to feel sorry for. If the policy changes, the direction of sympathy can be jerked around by a skillful news organization. The sympathy is highly appropriate, but the sense that policy definitely should be guided by the direction of one's sympathy at the moment is not.

The problem of assigning weight to sympathy, when whatever is done or not done is likely to have mixed results, emerges sharply in a case used by (among others) R. M. Hare (1981, 24–25). During wartime, some men go overboard from a ship that is subject to imminent enemy attack and is very vulnerable. The captain of the ship judges that to stay in the area to retrieve those men will create a very serious risk of death for a very much larger group of people on the ship (and will likely bring about the destruction of the ship itself). In arithmetical terms: if the ship steams away, the sum of the probabilities of death for each of the individuals whose lives are at stake will be less than it would be if the ship remains to pick up the men in the water.

This case may be unrepresentative in one important respect. It is plausible in it to regard the best decision as determinable simply on the basis of the sum of individual probabilities for serious harm: each individual counts equally in this. There can be other cases in which whatever is done or not done will have mixed results that look different from this. In them, promises or other commitments can be argued to give some individuals special claims. Or one might distinguish between people who had accepted the risks, on one hand, and innocent bystanders, on the other. Some would argue that the latter deserve more protection (see Donagan 1977, 177–180).

At this point, it is too early to deal with these complications. Let us agree that the case of the vulnerable ship need not be taken as a template for all cases in which results will be mixed. What it does share with them, though, is that sympathy alone cannot tell us what it is best for us to do. There will always be someone, on the losing side of our decision, to sympathize with. What we need is a way to factor in our sympathies in a reasonable assignment of weights to the various interests at stake. Again this is the sort of thing for which we can hope an ethical theory will provide direction.

The need is, if anything, greater in relation to sympathy than it is in relation to intuitions of fairness or the requirement of respect for persons. This is because sympathy can skew our judgment of a case. Sympathy generally tells us something important, that we should think about and consider. But sometimes sympathy is one-sided.

Here is an example. Suppose that you are a government administrator, who has to decide whether to relax environmental standards at a specific locale. If you do not relax the standards, the costs that these generate will result in about a thousand lost jobs, causing severe economic hardship for the affected laborers and their families. If you do relax standards (and save the jobs), the incidence of cancer in the area will increase, amounting to perhaps fifteen hundred additional cases in the next thirty or forty years.

Matters of this sort are often difficult to decide, in part because there can be so much collateral suffering, among the families, friends, and communities of those most directly affected. But a heavy reliance on sympathy risks inclining us, without adequate reason, more to one side than the other. If the administrator does not relax the environmental standards, we can see—and sympathize with—the people who lose their jobs. If the administrator does relax the standards, there will be no faces of those who will be affected to arouse our sympathy. First, the negative results will not be immediate, and indeed may well not emerge at all soon. But second, we never will be reasonably sure that someone's cancer is attributable to the administrator's decision. It always will be possible that so-and-so was one of the people who would have had cancer anyway. The power of sympathy is much more on one side here than on the other.

The conclusion remains that sympathy, like our intuitions of fairness and of the requirement of respect for persons, can be extremely useful in getting us to think twice about our adherence to entrenched (but possibly faulty) moral intuitions. Often the judgment that it pulls us toward is the right one. But in cases that are more complicated, we need something to supplement our sympathies and our broad moral intuitions, especially when they generate pulls in more than one direction. In these cases, especially, we can benefit from ethical theory.

PART II

ETHICAL THEORY AND QUALITIES OF LIFE

7

The Bases of Ethical Theory

The last chapter surveyed general intuitive ideas, yielded by a sense of fairness, respect for persons, or sympathy, that carry us beyond the particular moral intuitions we have been comfortable with. A practice that we regard as normal can be called into question by such questions as "Is that fair?" "How can you treat a human being that way?" or "Isn't what that is doing to X awful?" My argument was that the general intuitive ideas need interpretation, which should include a sense of the varying weight they have in particular cases. The general intuitive ideas carry us toward theory in two ways: first, in getting us to see the limitations of the particular moral intuitions we are used to; and second, in that the general intuitive ideas themselves need work of a systematic sort.

If we wish to be systematic, one natural move is this. We can take one of the three highly attractive general intuitive ideas, formulate a principle that seems strongly connected with it, and treat this as fundamental to ethics. Here are three ways in which this can be done.

First, if we take seriously the importance of fairness, we can look for a test of fairness. Our intuitions of fairness very often locate it in the context of accepted practices, which give people a right to expect certain forms of treatment. Not all accepted practices can emerge, after careful reflection, as acceptable. Many or all societies have some entrenched abuses that are part of almost everyone's sense of what is normal.

We need to look carefully at our first judgments of fairness, and reject those that simply reflect entrenched abuses. Despite this, fairness typically cannot be considered totally on a case-by-case basis. That is, it cannot be considered isolated from what is, or should be, a web of social practices and principles that condition what people reasonably can expect. Hence the importance of fairness points toward that of a valid moral order.

Second, if we take seriously respect for persons, we have to respect the rights of individuals. If X is done to Y, to which Y would not consent, this creates at least a presumption that Y's rights are being violated. In the end, any judgment of this will be determined by a number of factors, including how much difference X makes to Y's life, what the reasons for X are, what Y reasonably could have expected, and so on.

Y's lack of consent does not in itself show that X is unacceptable. It may be that Y is simply being unreasonable in refusing to consent to X (e.g., in refusing to drive on the same side of the road as everyone else). But lack of consent, particularly if it becomes widespread, is a warning flag about any established moral order. Indeed, very widespread lack of consent undermines any claim that there is an established moral order.

If we hold a society to a high standard in this, we might say that its morality should be part of a social contract to which everyone reasonably would consent (whether in fact they do or not). That everyone reasonably would consent does not imply that everyone will. But an established moral order can exist despite a modest number of those who reject or deviate from it. One way in which respect for persons is important is that it enables us to insist on an established moral order that takes adequately into account everyone's interests, that disregards nobody.

Third, our sympathy, along with whatever benevolence we have, can incline us to assign basic importance to people's, and also animals', well-being. We sympathize with them when they suffer. Also it can (and arguably should) bother us when their lives are constricted in relation to what they might be. It is not quite the same thing when a chicken spends its entire life in a narrow cage as when a bright person is blocked from higher education or employment outside the home, but a sense of loss that is somewhat allied to sympathy can distress us (in different degrees) in both cases. All of this can lead us to regard well-being (that is, quality of life in the sense of what makes life rewarding) as basic to ethics.

These natural reflections give us not one, but three, foundations to ethics. They also give us three kinds of ethical theory. Treating a valid moral order as fundamental can lead naturally to an ethics of principles, to which Kant's first and third formulations of the categorical imperative have a pronounced affinity. To insist on the primacy of an acceptable social contract is in some respects close to this, but it places more emphasis on regard for reasonable rights of individuals, an emphasis that can be read into Kant's second formulation and also John Rawls's theory of justice. It gives us a contractualist ethics. Finally, if one treats quality of life (in the sense of what makes life most rewarding) as primary, it is natural to evaluate choices—on some level—on the basis of whether they lead preponderantly to better or worse quality of life. This gives us a consequentialist ethics.

Three foundations may seem like two too many. On the other hand, each picks out something important that we may not want to discard. This chapter will begin the task of sorting out the appeal of these three foundations and examining how the considerations that they point toward might be combined in a single theory.

Why All Three Foundations Must Be Bases
of Ethical Judgments: A First Argument

The temptation is to insist that only one of the three can be an independent basis of ethical judgments, and that the other two either can be reduced to that one or disregarded. (A less full-blown and extreme possibility, which will be explored in later chapters, is that only one of the three can be a fundamental basis of ethical judgments; but that the other two are quasi-independent, and cannot be reduced to that one or disregarded.) A well-known theory that yields to the full-blown temptation of simplicity is act consequentialism, which insists that the best act to perform is always that with the best available consequences (or, in some versions, is the one that is most likely to have the best consequences).

Kant on occasion lapsed into a simplicity of an opposite kind, as when he endorsed "Do right even though the heavens fall," meaning, apparently, that consequences should not matter to morality. The dominant view in his work arguably is more complicated than this. Certainly the examples of the operation of the categorical imperative that he gives in the *Grounding of the Metaphysics of Morals* rely on what the predictable consequences will be of universal adherence to certain maxims. (For example, if everyone makes false promises, then no one will believe promises any more, and promising will wither away—making even false promises impossible. We know, he thinks, that people are not infinitely gullible.) Further, judgment of consequences is implicated in Kant's imperfect duties to aid (some) others in need and to develop one's talents.

What did Kant actually believe about the moral relevance of consequences? As J. S. Mill pointed out in *Utilitarianism* (1861/1979, 4), there is an apparent contrariety between Kant's official view and some of the details in his ethical writings. Perhaps the consequences that he wanted excluded from consideration are merely those about which one cannot be sure in advance? Kant's fuller view of consequences is a very large scholarly subject, which I will not pursue.

What is relevant to our inquiry is the standing temptation to which act consequentialists succumb and to which Kant may have succumbed. This is to assume that a valid ethical theory must be simple, resting a straightforward decision procedure on a single base. (Kant, to be fair, had three bases—three main forms of the categorical imperative—but he did suggest that they were equivalent.) In the wake of Sir Isaac Newton's achievements in physics, this must have seemed an especially tempting assumption. Even in physics things now look less simple. There is every reason for philosophers now to be open to a much more complicated account of ethical theory.

Here is one way of seeing that each of the three bases is ineliminable from ethical theory. We can, for the sake of argument, suspend any theoretical commitments any of us has and look at patterns of ethical justification. Here are some examples of justifications that would normally be found convincing.

(1) Smurf has a large lawn, and he regularly pays local teenagers $10 to cut the grass. Today, however, he pays Mabel, who has just cut the grass, only $5. Mabel says "That is wrong, because it is unfair. You always have paid $10, and that was what I had a right to expect." Smurf, let us suppose, replies that he is a little short of money and would like in any case to spend more on himself. But we think that Mabel is right, on grounds of fairness. Indeed it would seem peculiar to put the objection to Smurf's behavior in terms other than fairness.

(2) Smurf also plans not to pay his income tax. He has large expenses, he points out, and it should not be a "big deal" if he skips a year. His friends, trying to talk him out of this, say "What if everyone did that?"

(3) Hepzibah is administering a social services program in her community. The program mandates certain services for people who are below the poverty line. Hepzibah feels that some of the recipients are much too relaxed about their status. Accordingly, she issues an administrative ruling that says, "Those who receive welfare assistance must wear a badge that says 'I am useless.'" Objectors immediately say, "You can't treat a human being that way."

(4) The Zyklone culture has a rule that includes communal sharing of food, with the proviso that those who are crippled will have to get their own. A visitor from another culture remarks that this seems morally unacceptable because it excludes some people from the society.

(5) Bloggs is determined to get rid of a good deal of his property, including furniture, books, and recordings. His thought is to make a clean sweep, taking it all to a remote area and burning it. His friends point out that a number of people would like Bloggs's furniture, and many would enjoy the books and recordings. "It is wrong not to make all of this available to others," they say; "it is wrong not to make other people happier or better off at virtually no cost to you."

(6) Bloggs then finds out that he can sell the furniture, some of which is very old, for a considerable amount of money. If he does that, he will donate the money to a scholarship fund for bright adolescents who otherwise would not be able to attend a university (or would be able to attend only by working such long hours that they could not concentrate on what they were learning). But Bloggs still is inclined simply to burn the furniture. His friends now object, "You ought not to neglect a chance to give some people the opportunity for enriched and more fulfilling lives."

These six examples do not add up to a neat picture. Both (1) and (2), although they differ in some ways, can be assimilated to appeals to the requirement of a universal moral order that includes principles of fairness. (3) and (4) appeal to a moral order in which it is emphasized that no one should be left out or treated as negligible, although certainly respect for persons is a more explicit factor in (3) than in (4). (5) and (6) appeal to the importance of bringing about good consequences and avoiding less good ones.

So the examples look quite diverse. But there are ways in which someone could try to bring them (or most of them) under one heading. For example, an act consequentialist could argue that in all six cases, the behavior condemned generally has, on the whole, bad consequences. In the last analysis, it is bad consequences, and they alone, that matter. Act consequentialism usually is presented as a theory that accounts for all reasonable judgments (both moral and non-moral) of which choices are better or worse.

Conversely, some would argue that (5) and (6) do not concern what we would term moral choices. This would allow us to place (1) through (4) under the heading of respect for a universal moral order in which everyone is given due regard, with (5) and (6) pushed to the side. In this view, a poor choice in (5) or (6), while deplorable, is not positively immoral. Rather it is a failure of some other sort. Perhaps it is merely selfish in a way that remains outside the zone of morality?

Others might argue that (5) and (6) do concern moral choices, because in a way respect for persons (who might benefit from the use of Bloggs's former possessions) is a factor. Respect for persons might be held to include doing whatever we can to benefit them, especially if it is at little or no cost to ourselves. This move would enable us to place all six examples under the heading of respect for a universal moral order in which respect for persons is a key feature.

A first response is that all of these simplifying moves seem ad hoc. Let us look first at the act consequentialist simplification. It is easy to make pronouncements about consequences when no one knows the future all that well. But how can we know that fairness always coincides with good consequences? Perhaps, indeed, the unfairness of sometimes paying $10 for the grass cutting and sometimes paying only $5 may in some complicated way have on the whole good consequences? (Might it teach the teenagers something about social realities?) Some kinds of violations of normal intuitions about how people should be treated may on balance contribute more to human well-being than they subtract.

A thought like this is one of the reasons people still read Machiavelli. Some may argue, in particular, that sometimes (when a great deal is at stake) people with political power or leverage should have, for the greater good, what Sartre called "dirty hands." This is debatable, and perhaps a lot depends on just what is at stake. In the banal case of the lawn-cutting, though, what is at stake is not huge. Reasonable people generally would judge it as clearly wrong for Smurf to pay Mabel less than what had been the going rate, even if the consequences of this unfairness somehow were to look slightly better than those of being fair. It is highly implausible to dismiss this response out of hand.

Let us look now at the simplifying moves to bolster a unified theory of respect for a universal moral order. The examples that center on Bloggs's property raise difficulties of a different sort from those involved with judgments of consequences. A normal response to both (5) and (6) is that there is something really "off" in his simply burning his property, that he should not do it. On the other hand, it is far from clear that (given our normal ways of judging these things) anyone has a *right* to demand that he not do it. One may ask also to whom it would be unfair, or in what way it is a violation of respect for persons. Respect for persons is normally held to include not humiliating them, taking into proper account their wishes in matters that especially concern them, and in general treating them as autonomous, responsible agents. It is hard to see how Bloggs's burning of his possessions goes against any of this. To interpret respect for persons as requiring that we benefit others when we can is a great stretch in interpretation.

Attempts to assimilate these cases to standard ones of violations of rights or failure of respect for persons are bound to look artificial—rather like Wittgenstein's joke example (1953, no. 14, 7e) of someone who holds that all tools modify something (as hammers and chisels certainly do) and who, when asked about a measuring rule, replies that it modifies our knowledge of a thing's length. Twisting concepts to make our judgments come out all right has been, historically, the corruption of casuistry. When the issues are ones of ethical theory, it lacks any excuse.

The move that insists that the cases involving Bloggs's property do not raise *moral* issues (and hence do not have to be covered by a generalization that applies to all judgments of moral right and wrong) looks more promising. Even if we agree that it would be despicable for Bloggs to burn it all, we might well hesitate to say that it was immoral. There are many things that are despicable—such as deliberately hurting people's feelings or wantonly spoiling their minor pleasures—that we would not normally call immoral.

Hence, such a move might shore up a generalization that decisions of moral right and wrong all rest on an idea of a valid moral order. But the complications, pushed to the other side of the boundary between the morally wrong and other kinds of misconduct, would not disappear. If we want a general account of the bases of *ethical* judgment, in which the ethical includes all judgments of how people ought to behave, we need one that can fit the cases involving Bloggs's property.

Also, even within the territory of morality, it is far from clear that consequences do not matter. What if, on this one occasion, following a normally acceptable moral principle risks a catastrophe likely to kill millions of people? There also can be a problem of moral principles that had looked acceptable, but that now seem to be making more and more people's lives miserable.

All of this adds up to a negative first look at the notion that, after all, there is a single base of ethical judgment. The issues, though, require a closer look. In particular, we need to weigh factors relevant to the claim that diversity (illustrated in the six examples) of the bases of ethical judgments is irreducible.

We can begin by looking at one influential attempt to reduce all moral considerations to consideration of consequences, namely act consequentialism. Then we will look at the competing (but also, within its sphere, totalizing) Kantian morality of principles. The next chapter will examine, more broadly, attempts to base ethics entirely on some conception of a moral order. We will return to consequentialism, and to the justification of a mixed picture, in the final chapters.

The Hopes and Dreams of Act Consequentialism

Much of the debate over act consequentialism has centered on cases in which an action that is clearly unfair or that clearly violates what we normally would consider people's rights appears to have good consequences. These cases are advanced as counterexamples to act consequentialism. The act consequentialist response often has contended that the unfairness or violation of rights, despite appearances, would be likely to have bad consequences—because it would be likely to undermine trust, or support of the social order, and so on. Hence, defenders of act consequentialism claim, actions that we are confident (on seemingly independent grounds) are wrong—but that look at first as if they will have good consequences—will in fact generally have bad consequences. Thus they are not counterexamples.

If the question is whether the right thing to do is always that which will have the best consequences, here is one answer: Anything is possible. It might just turn out that in every case, what would be best to do (as determined on whatever basis seems reasonable) will have the best consequences.

This may seem like a massive simplification. But Leibniz in his *Theodicy* asserted one even more massive: anything that anyone ever does (whether good or bad, leading to salvation or damnation) has on the whole the best possible consequences. (Adam's sin, he says, was a *felix culpa*, but so are all of ours.) Leibniz did, however, have an ingenious cosmological/religious argument for his position. Lacking any comparable justification, any act consequentialist hope that whatever can be

reasonably be determined to be the best thing to do always will have the best consequences looks extraordinarily implausible. If what the act consequentialist offers is
an insistence, rather than merely a hope, then the basis for the insistence looks very
feeble.

One possible line of defense is as follows. It is a mistake, the act consequentialist can say, to hold that we are in a position to determine with anything like
certainty which of the alternatives open to us meets the act consequentialist standard for rightness. So there is a sense in which (given this account of rightness) we
never *know* what is right, even if we are sometimes able to make reasonable estimates. But often, given hindsight, we know what *was* right.

Hence, the defender of act consequentialism can say, the theory should not be
taken as, first and foremost, a theory about what we should do (given our limited
knowledge). Rather it should be taken as a theory of what, as it will turn out, was the
best thing to do among our alternatives (Bales 1971).

This may be less implausible. But let us look at the suggestion that often we
know what *was* right. Much depends on how much reasonable assurance we require
in order to say that someone knows something, rather than merely has an opinion. It
can look pretty clear that something done five or ten or fifty years ago has had good
(or bad) consequences. However, there is always the possibility that there will be
some rebound factor, or that the fact that things worked out well in the short run
causes missed opportunities in the long run. Chou En-lai, when asked whether the
French Revolution had been a good thing or a bad thing, remarked (more than a
century and a half later) that it was too early to say. Perhaps it will always be too early
to say? Consequences can extend to the end of time.

However, we sometimes can have some reasonable degree of confidence, years
later, that something that was done had the best possible consequences or, conversely, that it had bad consequences. This sense of how it worked (or failed to work)
requires judgments of what the probable consequences of various alternatives would
have been. Such judgments are often less difficult to make sometime after the
choice than they were at the time; various hidden forces may have had time to
manifest themselves.

There can be a running assumption that, by and large, in the further future the
consequences of what was done years ago usually will even out. This may be less
true of large-scale events like the French Revolution than of the moral decisions that
most of us make. Perhaps some events change history, but virtually nothing that you
or I do does?

How do we know all this about the further future? Readers of Hume know that
there is an argument for saying that none of our assumptions about the future meet
the standards of knowledge. On the other hand, up to now it does look as if consequences may tend to even out over time, so it may seem a reasonable running
assumption, even if it does not meet the standard required to count as knowledge.
Absent such an assumption, ordinary prudence as well as consequence-based moral
judgments would be called into question. It then might appear that, in the long run,
none of us ever knows—or even has a reasonable idea of—what he or she is doing.

Even if it is agreed that, given enough time, we can arrive at fairly confident
judgments of which of a set of alternatives had (or would have had) the best

consequences, this may not be enough to shore up act consequentialism. Here is one reason. Our ordinary discourse about what is right and wrong has features that require that we often be able, at the time, to say what is right and what is wrong. This can be appreciated if we focus on the function of this discourse.

The normal prescriptive function of providing guidance near to the moment of choice looks central to ethical, and especially to moral, discourse. Words like "right" and "wrong" very often are used to fulfill this function. Any function, on the other hand, of apportioning praise or blame decades later looks peripheral.

We can see this more clearly if we look at the word "wrong" and the ways in which its meanings might be taught to, say, a small child. This will be a complicated process with complicated results. No doubt, part of it is a connection of "wrong" with certain descriptive characteristics of actions. A well brought up child will learn to associate "wrong" with such things as highly selfish behavior, actions that make innocent people suffer, violations of trust, and so on. By now it is well-established that there is some latitude in these connections; different families or cultures (or even individuals) can lay out somewhat different descriptive connections.

But, as Philippa Foot has argued, there are limits to the variation (see Foot 1978a, 108–109). One can see her point in relation to an imagined case in which someone is taught (with no plausible hidden explanation) that what is wrong is such things as helping people who are sick or injured, or keeping promises, and so on. We would conclude that someone who learned this usage had a flawed understanding of the meaning of the word.

A range of descriptive features (sorts of things that might be considered wrong) forms part of the meaning of "wrong" that can be taught; and typically these will include behavior that harms innocent people. The meaning also contains a putative prescriptive element. In normal speech, to call something wrong is to recommend that it not be done.

This needs to be qualified carefully. Certainly there are subcultures and individuals for whom the word "wrong" carries no negative force. What is termed "wrong" may be seen as bold and exciting. Do they, then, really think it is wrong? It can be hard to say. Some philosophers would prefer to say that such people are talking about what is generally thought to be "wrong," in quotation marks, rather than what they themselves really think is wrong.

Be that as it may, even if not every use of "wrong" carries negative prescriptive force, the characteristic function of the word requires that it typically have such force. If we encountered a culture that generally had no negative attitudes toward what it termed "wrong," we would conclude that what they meant by the word is different from what we mean.

Given this typical prescriptive function, what can we say about the meaning of calling something wrong? Part of the answer has to be that, barring unusual contexts (e.g., we are at a club meeting of satanists), when someone speaks of something as wrong, we can presume it likely that part of what is being said is "Don't do it."

This prominent feature of the meaning of "wrong" would become extremely attenuated if we all agreed that judgments of wrong could be made only decades after the fact. At the least, the interpretation of act consequentialism that sees it as providing, at best, retrospective judgments of wrongness would seem to modify the use of "wrong" quite drastically. If the modification became widespread, we might well feel the need for a word that would tell us on ethical grounds—at the time— "Don't do it." A new word, say "rwrong," would have to be invented.

Because of considerations like this, the interpretation of act consequentialism as yielding merely retrospective judgments seems quite artificial. Even if it were accepted, most people—including most consequentialists—would want to move on, and to focus on how we are to decide what we should do.

It should be added that there are cases when, even if we know that a choice did turn out for the best, we would resist saying that it was the right choice. This would be especially true if it had carried serious risks. A nice example is that of the doctor who, in treating a non-fatal skin condition, prescribes a drug that has a 10 percent chance of killing the patient—but it doesn't, and the patient is cured (see Jackson 1991; Pettit 1997, 128).

A similar set of comments applies to R. M. Hare's (1981) highly ingenious move in treating act consequentialism as an account of how decisions would be made by archangels, thought of as perfectly knowledgeable, intelligent, and good. What Hare does here has considerable value in providing a perspective (through contrast with the limiting case of archangels) on our ordinary practice of ethical judgment. We (unlike the archangels) have to compensate for our limited knowledge of the future, and we have to safeguard against the human tendency to provide rationalizations for the normally forbidden thing that we really want to do. In the end, whatever might be true of archangels, we have to be concerned (as Hare does insist) with how we ordinary human beings should make ethical decisions. If what a human being (given limited knowledge) chooses to do were to turn out to coincide with what an archangel would do, that does not make it right.

Let us grant that often it can be meaningful to say, decades after a choice, "It turns out that the right thing to do was..." We do talk that way (although much more often in practical than in moral discourse). It also can be meaningful to say that the really right choice is the one that a perfectly informed, entirely benevolent being would make. But such uses of "right," along with the parallel uses of "wrong," have to be treated as secondary and parasitic on the primary uses, which are connected with recommendations of how to act.

Because of this, an act consequentialist theory will look far more relevant to the practice of ethical judgment if it can be used to provide accounts of what a reasonably intelligent and decent human being should do in various kinds of circumstance. The difficulty for the act consequentialist, then, is this. The function of an account of right and wrong includes the expectation that, at least in a number of cases, it will enable us to arrive at an assured judgment of what should or should not be done. If the best the account can provide, again and again, is along the lines of "Maybe such and such will work out, but who knows?" it will not be satisfactory. The typical prescriptive function that "right" and "wrong" fulfill does not require that we always know what is right and what is wrong, but it does require that we often know.

One special class of cases should be mentioned that may be exceptional. It has sometimes been suggested that act consequentialism is most at home, so to speak, in public policy decisions. Often, in these it is not clear that any leading option violates rights or respect for persons significantly more than any other, and social and economic consequences may be especially hard to predict. Budgetary decisions often have this character.

In this area, which is very much one of politics, there actually can be great advantages in a consequentialist stance that holds that (whichever option one favors) one cannot claim to *know* what the right choice is. Not claiming to know, it should be emphasized, is consistent with thinking that there are reasonable grounds of some strength for one's position. The advantage of a stance of not claiming to know, in this area, is that it is conducive to greater political civility and tolerance.

There would be no comparable advantages in a stance of not claiming to know, in terms of long-term consequences, whether a murder really is wrong or not. Anyone who adopted such a stance could be accused of not understanding what the word "wrong" means. Immediate guidance, which is firm and not hesitant, in some classes of case is a large part of the function of words like "wrong" and "right." Unless there were extraordinary features to the murder, so that at the time there was a reasonable case for defending it, it would verge on the unintelligible to say, "Wait a hundred years, and we might know whether it was wrong to murder so-and-so."

Further difficulties for act consequentialism will emerge in the remaining chapters. One, however, should be mentioned now. A familiar truth that emerges from practical experience is that there are certain things that are more likely to be attained if one is not always aiming for them consciously and directly. These include happiness, and also the most favorable balance of positive value over negative value.

This is one of the insights at the root of what has been called "restrictive consequentialism," a family of forms of consequentialism that restricts or forswears direct application of a standard of maximizing probable value (see Pettit and Brennan, 1986). We often can do better (overall, but not necessarily in each particular case) by relying on familiar maxims, moral rules, learned intuitions, or impulses guided by love, friendship, or a sense of professional obligation. In some contexts, sheer spontaneity can usually work better than calculation of consequences.

We can sum up the difficulties for act consequentialism as follows. If it is taken as a theory of what will turn out to have been right or wrong, or (in an even more extreme interpretation) as a theory of what we would know was right or wrong if we were virtually perfect, then it will not match the ordinary meaning of "right" and "wrong." Part of the meaning of these words is that they typically are used to provide guidance at the moment of decision. In particular, we can say (at least as an approximation) that if something is morally wrong, then we think that no decent, well-informed person should do it. If we were to assign "right" and "wrong" meanings in terms of what would be known only decades hence, or known only by archangels, then decent, well-informed people (decent and well-informed by normal human standards) could repeatedly do what in fact is the wrong thing, and it would often be hard to see how we could blame them for it.

If, on the other hand, we do equate "wrong" with "should not be done," it seems plausible that there often are better ways than sheer estimate of likely consequences for determining what is wrong. Some of these (e.g., following familiar moral rules, or acting out of love or friendship) are so well established that they generate their own pressures. There are many cases in which we would blame someone for trying to estimate likely consequences rather than following a familiar moral rule. Friends and loved ones also might wonder about someone who repeatedly decides how to behave toward them on the basis of estimates of likely consequences.

At this stage in the argument, we can leave open the question of whether there are cases (perhaps of an extreme nature) in which it is better to estimate likely consequences than to be guided by traditional moral rules or by love or friendship. Most choices to which traditional moral rules or considerations of love or friendship are relevant are not like this, however. Hence it is very implausible to maintain that consequentialism can claim to be the single base of ethical judgment.

Deriving Ethics from Respect for the Principles in a Universal Moral Order

Kantian ethics also, in my view, cannot claim to be (or to provide) the single base of ethical judgment. The argument that will begin here, and will continue in later chapters, will look in some respects unlike the one just brought against act consequentialism. That one went against the acceptability of act consequentialism as an ethical theory, and not merely against the claim that consequences are the sole basis for ethical judgments. The discussion of Kantian ethics will not be so flatly negative, for two reasons.

One is that there is no easily specifiable form of Kantian ethics that is as extreme and simplistic as act consequentialism, and that therefore can be simply argued against. The other reason is this. The argument later (especially in the final chapter) will be that consequentialist considerations of various kinds do play a major role (but not one so uniformly simple as act consequentialism suggests) in an acceptable ethical theory. In my view, some Kantian considerations also play a significant role; and this is a good place to begin to develop that point. Hence the argument that concerns respect for the principles in a universal moral order—a basis for ethical judgment advanced in the Kantian view—will be, to a degree, more positive than the discussion of act consequentialism was.

The argument will, however, limit to morality the domain of the Kantian claim. Within that domain, it seems mostly right, up to a point. The view, that is, that respect for a universal moral order (involving principles) is a basis for moral judgments is, I think, largely correct. My argument will be that it is not the sole base. Later I will argue that considerations of consequences are in some respects more fundamental.

If the position defended is that respect for a universal moral order is a basis for moral judgments, but not for non-moral judgments within ethics, then we need to look more closely at what is special about morality. We can begin with some banal truths about morality. These will lead us to the functions of morality that distinguish it from the rest of ethics.

Here is a banal historical truth about morality. It can be argued that it did not emerge as a distinctive separate category of choices in the development of Western philosophy until either the Middle Ages or the early modern period. It is sometimes said that there is no word that can be exactly translated as "morality" in classical Greek or classical Chinese philosophies. There is no sharp separation in the ethical philosophies of Plato or of Aristotle between what we would consider to be moral choices and non-moral choices. It should be emphasized that Confucius, Plato, and Aristotle all endorse some judgments (e.g., Confucius on filial impiety) that appear to have the force and flavor of what we would term moral judgments. What is being denied here is that these judgments were located in a way that sharply separated them from judgments of how to live that we would normally not regard as moral judgments (e.g., judgments of what constitutes Aristotle's *eudaemonia* or contributes to the poise of the Confucian sage).

By the time of Kant and Mill, there certainly is a sharp separation. It is marked in Kant by the distinction between cases to which only hypothetical imperatives (which tell us how to get what we might want) are relevant, and those in which we need the categorical imperative to test our maxims. Kant's ethics is concerned only with our treatment of the latter cases, which he regards as crucial to human dignity.

Mill's separation (*Utilitarianism*, chap. 5, par. 14) is between cases in which we feel (or should feel) that a poor choice deserves punishment—if not by the law, then by social pressure, and if not by social pressure, then by the agent's feelings of guilt—and cases in which a poor choice does not. The passage can be read as reserving the word "wrong" only for the former cases. The importance of the distinction had been explored in *On Liberty*, which argues that only behavior that directly harms others should be subject to the kind of societal pressure that, if extended more broadly (and thus misused), would constitute the "tyranny of the majority" (1859/1978, 7 and 9).

Mill concedes that we have a right to avoid and even admonish people who are not directly harming others, but who are tasteless or foolish (Ibid., 77). But he plainly thinks that this would not involve the pressure that moral condemnation typically brings. In a way, Mill's distinction between what he considers morality, and what he calls expediency, is between poor choices to which the appropriate response is a kind of hitting-out "penal" impulse, and poor choices to which the appropriate response is distaste or avoidance.

It is an interesting historical question why morality emerges as it does as a separate category within the wider group of judgments that give recommendations about how to live. Almost certainly there is no simple answer. Some of the reasons may be internal to the development of philosophical ethics. Certainly in Kant's case, the role of principles in some areas of life, but not normally in the pursuit of happiness or the style with which we conduct our social relationships, played a part.

There also may have been, for many thinkers, a dialectic involving heightened interest in the parts of ethics that can constitute a first line of social control, and on the other side a wish to protect a zone of private life that should be largely exempt from this control. In short, there may have been reasons both of a conservative sort (wishing to strengthen social order) and of a liberal sort (wishing to protect the spontaneity of personal life) for drawing the line.

Then there is also the matter of impartiality. It has been pointed out recently by a number of philosophers, notably Michael Stocker and some leading feminist thinkers, that many of the choices that are important in our lives presuppose special treatment of those near and dear to us (see Stocker 1976, Gilligan 1982). We may well feel that we owe various kinds of special consideration to our children, parents, partners, spouses, and friends. On the other hand, a legal and professional culture has developed in which it is understood that often such people should not be given preferential treatment. Examples are cases in which you are on a committee deciding whom to hire, or a bank officer deciding whether to approve a loan, or a judge passing sentence, or a medical officer deciding who is to get the last vial of vaccine. If your close relative or best friend were under consideration, you might well recuse yourself.

This can involve an intricate social sense of when impartiality is required and when it would be absurd. A clever example offered by the utilitarian Richard Brandt nicely illustrates this. He imagines a man who has saved money for his children's college education. But, when the time comes, it occurs to him that the money would do more good if it went to others of the same age who were more worthy and better qualified (see Brandt 1965, 109–110).

If the man in Brandt's example did deny the college money to his own children (and give it to others with much higher College Board scores), we would certainly be censorious. However, "immoral" is not the word we would reach for. Words like "inhuman" or "unfeeling" would be more likely.

Morality is a zone in which impartiality is required. It is not the only zone: various forms of professional ethics also require impartiality. (The two zones, it should be said, overlap. In some cases, we would consider serious violations of professional ethics to be immoral. But many violations are at most minor improprieties, not amounting to what we would consider immorality. And occasionally, cases arise in which adhering to professional ethics can look morally questionable.) Impartiality requires treating everyone's interests equally. It also requires that everyone be subject to the same laws or rules. Like the law, morality (and also any professional code) applies "irrespective of persons."

On the other side of the line, this is not true. Some people are cut out for the contemplative life extolled by Aristotle, and we might recommend it to them but not to others. We might in the same way recommend a trail to someone with considerable woodland experience that we would not to a novice. In general, the kind of person you are matters to what qualifies as a promising course—for you—of human fulfillment, or even as a desirable pattern of human relationships. But the kind of person you are cannot be allowed (with minor exceptions) to matter to what the moral requirements are that should govern you.

A first look at the phenomenon of morality suggests that it is widely taken to have many affinities with modern legal systems. Like the law, morality applies irrespective of persons and is widely thought to center on principles that one should hold on to despite temptations. In common discourse, someone thought to be extremely moral often is spoken of as a "woman (or man) of principle." Further, moral rules or principles are taught to the very young, who are expected to remember and retain them throughout their lives. No one believes that absolutely everyone in a society continues to endorse exactly the same set of moral rules. But there is a widespread expectation that a very large number of people will retain at least some respect for major moral rules. This contributes to the sense, entrenched in the law and also in the common view of morality, that virtually everyone "knows right from wrong."

Because of all of this, it is immediately very plausible to hold that something is morally right (or morally wrong) if and only if it would be endorsed (or condemned) as such in an acceptable societal moral code. What might be thought of as a moral decision in a specific individual case thus has implications for what should be universal law. If you have thought that something was right, but would be unwilling to have it implemented by everyone in a universal law, you need to reconsider.

All of morality, in this view, points toward the "realm of ends" that is central to Kant's third formulation of the categorical imperative. The realm of ends is the idealized matrix in which everyone follows moral principles that can be willed to be universal laws of human behavior. In the real world, of course not everyone follows moral principles that can be willed to be universal laws, and the patterns of human behavior diverge from the moral ideal. But, Kant contends, that is no excuse for any laxness on our part. If morality means anything, it means that one always should do what would be part of the moral order of the realm of ends.

The foregoing approximates what might be termed our society's "official view" of what morality is. Further, there is a lot of truth to it. Morality is largely learned, and to a large extent retained, in the form of general rules. We feel most comfortable when we can relate our moral decision to a general rule that everyone ought to accept. The prevalence of this mind-set seems on the whole very useful.

The investigations of the remaining chapters will poke some holes in this appealing picture, and also will bring out the roles—even in morality—of other bases of ethical judgment. Some of these roles already have emerged. As was just pointed out, the centrality of general rules in morality is quite convenient and useful. This amounts to a consequentialist justification for this centrality.

I have argued elsewhere (Kupperman 2002) that some features of Kantian ethics—including the insistence that all moral judgments be subsumed under general rules, and that morality apply irrespective of persons—cannot be given any logical justification. It is hard to see what other non-consequentialist justification there could be. Kant certainly does not provide any argument for the prominence in his ethics of broad maxims.

Also, it was pointed out in chapter 5 that one reason morality (unlike other kinds of normative recommendations) applies irrespective of the kind of person you are is that any other arrangement would undermine the effectiveness of a moral order. Envy and resentment would gather around thoughts such as "Why does that prohibition apply to me, and not to that person?" Again, this seems a consequentialist justification of a familiar feature of morality.

Finally, it is one thing to point out the centrality of general rules in morality. It is quite another to suppose that all moral thought focuses on the acceptance or rejection of moral rules. Recall the quote from R. M. Hare (in chap. 5) that mature people can arrive at some principles that defy formulation in words at all. This fits widespread experience. There is more to morality than its central element of general rules, and consequently there is much in morality that does not derive straightforwardly from respect for principles (of the general, articulable sort that Kant clearly intends) in an ideal moral order.

8

The Need for a Moral Order

The central argument of this chapter will be double-edged. It will be (1) that a necessary base of any acceptable moral judgment is that it can play a part in an acceptable moral order, and (2) that what counts as an acceptable moral order cannot be accounted for in purely contractualist terms. Hence contractualism is true, but it is far from the whole truth about ethics.

The reader will recall (from the lexicon in the introduction) that a real (as opposed to a notional) moral order involves at least a near consensus on a set of moral rules and on general considerations that have weight in moral thought. An acceptable moral order (whether real or merely notional) requires a set of moral judgments, along with principles intermediate between the judgments and the moral order's base, and also standard ways of interpreting cases, that (under the circumstances at the time) should be accepted by any reasonable person. In examining the role in ethics of the idea of an acceptable moral order, we need to understand how it is that any moral judgment, even a very quirky one that very few people would agree with, implicitly appeals to a moral order. The conditions for an acceptable moral order need to be examined. Much of this scrutinizes topics touched on in the fifth chapter.

Chapter 5 argued that to think something morally right is to think that it should be regarded as morally right throughout the society. The argument of this chapter takes this a step further, by deploying a contractualist conception of an acceptable social order. The argument then concerns the requirements for a moral judgment to be acceptable in its role within this.

The Primary Function of a Moral Order

The best way of appreciating what a moral order is, and why we need one, is to go back to classic social contract theories, especially that of Thomas Hobbes. The social contract theory is first and foremost political. It is an account of how we come to have the institutions of government and of law and (by and large) respect for law. But morality has to be part of the package.

It, or its absence, enters in two ways. First, life in the hypothetical state of nature would not be so nasty, brutish, and short if the great majority of humans had respect for what most of us would consider a reasonable morality. They do not, and Hobbes contends (against philosophers like Plato) that morality would be meaningless in a state of nature. Second, in the world of the social contract—our world—things can go as well as they do if the great majority have some respect for a reasonable morality. Hobbes is realistic enough not to hold that 100 percent acceptance of a reasonable morality, or even entirely consistent compliance among those who do accept such a morality, is required. This parallels his view of the power of law. That there is a social contract does not mean that we should not lock our cupboards.

There is abundant recent experience of how miserable life is in countries in which, even if there are modern systems of law, the number of people who are willing to violate them—and to harm their fellow citizens—is high. Law and the police cannot solve the problem. Often the police become part of the problem. This is a failure of respect for law, but at a more fundamental level it is a failure of respect for ordinary standards of decent behavior toward other human beings. Even if the police were incorruptible, if a sizable percentage of the population could be easily induced to harm others for personal advantage, no number of police would be enough.

This brief outline of a position like Hobbes's leaves out one element that was important to Hobbes. This concerned the motivation for the hypothetical agreement to the social contract. Hobbes (preferring a somewhat minimalist picture of human nature) portrayed the agreement as a choice of personal security and well-being: in short, as purely self-interested. This Hobbesian element drew considerable fire from subsequent British philosophers.

Bishop Butler contended that human nature is more complicated than Hobbes had suggested, and that in fact the most satisfying lives include concerned involvement in the lives of others. In such lives, altruism and self-interest do not conflict, and therefore Hobbes's conception of self-interest was far too narrow. Hume also argued that concern for others (such as members of one's immediate family) could be ascribed to even the most primitive human beings, and indeed that an important element of human nature is sympathy or benevolence.

My running assumption is that, even if (as I think) Butler and Hume were right, the other elements of the Hobbesian view outlined above are largely acceptable. In particular, even if sympathy and benevolence are elements of normal human nature, and even if (as Hume argued) such elements have given rise (at least under appropriate conditions) to morality, that does not mean that those living in a hypothetical state of nature would have moralities. One can easily imagine very primitive human beings who care about their partners and children but have no awareness that it is *wrong* (in anything like a moral sense) to harm others (and hence would not think twice about harming those who are not members of their little group).

Some people's concern and sympathy are extremely narrow. In some cases, we think they have an excessively narrow conception of the scope of morality. But still they generally have some sense of what morality is. This includes understanding that there can be things one wants to do that nevertheless should not be done, in large part because of acceptable community standards.

Part of what I am suggesting is that (in contrast) primitive human beings, given a narrow range of sympathy, would not have the very idea of morality, with its demandingness that can be guided by generalizations. Even if it does not make sense to speak of an actual historical social contract, the social contract story is an "as if" story that explains, among other things, how membership in a society would enable even people with very narrow sympathies to have a sense of how demanding, moral-like judgments function.

The largely acceptable Hobbesian elements suggest the following. The primary function of morality is to protect us against harm. Without the protection of widespread social acceptance of moralities, we would be far more vulnerable than we are. We would lose our security and, with it, our willingness to take on projects that might bring satisfaction or a sense of meaning to human lives, because completion would be so unreliable in a drastically insecure world.

Often, form follows function. If the primary function of morality is the one just described, then it is reasonable to suppose that a good morality (that is, one that is both reasonable and also effective at accomplishing what one would expect moralities to accomplish) will have features that lend themselves to fulfilling the function. In what follows, we can continue to examine the nature of morality with this in mind. It is important that we keep the primary function of morality in mind, but it will be important also to be alert to secondary or peripheral features of morality that may not be simply derivable from the primary function.

Morality as Protection against Harm

A first step is to think about the varieties of harm. The most obvious cases are murder, rape, torture, having your money stolen, and various kinds of physical injury. There are other forms of harm that in practice can be less obvious. Being steered into a life that is stultifying, and that allows minimal development of one's capacities, is arguably harm. But it lacks the dramatic quality as a discrete event that the examples above have. It might not even register (either for the persons who do it, or for the one who is steered, or for most onlookers) as a kind of harm. This is true also when someone, through a series of personal interactions, is made to feel worthless and to lose all self-confidence. That is serious damage, but what is happening can be so diffuse and subtle that it hardly registers on anybody.

There are reasons why, in practice, morality (even a very reasonable morality) is not designed to protect people against the full spectrum of harm by others. To protect against the more subtle kinds of harm referred to above, a morality would require communal intrusiveness into the personal lives and interactions of everyone. Further, the risks of mistakes and abuses—say of people being denounced on the basis of an insensitive reading of how they interact with others—would be great.

The protection that morality offers therefore is mainly against the dramatic kinds that were first mentioned. It is relevant that they typically involve a single event (rather than a continuing pattern), and that the nature of what is done is usually visible even to a casual and fairly insensitive onlooker. If morality fulfills its function partly by organizing social pressure, then the ease with which the harm that is interdicted can be recognized and agreed upon is vital.

There is a traditional device that is brilliantly adapted to ensure that some varieties of harm can be easily recognized and agreed upon. This is the code of simple general rules. Because protection against harm is the principal focus, most of them can take the form "Thou shalt not . . ." As Julius Kovesi (1967) has pointed out, the categories encapsulated in these rules structure our perception of the world, as well as our avoidance of certain kinds of behavior. In a scene in which a lot is going on, and there is a riot of colors and shapes, if a major traditional moral rule is being violated, it is especially likely to be noticed—and to be noticed as a transgression.

The training to notice such things begins in early childhood, and part of the brilliance of the simple general rules is that even very young children can grasp them. Also, they are easily remembered. It helps that there are typically only a small number. Even dim-witted adults can be presumed to remember the major sorts of things that are generally wrong.

Usually children do more than merely memorize the rules. Loyalty to them is inculcated. The process varies from case to case, but generating loyalty to these core standards often fits what Aristotle says when he speaks of steering children "by the rudders of pleasure and pain" (1984, bk. 10.1, 1852). Parents and teachers will make sure that the thought of following the moral rules becomes a pleasant one, including pride and satisfaction with oneself, and that the thought of violating them becomes unpleasant. Creating the capacity to feel guilty will be an important part of this.

It is assumed that many of us as adults will be tempted to violate the central moral rules, and that normal wishful thinking might incline us to think that we could get away with it. Childhood training will seek to create countervailing psychic forces. The capacity to feel guilty is one of these. More basic, perhaps, is a structure of inhibitions, so that when we are tempted (say) to steal or to cause physical harm to people who are disagreeable, these actions don't feel at all comfortable to us, and we actually would find it hard to get ourselves to behave in this way.

To summarize: morality's central characteristics can be understood in relation to a Hobbesian function of protection against some of the varieties of harm in a society. The function helps to explain the prominence of simple general rules. It also explains the essential roles of inhibitions corresponding to the rules, and of the capacity to feel guilty.

Does this picture entirely capture the nature of morality? It is important to ask such questions, because so often philosophers articulate important truths and then stop, ignoring qualifications and complications around the edges. In this case, some of the qualifications and complications are fairly obvious. It has by now become widely accepted that many moral decisions cannot reasonably be made merely by appeal to simple general rules. Certainly Kant, who in the *Grounding of the Metaphysics of Morals* makes it sound like the maxims to be tested by the categorical imperative are all simple and highly general, knew that. In the second part of the *Metaphysics of Morals* (also translated as the *Metaphysics of Virtue*) he speaks of hard cases in morality, in which it may not be clear whether a case falls under a general rule. These require, he says, casuistry as the method of examination.

Beyond this, rigorism—the doctrine that at least some general moral rules do not admit of imaginable exceptions—is less widely accepted than appears to have been the case in Kant's time. Might there be a case in which, say, murder was justified? It is peculiarly difficult to discuss such questions, for two reasons. One is that the plausible examples (in which, say, a murder of a very likely future evildoer might almost certainly prevent very great evil) are so removed from real-world experience that it is hard to get a clear sense of what would be involved. The other is that most of us have strong inhibitions in relation to the moral rules involved, so that even if we were convinced that violating a rule was justified, we might be unable to bring ourselves to do it. Putting this to the side, though, we can see that there can be cases in which one starts with a generally valid moral rule and then, through a process of reflection, decides that the present case counts as an exception. It is probably easier to see this in relation to theft than in relation to murder.

Because we have the habit, since early childhood, of thinking of morality in terms of general rules, it is tempting to look for general rules that somehow incorporate the exceptions that we have reflectively arrived at. In the murder case above, such a rule would be "Do not commit murder unless the victim is a very likely future evildoer, and the murder is to prevent massive evil." The trouble is that the process is unlikely to end with this one step. There may be cases in which the victim is a very likely future evildoer and to murder is to prevent massive evil, but there still can be special reasons (e.g., there are other ways of constraining the potential evildoer, and possibly hidden risks in taking drastic action) for thinking that the murder is unjustified. There can be cases, on the other hand, in which the victim is not a very likely future evildoer (but is hardly blameless), and the potential evil is extreme indeed, and so on. In the end, a reasonable person might decide that there simply is no articulable general rule that can yield an appropriate answer to all imaginable cases. To quote R. M. Hare again, mature, reflective people often arrive at principles "that cannot be put into words."

There is a legal maxim that hard cases make bad law. The moral analogue would be that whatever reflection on hard cases gives us should not be taught to children. Simple general rules, and the resultant inhibitions and capacity for guilt, are very useful in a Hobbesian way, even if there then is more to morality than that.

What is simple at the core can become elaborate in a variety of ways. Let us begin again with the Hobbesian story of a set of moral rules that prohibit the most obvious kinds of harm that might inflicted on someone in a society. The moral judgment that such-and-such should not be done will have some striking features beyond those just mentioned. The main one (see chap. 5) is that the judgment will imply that it represents an appropriate social understanding. Hence, although any individual can arrive at the judgment, there will be the standing implication that whatever is morally wrong is everyone's business. It should be seen by everyone as morally wrong, and conversely what governs an upright individual's conduct should govern everyone's conduct.

All of this is implicit in the social contract story. Presumably we not merely (hypothetically) sign up to obey the laws and dictates of morality, but we also sign up to respect them. This includes support, which in the case of morality would involve the willingness to hold other people to the same standards that we have signed up for.

Cases Near the Boundary of Morality

Once morality is established as a class of high-pressure judgments in cases in which what someone chooses is everyone's business, and what is right for you is presumed to be right for everyone, it is easy to extend these features to cases lying outside the core of general harm-preventing rules. There may be a lot of things that we do, or fail to do, to others (or even to ourselves) that need to be taken seriously. Some of these also can be regarded as everyone's business and eligible for high-pressure judgments in which what is right for you is presumed to be right for everyone.

Indeed, it always has been possible for the kind of pressure, and also the appeal to what (it is held) should be the order in society, associated with morality to be extended to judgments that do not in any normal sense involve harm. Various kinds of sexual relations between consenting adults, if there is no wronged partner in the wings, might not in any obvious way involve harm. But they frequently have appeared among the forbidden items in moral codes.

It may be uncontroversial that the core of traditional moralities is designed to prevent obvious kinds of harm. But it is deeply controversial whether morality should have other concerns as well. Mill's *On Liberty*, which argues for a negative position on this, does so on the basis of what (at least in societies like his or ours) is claimed to be most conducive on the whole to human happiness. It recommends narrowing the scope of morality for the greater good. Various actions and characteristics thus could become objects of "distaste" rather than the aggressive pressure normally directed toward what is considered immoral (1859/1978, 77; see also Mill 1861/1979, chap. 5, par. 14).

An especially troublesome non-sexual example of a choice that perhaps does not involve harm but that many would judge morally grows out of a notorious Monty Python skit. A young man goes to a funeral director, reports that his mother has died, and asks about an inexpensive way of disposing of the body. The funeral director recommends cooking and eating. That, of course, is thoroughly disgusting, and the skit at this point dissolves. But the interesting philosophical issue is this. Imagine a world in which people sign consent forms, saying that anyone can do anything they want with their bodies after they die. It would appear that, in such a world, entirely disgusting things could be done to corpses without anyone, at least in any obvious way, being harmed. Would this be tolerable?

Many of us would say "no," and some of us might say that this is so seriously wrong that it is everyone's business and should be subject to public condemnation. But then we need to find a reason. A reason may not be readily available to a John Stuart Mill–style liberal. That whatever was done to the corpse was thoroughly disgusting does not seem to pass Mill's tests for moral condemnation.

Alternatively, it could be argued that allowing corpses to be treated in disgusting ways undermines and coarsens our attitudes to life and death in ways that could have important ramifications in social behavior. Therefore, it could be argued, it would involve such indirect harm to society that it should be subject to both moral and legal prohibition. This is a broader argument than Mill seems to allow in *On Liberty*. He insists that public moral pressure can be appropriate only when someone is harmed directly, or when the action fits into one of a few special categories (public indecency, being a "nuisance," or creating imminent danger of harm) that are presented in an ad hoc way. Even if the argument against allowing corpses to be treated in disgusting ways does not fit anything that Mill says, it does seem plausible to me.

There is a problem, though. Empirical tests of how bad the indirect consequences of allowing abuse of corpses would be are, for reasons discussed previously (in relation to the unevenness in our inadequate knowledge of the future), very unlikely to yield a clear and decisive verdict. What may seem obvious to some of us is unlikely to be established to virtually everyone's satisfaction.

If, as I guess, most people would hold that lurid treatment of corpses should be morally (and legally) interdicted, this may be because most would share my hunch that the indirect consequences of such kinds of behavior would be very bad. This certainly lacks a strongly assured empirical base. But it naturally leads to a sense that practices like that recommended in the Monty Python skit should be taken seriously, and thus should be subject to high-pressure judgments centering on general rules.

Here is a different example of a choice that lies near the boundaries of morality, and that may or may not involve issues of harm. Widgets International has been making modest profits with a large workforce, the great majority of whom have been with the company for many years. It is pointed out to the CEO that the profits would increase drastically, bringing more benefits to the shareholders, if about a third of the workers were dismissed. Some of the work could be done by contract workers, who would be paid less and not offered the medical insurance benefits that are standard for the regular workers. The remainder of the work could be handled if the remaining two thirds of the workforce (now in fear for their jobs) are pressured to increase productivity.

There are two linked contentious issues in relation to cases of this sort. One is whether there is a moral issue (as opposed to merely a business decision). The other is whether anything that might result counts as harm.

The linkage can be understood in this way. To say that someone has been harmed implies two things. One is that something seriously unfortunate has happened to that person. The other is that it happened as a result of wrongful, or at least inappropriate, behavior. Many seriously unfortunate things that are the foreseeable result of human action do not constitute harm. If Bloggs and Smurf are competing for the one job that Smurf needs in order to carry on with his career, and Bloggs gets the job (thus in effect forcing Smurf to replan his life, with lower expectations), we would not normally say that Bloggs harmed Smurf—unless Bloggs had competed unfairly. Much the same holds when two people compete for the same marriage partner.

Similarly, if a normal and perfectly appropriate business decision happens to cost Smurf his job and his happiness, we would not normally say that the person who made the decision had harmed Smurf. For us to say this, the decision would have had to have been inappropriate or wrong. If we assume in the case at hand that the decision was made in the normal business way, then it looks as if we can speak of harm if and only if we judge that (all the same) it wronged the dismissed workers. Given the seriousness of what is at stake, it would be plausible to hold that if it was wrongful, then it was morally wrong.

In my view, there is a strong case for holding that it is often morally wrong to dismiss numbers of employees in order to increase profits. The kinds of reasons that would constitute this case will become more apparent as our exploration of ethical theory continues. They have to do with the disadvantages of a moral order in which the well-being of employees (and others who depend on you) is not given moral weight, as compared to a moral order in which it is given moral weight.

These disadvantages involve the damage done to numbers of people by policies such as the one at issue, and the ways in which they undermine the stability of lives and people's ability to identify with the places in which they work. Because of the seriousness of these results, it seems appropriate to me that some decisions of this sort be subject to the pressures characteristic of morality.

Perhaps my view here is a revisionist one, in that decisions like the CEO's are very often not placed squarely under the heading of moral decisions. At the least, one might say that the classification of the decision is contentious. Whichever side of the line that divides morality from other kinds of judgments one places it at, it assuredly is close to the boundary. There is considerable consensus in classifying judgments about murder, torture, and so on as moral judgments. But they are at the core of morality, far from the boundary. Closer to the boundary is less consensus.

Let us return to the complications in judging the CEO's decision. I suggested that it is often wrong to dismiss employees in order to increase profits. I qualify by using the word "often": cases in which numbers of employees are dismissed in order to increase profits can differ significantly among themselves, and the differences can affect the justification of decisions like the CEO's. In some cases, the employees concerned are useful and at least moderately productive, but in other cases, they have little to do. Arguably this makes a difference. The competitive pressures on the company also can make a difference. There may be cases in which the competitive pressures are not great, and the main motive for the firings is greed. In others, the competitive pressures are quite serious, and there is every prospect that (unless something is done sooner rather than later) what is now a modest profit could turn into a loss, threatening the very future of the company.

Finally, in cases in which one might think that the decision could be classified as a moral one, the alternative prospects for the dismissed employees matter. If there are a fair number of comparably decent jobs available in the area, this will make what is done to dismissed employees look less like harm (and will make the decision look less like one in which moral issues are involved). If, conversely, there are very few comparably decent jobs available in the area, we might begin to think that a truly humane CEO should stretch at least a point or two to protect the jobs. The next thought might be that the drastically inhumane option, in light of the damage it would inflict, should count as immoral.

Part of the suggestion here is that enough factors are relevant to an appropriate decision by the CEO to make it seem implausible that some general rule could be formulated to determine what is morally acceptable in all such cases. There can be many variations in the present positions of the workers who might be dismissed, and in their prospects if they are dismissed, and in the competitive position of the company, all of which could be relevant to the appropriateness of a decision. A further complication is that there can be a great many more than merely two main options. Some workers, for example, might be shifted to part-time work (but with benefits); and there might be other arrangements that would diminish the payroll but fall short of the drastic cut that might have been considered. In the end, a CEO who is both prudent and humane might well think that the principle underlying a good decision was one that, as Hare said, could not be put into words.

An Expanded View of What a Moral Order Is

Here is what we have seen thus far about moral orders. A moral order is a morality that is widely accepted within a society (or is being considered for wide acceptance). The special features of morality, in contrast with other kinds of normative judgments that fall within ethics, include a typical appeal to social pressure against those who do what is morally wrong, the requirement that morality (like the law) apply irrespective of persons, and the centrality to morality of general rules, including very simple rules that are taught to children.

These simple general rules, mostly designed to prevent harm, are most central. Despite their dominance, it would be wrong however to picture a moral order as entirely tight and cohesive. There are many tolerances built into the system. First, there need not be 100 percent compliance with (or even respect for) central moral rules. Second, there is room, around the edges so to speak, for moral judgments that are inherently contentious, so that there is no reasonable prospect that they will be widely shared. Some of these judgments may involve such complicated intuitive balancing of relevant factors that they do not admit of formulation in general rules.

Third, a moral order normally will not be static. The understanding of some of the rules can adjust over time: what counts as theft, for example, can be modified. New moral rules can evolve. How many people living 150 years ago would have anticipated a moral order in which rules against racism and sexism would play a major role?

If we look at the process of such moral change, elements such as a sense of fairness or the functioning of sympathy begin to loom large. It was argued previously that what counts as fairness, or as an appropriate object of sympathy, is very much subject to interpretation. It would be wrong to explain our rules against racism and sexism by saying that our ancestors did not care about fairness but now we do. Rather, we have arrived at a broader sense of what fairness requires.

This change clearly is progress. That itself is an ethical judgment, one in favor of a societal climate in which there is pressure to treat all races and both genders equally. What we have now, of course, is not entirely equal treatment, but a widespread presumption (accompanied by some pressure) that there should be equal treatment. That is how moral orders work.

The Value of a Moral Order

The obvious next question is how we can demonstrate that our current moral order, in which rules against racism and sexism play an increasing role, is superior to the moral order of about 150 years ago. There are many particular advantages of the new order that can be pointed to immediately. However, it would be good to have a general solution to the question of how a moral order can be judged. Elements of such a solution will be developed in the remaining chapters.

There is the separate question of whether there is any great value in having a moral order at all. Most people nowadays are quite satisfied with the understanding that questions of what is most worth pursuing in a life can admit of many different answers. The widespread assumption in predominantly secular societies is that we can be "pluralistic," that there is no reason to press for anything like consensus about what the major goals of a satisfying life should be. Indeed, in countries such as the United States, many people seem to favor a public stance of neutrality on such questions. Why, then, one might ask, could we not be equally happy with a comparable pluralism in morality?

The answer is complicated. First, the latitudinarian attitude, with regard to judgments of what the goals and values in lives should be, does extend to many areas of morality: all of them in what I have characterized as the periphery rather than the core of morality. There is a widespread willingness to have a wide variety of responses to moral questions involving such things as conspicuous and unusually heavy use of natural resources, abortion, and the rights of animals. But in relation to the central cases of murder, rape, torture, or theft, many people's willingness to have a pluralistic social climate stops short.

The Hobbesian reasons for this are clear. Murder, rape, torture, and theft are threats in virtually any society, because compliance with even the most effective moral order is never 100 percent. But it is predictable that any society that maintains a pluralistic climate with regard to such matters will have a higher incidence of such harmful behavior than we normally would tolerate. Because of this, even those in our society who are most adamant that public education should be "value neutral" usually do not object if children are urged to regard such things as murder, rape, torture, and theft as impermissible or unthinkable.

In short, any human society needs a moral order, one that includes the familiar prohibitions just discussed. There is a case for saying that any human society should have, not merely this core, but also a periphery in which there are moral issues that are widely regarded as "up for grabs." If moral progress, such as that which has contributed to greater racial and gender equality, is important, then it is important that there be a zone within moral orders in which additions to or subtractions from moral requirements, or new understandings of familiar rules, can be argued and thought through.

Is Contractualism the Whole Truth about Morality?

Finally, we can consider whether the contractualist view provides the sole base of morality. The main reason for answering "No" is this. We have to look at standards for what people can "reasonably" agree to. Can these standards themselves be given a contractualist justification, it being contended that everyone reasonably should agree to them? If so, then we can ask why everyone reasonably should agree to the standards. This points toward difficulties for contractualism. My view of the difficulties parallels at one or two points that of an interesting and important recent paper (Kumar 2003).

We cannot justify a moral order by simply saying, "Everyone would reasonably agree to that," every time something is questioned. We need to explain why it is reasonable to agree. This explanation must go beyond contractualism.

The words "reasonable" and "reasonably" have many meanings. In some contexts, there is a strong connection between being "reasonable" and being accommodating. In much philosophical writing, "reasonable" can mean something like "This is what an intelligent person would say" or perhaps "This is OK; you should agree." In relation to a moral order or its elements, though, there can be a strong connection between "reasonable" and what would count as good supporting reasons. A moral order that can be reasonably accepted, then, is one that has decisively good reasons to support it.

Not just anything can count as a reason in support of a normative conclusion. Philippa Foot's (1978b) illustration of this point was the absurdity of saying that someone was a good man because he clasped and unclasped his hands three times an hour (absent some story that would indicate that there was a purpose, related to human needs or benefits, to this activity). Her contention was that sometimes it is not an "open question" whether something can count as a reason for a normative conclusion. But she also held that there was a range of possible views that could be intelligible as a morality (see the discussion of Nietzsche in Foot 1978a). In other words, her view of normative discourse left what amounted to a zone of contestability.

All of this seems right. Is there an objective logic of what counts as reasons in support of normative conclusions? I have argued elsewhere that the answer is "yes and no" (Kupperman, 2005b). We often recognize that someone whose normative conclusions are different from ours nevertheless does have some good reasons for her or his views. However, we may well differ on how strong these reasons are.

One model of a logic is provided by deductive logic. It is commonly said that in valid deductive inferences, the conclusions are implicit in the premises. It becomes plausible to say that there is a logic connecting "is" and "ought" statements if the meaning of normative conclusions can include elements found in primarily descriptive premises.

There is a strong case for holding that there are two elements that are normally (although not in every single use) contained in the meanings of normative terms such as "good" and "right." One is the prescriptive element of guidance that typically (but not always) is involved in judgments using such words. The other is the positive connection between what is good or right, on the one hand, and, on the other, the satisfaction of human needs and accomplishment of human purposes. Both elements are clearly visible in the most common forms of teaching small children the meanings of such words. Typically the child learns that to call something "good" or "right" is to recommend it. The child also, in the vast majority of cases, learns to associate such words with such activities as cooperative and helpful behavior, relief of suffering, and so on.

It would seem that this second element has, as Foot maintained, a great deal to do with why some primarily descriptive accounts can be read as reasons that do support normative conclusions. The connection of meaning between the descriptive elements and the normative conclusion would appear to be doing the work. However, because of the zone of contestability that is implicit in moral views that can count as intelligible, the connection is not tight, and the strength of any particular recognizable reason remains contestable.

Let us return to Foot's contention that good reasons point to relations between what is evaluated on one hand, and human needs or benefits on the other. Such an account suggests that whether elements of a moral order can be "reasonably" accepted depends a great deal on whether they further or thwart the satisfaction of human needs and accomplishment of human purposes. There is room, but not unlimited room, for contestability in the answers to these questions. The point that is most relevant to the argument of this book is as follows: Whether elements of a moral order work in ways that benefit or thwart people in their lives is a consequentialist consideration. What it amounts to will be investigated further in the remaining chapters.

9

The Logic of Consequentialism

The conclusion thus far is that ethical judgments have more than one basis. This suggests that any nearly adequate picture of the structure of ethics will be neither elegant nor neat. Against this background, my view is that consequentialist considerations have a special importance in ethics. This chapter will explore this contention.

The argument will be that there is a logic embedded in ordinary normative discourse that makes consequentialist considerations decisive. The logical case, though, like many logical cases, will skirt the real-life difficulties of making the judgments required. A more complex (and less thoroughly positive) assessment of consequentialism then will be developed in the remaining chapters.

Logical Claims

Here are three logical claims that constitute a preliminary argument for consequentialism as a base for judgments of how one should act. These all concern relations between, on one hand, which of the actions open to us would be for the best (i.e. would have the best consequences) and, on the other hand, which of the possible actions would be the best to perform.

LC1. If what would have the best consequences is not the best thing for X to do, there must be a reason.

LC2. There are constraints, depending on the seriousness of what is at stake, on what can count as a reason for X's not doing what would have the best consequences.

LC3. The only possible reason for not doing what would have the best consequences would be one that appeals to systems of attitudes, habits of mind, and/or policies (of which morality is one) that themselves promote important values (most of which can be put under the heading of human flourishing). These systems themselves are open to question, and it counts against any one of them in its present form if its existence (as prevalent in a society) is not for the best.

All three claims are concerned with the possibility that what has the best consequences is not the best thing to do, which act consequentialism denies is possible. An argument against act consequentialism has already been given in chapter 7. Nothing in this chapter need rest on that argument, however. It is enough if we assume that it can be claimed coherently that an action will have (or did have) the best available consequences and still is not (was not) the best thing to do. Even an act consequentialist—at least one who does not claim that act consequentialism is true by definition—could concede this.

All the same, the argument for the three claims will add up to a case for consequentialism (at least in the abstract) that points toward an indirect consequentialism. The argument is recursive (see Kupperman 1981). That is, possible objections turn out to rest on consequentialist considerations.

LC1 in effect claims that to say that something would be for the best creates a presumption that it is the best thing to do, which holds unless it is defeated. The logical support for this can be gauged if we consider the conjunction of "X would be for the best, but would not be the best thing to do" with:

E1. "There is no reason (in this case) why it would not be best to do what would be for the best. (Nevertheless it would not be the best thing to do.)"

My argument will be that the conjunction verges on contradiction.

If this seems too abstruse, consider the following case. Betty has an opportunity to make some worthy person (perhaps Betty herself) happier, at negligible cost to anyone or anything else. Betty says that this is so, and yet also says, "It would not be the best thing to do; there is no reason for this judgment, and yet it would not be best to do." Are Betty's conjoined statements self-contradictory, or are they merely odd? Neither response seems entirely satisfactory. It may seem implausible to label them as self-contradictory absent a formal logic in which we can demonstrate a contradiction. On the other hand, what is involved goes well beyond ordinary oddity. What we are confronted with is not merely something unusual and unexpected, but rather a pair of claims whose conjunction prima facie is incoherent.

There is a mystery that could be dispelled. Perhaps there is some reason that Betty should not do whatever it is, and that reason (which, with help, she might articulate) is subliminally registering on her, creating uneasiness and reluctance. All the same, if there really is no reason, and if Betty really does think that what she says is not the best thing to do would be for the best, there is a strong logical strain that looks very like a contradiction.

Any initial resistance to this point may be connected with the thought that if Betty decides not to do whatever it is, that may well be her business. In this sense, even if X would be for the best (and Betty knows it), there may well be no compelling reason either for her to do it or not to do it. Phrases such as "compelling reason" have associations both with logical compulsion and social compulsion, the latter arguably being a feature of judgments of moral obligation. Let us assume that Betty's case is not one that involves a moral obligation. Someone may well then deny that "X would be for the best" creates a reason for saying "Betty should (or ought to) do X," even if Betty and we agree that there is no reason not to do X.

Some of this resistance can be removed by the following consideration. There are many judgments of what it is best to do which do not have the force of moral judgments, or indeed much force at all. Examples are bits of advice on how to begin a letter accepting an invitation or on how often the engine oil in a car should be changed. Sometimes what is at stake is so inconsequential that we would hesitate to use the words "should" or "ought to." Arguably, you should change your engine oil every five thousand miles or so, as opposed to changing it only every five years. If someone asks, "Is it better to change it every five thousand miles or every six thousand miles?" a reply might take the form of "It is better to . . ." rather than "You should . . ." or "You ought to . . ."

In light of this, if Betty's case is one that does not involve a moral obligation, it may well also be one in which words like "should" or "ought" are out of place. Indeed, it may be one in which people with decent manners keep their judgments to themselves. They may say, to themselves or to friends, "In her place, I would . . .," without being willing to offer this opinion to Betty.

Further, even if what we would (if asked) recommend does not fulfill anything like an obligation, other terms are available. It may simply be a nice thing to do. Or (if the interests involved are mainly Betty's own), not to do it may be mildly impractical. Or it may be what a civilized person/responsible member of the community/good friend would do. If Betty chooses to do what is mildly impractical, or not to do what (all things considered) would have been nicest, we very likely will not condemn her, and possibly will not even think less of her. Nevertheless we still can have the thought that it would have been best if she had done whatever it was.

Remaining resistance may crumble if we confront this line of thought. A reader may think, "Even if all of this is so, suppose that Betty simply does not feel like doing X? Doesn't that make a difference?" The answer that I contend is built into the structure of our normative discourse is that it depends on the case. If what is at stake is merely that a friend will have the pleasure of Betty's company for coffee (where, we will assume, the friend's pleasure will outweigh whatever negligible discomfort or boredom Betty will experience), then the answer arguably is that the fact that Betty does not feel like it is an adequate reason for not doing what (she may agree) is for the best. If what is at stake is someone's life or happiness, then the answer of course is no.

Let us examine this more closely. Why should the fact that Betty does not feel like doing X ever be a reason for not doing what (we will stipulate) would be for the best? Could we not instead, in the case in which Betty decides not to join her friend for coffee, say (or merely think) that of course it would have been (very slightly) better if she had, but that so little is at stake that any further normative thought is hardly appropriate?

I want to accept elements of both sides of this argument, for reasons that have a great deal to do with the structure of any consequentialism that (at least in the abstract) is acceptable. We may begin with a widely shared judgment of value: that a life with considerable space for spontaneity, acts by and large not reflected on and usually not judged, is (generally speaking) more desirable than one with little or no room for spontaneity. This point of view comes through in J. J. C. Smart's remark (1977, 128) that when he plays field hockey, he never thinks of the greatest good of the greatest number. If spontaneity really is important to human flourishing, this supports a general policy of not approaching reflectively decisions in which not a lot is at stake. Reflective judgment has spontaneity costs. Hence we by and large will not engage in it unless there is some signal that the situation especially warrants reflection. To follow such a policy is for the best.

This chapter is philosophy, and as such provides a reflective pattern of discourse. T. M. Scanlon (1998, 108 ff.) has pointed out, in my view quite correctly, that in ordinary life we usually do not relate our choices to questions of what would enhance personal well-being. A similar point applies to questions of what is for the best. For most of life we more or less carry on, or act out of love, friendship, moral conviction, or a general sense of what feels right. The real-world situations in which judgments of what is for the best are likely to enter tend to be either ones in which a particular choice looks both serious and problematic, or a path of life or pattern of behavior has come to look unsatisfactory, or choices have been questioned in a probing way (say, by a philosopher).

Hence, unless Betty is unusually pompous or is a philosopher, she will be very likely to treat "I don't feel like it" as the last word on why she can decide not to meet her friend for coffee. All the same, reflective examination discloses that there is a good reason having to do with the value of spontaneity. The argument from the consequences of a policy underlies both levels of response to Betty's decision not to join her friend for coffee. First, we would not want Betty (or ourselves) to follow a policy of, by and large, subjecting such decisions to normative scrutiny. In the absence of normative scrutiny, doing what you feel like doing becomes the default position. Second, this does not preclude the possibility that Betty's decision might be singled out for philosophical or psychological analysis (both highly artificial activities): decisions that by and large are not subject to normative scrutiny might be, on special occasions, looked at more closely. Betty then easily can produce the reason "I didn't feel like it." Given the structure of normative discourse, this trumps any evidence that there would have been very slight advantages (overall) in Betty's having coffee with her friend. Indeed, we might go so far as to say, "She shouldn't do it if she does not feel like it."

Let us go back to the underlying consequentialist justification: that it is better (by and large) to encourage spontaneity in ourselves and in others. Note that this states a policy, and not in any normal sense a rule. Normative rules frequently have imaginable exceptions, and often it is impossible to specify clearly in advance what these will be. A policy, on the other hand, admits of looser and more flexible formulation: one might have a policy of drinking heavily only on very special occasions, or of never breaking promises lightly (i.e., without compelling justification). A policy can be deviated from on occasion without a significant sense of transgression (if not very much is at stake); but if a policy is oriented toward important goals or standards, a readiness to deviate from (or change) it because of immediate prospects of good consequences can undermine any sense that one has a policy at all. (This was the burden of complaint against what Marxist consequentialists used to call opportunism.) Adhering to a policy has the useful feature of stiffening resistance to temptations and other pressures that can arise in particular cases.

The Act-Consequentialist Retort, and a Refutation

It can be argued that if a policy in general has good consequences, and if a deviation or transgression undermines the policy, then one ought to be able to assess the bad consequences of the deviation or transgression and weigh these against its putative good consequences. This is a point especially likely to be made by an act consequentialist. The further claim can be that, if the weighing is accomplished and if the good consequences (of the deviation or transgression) genuinely outweigh the bad consequences (of undermining a useful policy), one should deviate from the policy. (It would be irrational not to.) If the bad consequences of undermining it outweigh the good consequences, then one should not deviate. This seems to lead to the conclusion that an intelligent version of what might be termed policy consequentialism collapses into act consequentialism.

One of my objections to this argument is that it assumes that there is a clear way of distributing the cumulative costs to the effectiveness of a policy among deviations from it. Suppose that deviation A encourages deviation B, and that A and B encourage deviation C, and that the subsequent workings of the policy are impaired to a total of X units of value. (Anyone who works with value in real-world terms will find the mock precision of this ludicrous, but I hope will forgive it: here it is merely a quick way to make a point.) Do we assign the full loss of X units of value to deviation A, without which B and C would not have occurred, and then assign correspondingly lesser amounts to B and C? There may well be a sense of double or triple counting of demerits, especially if A, B, and C all are committed by the same person. If this disturbs us, we might wish to assign only part of the loss of X units to A, with the remainder shared by B and C. How should the moral demerit be parceled out? There may be no solution that is clearly the most appropriate.

Here (as so often), attempts to arrive at something like a consequentialist "calculus" founder. There is another reply that more directly refutes the act consequentialist's attempt to collapse policy consequentialism into act consequentialism. This will move from consideration of what will be called illocutionary costs—of statements that something is, or would be, the best thing to do—to examination of whether (and how) such costs are relevant to the assessment of these statements. The argument will be that one kind of illocutionary cost is largely irrelevant in some kinds of case but essentially relevant in others. These latter cases are the ones in which policy consequentialism most clearly cannot be collapsed into act consequentialism.

Statements that such-and-such is the best thing to do often model what is recommended in a way that may influence the conduct of others (and also our own future conduct), perhaps in situations not entirely like the one at hand. (We may put to the side the issue of whether this is always—or, as a weaker claim, normally—the case, along with the question of whether its being always or normally the case is implicit in the logic of ethical discourse, as some prescriptivists have claimed.) Given that statements of what is the best thing to do sometimes do influence future conduct, we can see that evaluation of such a statement could involve more than one sort of consideration. On one hand, there are the reasons we normally give, a mixed group that often includes estimates of the likely consequences of the action recommended and of the alternatives, and can include also appeals to morality, professional responsibilities, the demands of friendship, family, or one's lifework, and also to what one feels like doing. On the other hand, the recommendation itself, in thought or in speech, is an event that may have consequences, possibly contributing to a habit of mind on the part of the recommender and some who hear of it (or witness the conduct it recommends), and perhaps also contributing to a climate of opinion. (It is important to bear in mind that although the primary subjects of any consideration of How To Do Things With Words will be spoken or written words, we sometimes also do things with words merely whispered or thought or acted out in a kind of charade.) This very different sort of consideration yields its own reasons, which point further toward the wider risks or advantages of the recommendation's acceptance. The classic expression of this concern is "What if everyone acted like that?," which sometimes unpacks into a worry about the increased likelihood of others (not necessarily everyone) doing the sort of thing that is recommended.

The phrase "sort of thing" is deliberately imprecise. If Betty says that the best thing to do in situation A is Y, then her friend Joe may be more inclined to do something like Y (something in broad outline like Y, although not every feature will be identical) in situation B, which seems much like A. The differences between what Joe does and what Betty did, or between B and A, may or may not be significant. The point is simply that imitations, or behavior that is in part the result of influence, will never be entirely identical with the original source of influence.

Even if Betty, imitating R. M. Hare's caution in presenting the thesis of universalizability (1963, 17 ff.), avoids general terms and says, "The best thing to do in a situation that is in all relevant respects like the one I am now in is something that is in relevant respects like what I am now doing," Joe may imitate the conduct that he sees. Depending on the context (which includes how suggestible Joe is, and the seriousness of what is at stake), Betty may share some responsibility for the imitation. Think of the case in which Betty carefully and competently checks that a gun is not loaded, and then (to make a point) aims it and pulls the trigger, and in which Joe later quickly looks at the gun to verify that it is not loaded, aims it, and pulls the trigger, killing someone.

Often, spoken judgments of what is the best thing to do, or unspoken ones manifested in behavior (ranging from evident choices of conduct to facial gestures), have serious consequences. In the most dramatic cases, a judgment leads to other behavior (beyond that which was its immediate concern) which we judge to be unfortunate. There also can be costs which go under the heading of intrusiveness or disruption. We already have touched on the risks that judgments which provoke unnecessary reflective self-consciousness will undermine spontaneity. Judgments (especially those that make demands on people) also may disrupt or undermine the central projects of someone's life. Bernard Williams (1973, 108–118) noted this in a well-known attack on utilitarianism.

Because of all of this, we can rate judgments of what it is best to do in different ways. If Betty holds that the best thing to do in case A is Y, this can be assigned:

1. A consequences rating. We can try to estimate whether Y is likely to have better consequences than any of the available alternatives would.
2. A rating in relation to good systems of attitudes, habits of mind, or policies. We might ask whether Y goes against the requirements of morality or of professional ethics, whether it slights the demands of friendship or family life, or (more modestly) whether it undermines Betty's spontaneity.
3. An illocutionary rating. We can ask whether Betty's judgment, in the circumstances, itself is likely to have unfortunate consequences. We can ask further whether *our agreement* with Betty's judgment carries with it risks or advantages.

The last element of the illocutionary rating is part of the key to refutation of the act consequentialist's attempt to collapse policy consequentialism into act consequentialism. The consequences of Betty's judgment will be part of the act consequentialist's reckoning of whether she has acted for the best, at least when the judgment that Y is the best thing to do is part and parcel of her doing Y. But as this reckoning normally is made, the consequences of our agreeing with Betty's judgment fall outside of it. It can be that, as these things normally are reckoned, an action of Betty's had (or would have had) good consequences, but that our thinking that it was the best thing to do would have poor consequences. What worked well this time (even factoring in the consequences of Betty's favoring it) may be such an unfortunate model that we have to reject and condemn it. Is it the best thing to do? The argument is that in some kinds of case illocutionary costs may force us to answer "no."

Here are two examples of kinds of cases in which reversals of judgment based on illocutionary costs are standard practice. One is the military practice of court-martialing those who, because of predictable good effects in the present case, broke a generally useful rule. The alternative is seen as not rejecting their rule-breaking judgment, and not to reject would undermine a useful rule in a damaging way.

The other example is this. Let us suppose that Raskolnikov can reasonably estimate that his robbing and killing a very sour old lady pawnbroker will have, on balance, good consequences. (It is true that he will be punished, but this will lead in the end to a very valuable spiritual redemption; and more immediately, her money can lead to a great deal more happiness than will be lost by her death.) Even if we factor in the illocutionary cost of Raskolnikov's judgment, the balance remains favorable. (It helps that Raskolnikov is not much of a role model.) Do we then agree that it is right for Raskolnikov to kill her? The illocutionary costs of *this* are both great and incalculable. It would undermine a very useful moral order.

An act consequentialist might want to object here that we should not separate an act and its consequences from our consequent judgment of the act and its consequences (which would be further consequences of the original act). The consequences of Raskolnikov's murder along with our judgment that it was morally acceptable would be very bad indeed; it can be urged that hence the act consequentialist can consistently condemn it. This defense, however, misses the point. It is predictable that we will condemn Raskolnikov's act, and indeed to judge otherwise would have bad consequences. But this leaves us with a murder that (as we have assumed) happens to have good consequences, and the judgment that it is morally wrong (which also has good consequences).

Perhaps we have been going too fast here and need to look more carefully at the varieties of judgment of what is the best thing to do, and at the ways in which illocutionary costs (especially of the second kind) are relevant or irrelevant to their assessment. On the face of it, we have a puzzle about the relation between the three kinds of rating of a judgment of what it is best to do, on one hand, and what counts as the proper conclusion, on the other. A simple point is that in much of our normative life these three ratings do not pull in radically different directions. We all, of course, are familiar with cases in which a proposed action gets a high consequences rating and a low rating in relation to good systems of attitudes and so on (including cases in which what seems likely to be for the best simply is immoral). But such cases, although not rare, are hardly the norm. Ones in which a proposed action gets a favorable consequences rating but the judgment it represents gets a low illocutionary rating may be even less common.

Nevertheless they exist. And as we have seen, there are imaginable cases in which the illocutionary rating is very negative of our agreeing with a recommendation of a particular action that will have good consequences. One traditional way (see Sidgwick 1907, 489; also see 413) of handling this is to say that our agreement (and the act consequentialism on which it would rest) should be kept from the majority of the population. This presumably will diminish the illocutionary costs. The thought is that the illocutionary costs will be minor among educated, reflective people, who can employ act consequentialist decision procedures responsibly, but would be catastrophic among the general population.

Some have objected to the elitism of this strategy and to the patronizing attitude that it would create or reinforce in educated act consequentialists toward the non-act-consequentialist bulk of the population. Beyond this, though, it has to be noted that Sidgwick's strategy would have some costs and very limited effectiveness. Moral orientations can hardly be kept a complete secret, and in hierarchical societies (which is what Sidgwick's strategy to some extent requires) there is normally some tendency for people to imitate their "betters." Further, anyone who believes that he or she has a special license to violate the morality that most people have (to some degree) internalized is liable to be unreliable or dangerous. Hence any distinction between a publicized morality for the masses and a covert "true" morality for an elite is both corrupt, risky, and unstable.

Nevertheless we can continue to ask whether illocutionary costs of the second kind should be counted against any judgment of what is the best thing to do. One possible position remains that we can distinguish between criteria for truth or warrant, on one hand, and the criteria for the desirability of expressing or promulgating a view, on the other. There is no logical reason why there cannot be harmful truths and useful lies. If some applications of this distinction (e.g., the one suggested by Sidgwick) themselves might have harmful effects, those who maintain the distinction can consistently refuse to charge its own illocutionary costs against its correctness.

It is always tempting in philosophy to give general answers to general questions; but sometimes, including now, it is important to resist this. Perhaps illocutionary costs of the second kind matter in some kinds of case in a way that they do not in others? Rather than look for general principles, we may need to look at the special logic of some kinds of judgment.

Here are some examples of judgments of what is the best thing to do.

A. The best thing to do in response to that written invitation is to reply in writing.
B. The best thing to do, in trying to get that nail into the wall, is to use a hammer.
C. If a good friend needs you, and if there are no competing demands on you that are pressing, then the best thing to do is what your friend needs.
D. If you are a lawyer and a client tells you something that is highly compromising, the best thing to do is to keep it confidential.
E. If you have an opportunity to murder an unpleasant old person who will not be missed and whose murder predictably will lead to happiness for a number of people, the best thing is to do it.

The reader can recognize major kinds of normative judgment relating to etiquette, practical mattters, the demands of special relationships, professional ethics, and, finally, moral judgments. We can ask for each what the role would be of illocutionary charges, especially of the second kind.

The answer for judgments of etiquette surely is that it is negligible. There may be cases in which special circumstances might lead a knowledgeable person to recommend or endorse something that normally would not be acceptable (e.g., replying to the invitation in sky writing, or by a loud shout in the direction of the person who issued it). Even if what is recommended in an unusual case might provide a bad model for the more usual sorts of case, the costs are very unlikely to be serious. If an etiquette recommendation somehow does lead to disastrous consequences (e.g., someone's death or severe depression), the most likely response will be either (a) the disastrous consequences were a fluke and could not have been anticipated, or (b) to the extent that they could have been anticipated, this riskiness would ground a moral recommendation that would run counter to (and trump) the normal demands of etiquette; but even if this is so, the original recommendation can be correct qua judgment of etiquette.

The important thing is that judges of etiquette sometimes are willing to be flexible in their advice, allowing not only for the importance of particular circumstances but also for flourishes of individual style. If what is recommended in one case would not work well in others, there is no incoherence or logical strain in saying, "This was the best thing for her to do in those special circumstances, but normally . . ." Indeed, there is no incoherence in saying, "Do X if that is what you would be most comfortable with, and otherwise do Y."

This contrasts with morality. We would not normally say, "On moral grounds, the best thing to do is X if it is what you would be most comfortable with, and otherwise it is Y." For that matter, although we sometimes do allow for special circumstances in our moral judgments, there is some built-in reluctance (which we will shortly explore) to do this very freely.

The role of illocutionary charges normally would be negligible also in relation to ordinary practical judgments. An exception would be if they occur within a "how-to" book: one could imagine something being recommended which would be difficult and disastrous for any but the most skilled reader to attempt. The normal reaction would be that the recommendation was out of place in the book or should have been accompanied by dramatic warnings. But there would be no inclination to go on to deny that what was recommended was the best thing—for the right kind of craftsperson—to do. It was right for Raskolnikov (who, let us say, is unusually skilled at this kind of thing) to do what is described on pages 129–132, but it should not be recommended for the rest of us. The contrast with morality is obvious.

Judgments when special relationships are a significant factor, of what it is best to do, bring more than one complication into the discussion. They readily can place major demands on us, much more often than is the case for ordinary judgments of etiquette and practicality. They also, insofar as there is enormous variety in close human relationships, may be especially resistant to attempts at generalization.

There is room for worry here about two opposite kinds of illocutionary costs. One is that judgments comparable to (C) will set up a social pattern in which people's engagement in central projects in their own lives will be routinely curtailed. The old-fashioned practice of unmarried daughters subordinating their own lives to the needs of aged parents is a case in point.

The opposite kind of worry is this. If we deny (C) in cases in which, all relevant factors considered, it is likely that not helping the friend in need will have slightly better consequences, then (it will be claimed) we are contributing to what is in effect a climate of selfish individualism, in which special relationships are devalued. These are serious illocutionary costs. Hence the act consequentialist position here—that the demands of special relationships can be decisive only in cases in which the overall consequences of fulfilling them are better—itself has poor consequences. It is, if not immoral, inhuman.

The issues here are rich and complex, but I will be brief. This is in part because, while my own inclination is to believe that illocutionary costs of the second kind can be a significant factor in cases featuring demands of special relationships (i.e., that agreeing that what is likely to have the best consequences is the best thing to do can itself have highly negative consequences not already factored into the assessment of the original judgment), I think that the matter is more clear-cut when professional ethics or morality is at stake. Hence the objection to the attempt to collapse policy consequentialism into act consequentialism will rest on analysis of these two areas.

I should point out, though, the reasons that issues relating to (C) can seem intermediate in character between those relating to (A) and (B) and to (D) and (E). On one hand, the demands of special relationships are normally thought to allow more consideration of individual circumstances, and also more attention to the roles of style and nuance in the execution of whatever is done, than usually is the case for professional ethics or morality. The differences here arguably are of degree and scope, rather than being largely of an all-or-nothing character. The greater looseness and flexibility of the general demands thought to be attached to special relationships diminishes the importance—as a precedent—of any judgment in a particular case. On the other hand, the demands of special relationships are normally taken much more seriously than those attached to etiquette or to ordinary practical judgments. The greater pressure makes the role of any particular judgment in relation to social consensus look more serious.

On the other hand, it should be clear that demands of special relationships are entrenched in our normative discourse. We blame people for not being kind to their parents, not being loyal to their friends, not adequately combining affection and responsibility for their children, and so on. What should be noted is that the structure of normative discourse also contains features designed to diminish some of the illocutionary costs attached to this. One is that there are certain kinds of sacrifice that we may judge represent the best thing to do in a given situation but are too much to ask. Some of these cases are ones in which the judgment based on conventional views of special relationships coincides with the act consequentialist verdict (e.g., it does seem very likely that the aged parents would benefit more than the unmarried daughter would lose); others are not. The structure of normative discourse is a complex bit of conceptual engineering (more complex than many ethical philosophers are willing to recognize), in which there are strains that are inevitable but can be (within the structure) alleviated or balanced. At present, though, we are concerned principally with the logic that is built into the structure.

Let us turn now to recommendations in which considerations of professional ethics or of morality can play a significant part. Professional ethics is not clearly the same as morality. For one thing, it is arguable that some of its recommendations in some circumstances represent a moral mistake; for example, it might be argued that there are times when it would be morally wrong to respect client confidentiality. This is linked to another difference between professional ethics and morality, which lies in the ways the two are enforced. The enforcement of professional ethics is in large part institutional and formal, whereas the enforcement of morality is primarily social and informal. Because of this difference, it is far more difficult for a professional ethics to allow for individual judgment of exceptions to rules than it is for a morality.

Nevertheless, the two systems of recommendations share some features. One is that they are intended to govern everyone within a class: all human beings (or rational beings), all doctors, all lawyers, and so on. Another is that someone can have a sense of, as it were, having signed up for the entire system. Moral psychologists often have suggested that actual moral virtue is "specific"—that is, that many or most people are more virtuous in some areas of their lives than they are in others. Be that as it may, a great many people, whatever their actual behavior, have a sense of some general resolution to be a morally decent person. And doctors, lawyers, morticians, and so on are highly unlikely to feel that some parts of their codes of professional ethics can be disregarded by them even if they are governed by other parts.

Both of these features are shared with etiquette, but the first especially generates worries in morality and in professional ethics that are unparalleled in relation to etiquette. We are disturbed if someone considers himself or herself above the demands of morality, or above those of a profession, in a way that goes beyond the normal irritation with someone who seems to feel exempt from etiquette. What is at stake is thought of as an important aspect of the social contract or as the ground rules of a profession. These are less likely to gain lasting widespread acceptance if they are perceived as intrinsically favoring some person or persons over everyone else. We do recognize special circumstances in some moral judgments; but this is against a background of suspicion of people's tendencies to plead special circumstances (it may be thought) as a way of gaining exemption from what is meant to apply to everyone.

One difference, not yet mentioned, between professional ethics and morality is that the former becomes a clear subject of appeal or argument only when a professional ethics has been widely agreed to. A pioneer in a profession can propose or attempt to formulate an ethics that is to govern the profession, but we normally are most comfortable in speaking of so-and-so's professional ethics when there is already one that is widely agreed upon. (i.e., to have a professional ethics is not necessarily to have the one that is widely agreed upon, but generally presupposes that there is one.) In contrast, we readily can speak of Betty's personal morality even in a society in which there is no moral consensus. A fortiori, we can speak of Betty's personal morality even if very little in it would draw agreement from many people.

Nevertheless (as noted in chap. 5), it is part of the nature of morality that to hold that X is morally right, wrong, or acceptable is to hold that such a judgment should be included within a morality widely agreed upon within a society. (For a suggestive discussion of this, see Strawson 1961.) Any personal morality, thus, has to be seen as a candidate for a social morality. Hence both moral judgments and those of professional ethics reach beyond whatever is the particular case at hand. It is an interesting question why both are designed to have this characteristic. A short answer is that both meet pressing needs of very reliable social coordination (as opposed to ordinary practical judgments or judgments of personal ideals, which are not much concerned with social coordination, and to judgments of etiquette, in relation to which the needs of social coordination are not so pressing).

Bearing all of this in mind, we can understand why illocutionary costs of the second kind would play a special role in relation to judgments of what is the best thing to do in which the primary consideration is moral or concerns professional ethics. For the sake of brevity, I will concentrate on morality in what immediately follows. Suppose that Betty judges that X would be the best thing to do in circumstances A; suppose also that X seems morally questionable. We can ask whether the consequences of Betty's doing X would be optimal or not, including in this reckoning the primary illocutionary costs of Betty's (explicit or implicit) judgment that X is the best thing to do. These illocutionary costs, it should be said, might be fairly minimal. Betty's future attitudes and behavior perhaps are hardly affected, especially if she regards doing X now as a one-off thing. If she keeps it secret, also, the illocutionary effects on others might be limited to the subtle influences of slight (not easy to notice) changes in comportment and would be minimal or nonexistent.

Suppose further, though, that there would be significant costs if a morality widely accepted throughout the society were to include the judgment that X is the best thing to do in circumstances A. Do we charge these to Betty's judgment? This might seem unfair, especially if Betty is perfectly willing to keep quiet about the whole thing, and also if Betty's own morality hardly represents the dominant view in the society.

Nevertheless, the answer is that the secondary illocutionary costs in this kind of case are chargeable, that is, count against Betty's judgment; and this answer is based on the logic of normative discourse, not merely on some normative intuition. If Betty, explicitly or implicitly, holds that X is morally acceptable in circumstances A, this *means* that the judgment is worthy of inclusion in a prevailing social morality. If the consequences of our agreeing with Betty's judgment would be poor, this would normally be held to show that it is not worthy of inclusion; and this counts decisively against the judgment.

This refutes the claim that a rational policy consequentialism must collapse into act consequentialism. In at least two kinds of case—one involving moral considerations, the other involving professional ethics—a judgment that X is the best thing to do can be such that a person's accepting it and acting on it would have optimal consequences and yet be unacceptable on broadly consequentialist grounds because the judgment implicitly endorses a (moral or professional) policy which, if used widely, would have poor consequences. Hence if the act consequentialist insists that violating a generally useful policy in a particular case is rational if it would have (even when primary illocutionary costs are weighed), on the whole, good consequences, the reply is that this fails to take account of the logical character of moral judgments and the judgments of professional ethics.

It should be emphasized that this argument does not entail that policy consequentialism collapses into some kind of rule consequentialism. In talking about Betty's case, we could hold (1) that X is generally unacceptable and should not be done lightly, (2) that there are some cases a bit like Betty's in which doing X seems acceptable, and (3) that Betty's is not such a case. This need not include any suggestion that a rule could be formulated that would demarcate exceptions to the general condemnation of X.

Underlying the unacceptability of act consequentialism is the shallowness of an atomism of life, especially of moral and professional life. The assumption that judgments in particular cases systematically can be viewed in isolation from the agent's ongoing habits of mind and policies is psychologically unrealistic. (It can be done on occasion, especially at a dramatic crossroads, but not systematically.) Because of this alone, act consequentialism could not work—either as a systematic decision procedure, or as a reconstruction of how morality functions—for human beings, although this would not prevent it from working for Hare's archangels (see Hare 1981). Archangels, of course, would not have needed to construct the structures of morality and professional ethics. We, however, have these structures and their logic. The assumption that judgments in particular cases that involve issues of morality or of professional ethics systematically can be viewed in isolation from the social practices that they (explicitly or implicitly) endorse or reject is not only unrealistic; it also goes against the logic of these kinds of judgment.

Agent-Centered Prerogatives and Agent-Centered Restrictions

My view, as developed above, should be placed in relation to the influential discussion of "agent-centered restrictions" and "agent-centered prerogatives" in Scheffler (1993). Scheffler finds a clearer justification for the latter than for the former. The view of this chapter is that both agent-centered restrictions and agent-centered prerogatives have consequentialist justifications. This still leaves an asymmetry between the restrictions and the prerogatives. The restrictions by and large are quite specific. Acts of certain kinds (e.g., murder, rape, and torture) can be ruled out even in some cases in which they predictably would have, on the whole, good consequences. The prerogatives, in contrast, by and large do not fall neatly under such a set of headings, rather amounting to a consequentially justified zone in which it is acceptable not to choose what would have the best consequences.

Consequentialist justifications here have to do with mind-sets, habits of mind, attitudes, and practices, and they can be understood against the background of two facts. One is that we are not archangels and would not function well if we had to make all moral decisions on a case-by-case basis. The other is that a viable moral order relies on agents' internalizing constraints on their tendencies to prefer their own perceived interests to those of others, but the constraints will be more widely accepted if they are not extremely stringent and instead allow some latitude.

Suppose that there were an Infallible Optimizer (Scheffler 1993, 111) who could always tell us whether, say, a killing really would have suboptimal consequences. Would the existence of such a person eliminate any justification for agent-centered restrictions? One might equally ask whether the existence of such a person would eliminate any justification for an agent-centered prerogative. To answer these questions, we would need more information about the rest of the population. Are they what we think of as normal human beings? Will they, in each decision they make, unhesitatingly accept the guidance of the Infallible Optimizer without the slightest hesitation or regret? Unless the population uniformly consists of archangels or of beings that are infinitely docile and robotic, it is hard to imagine a viable moral order—even given the presence of an Infallible Moral Optimizer—that rejects agent-centered restrictions or agent-centered prerogatives.

Constraints on Reasons for Non-Optimific Choice

It is a commonplace in recent ethical philosophy that many imaginable reasons that could be offered to justify conduct fail because they are simply irrelevant or lack sufficient weight. Thus, the fact that your last name has a certain number of letters does not make it acceptable for you to kill the neighbors. "I feel a bit tired" could support Betty's judgment that it would be best not to meet her friend for coffee, even if on this occasion the friend's pleasure would outweigh Betty's discomfort or boredom. But it would not qualify as a reason that supports such a judgment as "The best thing to do would be to let so-and-so drown."

Cases of this sort are enough to establish the second of our three claims about the logic of consequentialism, LC2. What follows will give a fuller picture, and in particular will begin to make a case for the third of the three claims. The reader may wish to be reminded that the first half of LC3 states that the only possible reason for not doing what is optimific (would be for the best) is one that appeals to systems of attitudes, habits of mind, and/or policies (of which morality is one) that themselves promote important values (most of which can be put under the heading of human flourishing).

As an illustration of this, we have already seen that the cogency of "I don't feel like it" as a reason for not doing what would be for the best, in cases in which very little is at stake, is underwritten by the usefulness of zones of spontaneity in human life. It is in fact for the best that people not feel under continuous pressure to do what would be for the best. Implicit in "I don't feel like it" (at least in the cases in which it is an adequate reason) is "There are areas in life in which, when very little is at stake, it is desirable that people often do what they feel like doing." Although it has good consequences that there be zones of spontaneity, if these are made unreasonably large, the advantages become counterbalanced by major disadvantages, which is why "I don't feel like it" would not be counted as a reason for not doing what would be for the best when something significant (such as someone's life or happiness) were at stake.

Other major sources of reasons, on some occasions, for not doing what would be for the best already have been mentioned. These include the attitudes, habits of mind, and policies demanded by family life, friendships or love relations, professional ethics, and morality. The most obvious point is that attachments to family members, friends, and loved ones contribute considerably to the quality of most human lives: these generate reasons for doing what otherwise there would be little reason to do, and ethical common sense holds that the reasons often justify doing what in a particular case would not be (everyone's well-being considered equally) for the best. The advantages of the cooperative and somewhat predictable systems of behavior that professional ethics and morality promote do not need to be insisted upon. Above and beyond this, the content of acceptable morality clearly has something to do with a general pattern of good consequences from certain sorts of attitude and behavior. When Judith Jarvis Thomson (1997, 282) endorses the idea that "there being people who possess the virtues is good for us," it should be clear that this has everything to do with what makes these qualify as virtues. My view of the virtues has much in common with the account recently advanced by Julia Driver (2002), and my view of the virtues of friendship, in particular, is very close to Robert Card's (2004).

Here is an argument for LC3: The *only* possible reason for not doing what would be for the best would be one that appeals to some system of attitudes, habits of mind, and/or policies that promotes important values. A fully conclusive argument would require that all alternative kinds of reason be explored and disqualified. The argument that follows is not intended to be conclusive, but it does create a case for holding that other kinds of reason should be disqualified.

What (besides the beneficial systems that have been nominated) could provide a reason for not doing what would be for the best? Particular goods can serve as reasons for not doing what we might otherwise be inclined to do. But this is the case when a good that would otherwise be missed outweighs, or seems more important than, the goods that we are aiming for. We then, however, might say that allowing the good that might be missed to determine our conduct is for the best.

How else can a particular good provide a reason for passing up other goods? Here is a leading possibility. It might be urged that if it is a good for the agent, and the competing goods benefited others, then an agent might be justified in pursuing what was good for her or him, even if from a neutral point of view this was not for the best.

Our ordinary normative thought about the claims of egoism (to put matters in this general way) is far from simple. We sometimes condemn people for being selfish or greedy. But we sometimes also comment adversely on people who seem to lack self-respect, who are too deferential to the needs or desires of others while insufficiently representing their own. My concern here is not with saintliness, which in a number of ways is a special case. (Powerful self-denial is typically a form of self-realization, and anyway—to put it crudely—to be a saint can be an ego trip.) My concern is with more ordinary cases, in which people are willing to neglect their own interests without there being much joy in it or compensating satisfaction. People of this sort often are not much respected, and this is rooted in a sense that the quality of their lives is not what it might be. We tend to think that widespread policies of the kind of self-denial that they represent would deprive a society of its energy and joy and would not be generally useful.

The thought seems to be (a) that a modest and circumscribed self-favoritism is useful to the energy and prosperity of a society, (b) that the absence of self-favoritism would not be at all useful, and (c) that pressure to radically diminish self-favoritism would be (given human beings as they are) counterproductive.

What is a modest and circumscribed self-favoritism? It is modest in that we condemn self-favoritism when the stakes are high, as, for example, when pursuing one's own interests causes one to ignore the person who is drowning or who will be directly and seriously hurt by one's actions. It is circumscribed in that there are areas of public life in which scrupulous fairness and the denial of self-favoritism (or of favoritism of loved ones) are expected. (Think of the professional activities of judges, bankers, etc.)

It would be wrong to make the nature of ordinary normative thought seem more definite than it is: often it presents a circumscribed range of possibilities rather than anything like a normative convergence. The degree of self-favoritism that is acceptable is contestable, as are the boundaries between areas of life in which some degree of self-favoritism is acceptable and those in which it is not. Even if (as many writers since Mandeville have urged) societies tend to be more prosperous and happy if their members give some special attention to their own well-being over and above that of others, the degree and kind of special attention that is allowed (and perhaps encouraged) can be adjusted through time. It may be that an allowance of self-favoritism that is both large and broad can come to be seen as having consequences that are not nearly as good as they might be, if the lives of the less able or the less well-connected become too miserable. In short, we can see limited self-favoritism as expressing attitudes, habits of mind, and policies that can contribute to human flourishing but also may have serious costs; this leaves room for arguments that modifications will largely retain the advantages and significantly lessen the costs. The immediate point though, in relation to the general argument, is that limited egoism, like the zone of spontaneity, can itself be given a consequentialist justification.

There is one aspect of limited egoism that especially deserves notice. This is the policy of encouraging people to get on with their lives without, by and large, very prolonged or continuous disruption. Traditionally, wars and other societal emergencies have been treated as exceptions to this; the societal utilities clearly create consequentialist grounds for treating these as special cases. Whether what Loren Lomasky (1983, 272) has called "moral black holes" also would qualify raises interesting questions. Lomasky's examples in a presentation were aged parents and a perennially desperate Third World country. Part of the problem, as he presents it, is that whatever one does is in some sense not enough, so that ethics (and especially a consequentialist ethics) can seem like a losing game. But the persistence of the need—also is relevant.

This leads to a mixed verdict on Bernard Williams's well-known point about what he calls "integrity" (1973). If a morality, or a set of social relations, on occasion demands a great deal of one, it may not seem persuasive (it may, in fact, seem unattractively selfish) to complain about the integrity of one's life being under threat. If the demands, on the other hand, are constant and seemingly endless, and amount to a disruption of one's life, that is another matter. These cases force us, at the least, to balance the usefulness of a general policy of encouraging people to get on with their lives, without prolonged or continuous disruption, with the seriousness of the needs that might be addressed.

One way of attempting to work out the balance as favorably as possible is to limit the disruptive-to-personal-life benevolence that we expect of people while still holding, in a different tone of voice, that it would be nice if they did more. It also helps if burdens of disruption are shared. Here, issues of justice intersect with those of benevolence: "Why me?" can be a pertinent response, when someone who has already done a great deal (while others have done very little) is asked to do more. Surely it is useful to have a policy of not expecting too very much more of some people than of others. Different issues of justice are relevant if what is demanded has a gender bias, as in the traditional tendency to expect an unmarried daughter to do most of the work of caring for aged parents. Here again, someone can agree that (all interests balanced) it would be for the best if she did what was asked, and yet reasonably appeal to a (generally useful) consideration of justice in judging that it might be best if she did not.

If it is accepted that policies that encourage modest and circumscribed self-favoritism by and large have good consequences (even if it is not always clear how such policies best should be adjusted), is there any reason for not doing what is for the best that does not rest on consequentialist grounds? A temptation is to look for such a reason within resolutely non-consequentialist morality. Can there be moral justifications, that themselves cannot be given a consequentialist justification, for not doing what is for the best?

What would fill the bill here is a moral reason for doing what would not have particularly good consequences, and which is such that the moral reason is not integrally connected with a system of attitudes, habits of mind, and or policies that promote important values. Those whose view of morality is dour will have no trouble imagining that such a reason could be found. Even a brief examination of how morality functions, though, is enough to create strong doubt.

We need to bear in mind that the attitudes that play a part in acceptable morality include what might broadly be termed fairness, along with respect for persons (including other people's autonomy). Surely it is highly useful that these attitudes be widespread in any society. Any morality-based attack on a sophisticated indirect consequentialism must find a valid element or portion of morality that, unlike these, is useless or counterproductive. There has been some past success in finding useless elements or portions of accepted morality. Think of Hume on the "monkish virtues" (1751/1975, nos. 219, 270). This success, however, has always contributed to a case for eliminating these elements. Hence the prospects for this escape route from consequentialism do not look bright. Whether there are other possible means of escape will be explored in the next chapter.

10

Some Difficulties
of Consequentialism

One way of seeing the argument of the last three chapters is this. It points straightforwardly to a multi-level indirect consequentialism. In the area of morality, a fundamental test of judgments is their ability to be included in a moral order that a reasonable person would accept. Below this foundation, though (it might seem), is another (ultimate) foundation that is consequentialist. The test of all of the elements of an acceptable moral order would seem to be consequences.

The line of argument of this and the final chapter, however, will lack this appealing simplicity. It also will lack any sense that, when consequences do count, they count in a precise way. Indeed, we will be very far away from Jeremy Bentham's "calculus" of values.

Our Imperfect Knowledge of Consequences

Let us look first at reasons for lack of confidence about consequences. These include some that are in a sense logical. We are not in a position to evaluate the consequences of a practice (e.g., promise keeping) until it has developed, but a practice like that of promising cannot develop unless it is generally accepted to be good (see Rawls 1955). Because of such cases, we may want to distinguish between a logic of justification (which perhaps is consequentialist?) and the logic of discovery (which sometimes cannot be consequentialist).

Other reasons have to do with the complexities of the future. A change in one element of the moral order (and social fabric) may prove workable only if there are appropriate related changes. But what these will be, and how well they will work, may be beyond the ability of even the most intelligent people to forecast.

All of this may seem to point toward a consequentialist logic of justification (but not a consequentialist logic of discovery). Intuitively, it does seem that there is an important difference between the role of consequences in determining what will be the best choice, and the role in justifying (or deploring) a choice that was made.

Often we have no idea what will work best, but after the fact we think we know whether or not the choice had good consequences.

However, any judgment, after the fact, that a change in the moral order has had good consequences implicitly compares what has happened with what the consequences would have been had there been a different change. How can we be confident of hypothetical judgments of the consequences of a complex set of events that did not occur? There is a limit to the degree of confidence that we should have even of retrospective judgments of what would have had the best consequences.

The logic of consequentialism that was examined in the previous chapter certainly (I claim) governs the implications of judgments that something would be for the best. That is, someone who makes such a judgment needs a reason for judging that whatever would be for the best is not the best thing to do (or the best policy or stance to adopt), and there are constraints on what can count as such a reason. This is well and good, but then we have to ask what logic governs someone who says, "X seems likely to have the best available consequences, but it is hard to be entirely confident of this." When X is a policy or stance rather than a single action, and its effects will be widespread and prolonged, this becomes an especially worrying question. No plausible answer can be either crisp or simple.

One way to see the complication is this. The simple model (toward which the previous chapters may have seemed to point) involves being able to make a judgment of which possible action has the best consequences, and then perhaps being aware that there are acceptable reasons for not acting along those lines. These acceptable reasons include those provided by morality; and central moral ideas, such as fairness or respect for persons, can play a major part. A consequentialist, though, will want to argue that any idea of fairness or of respect for persons itself has to pass the test of consequences: if, on balance, it subtracts from the values of the world rather than contributing to them, then it is not an adequate idea of fairness or of respect for persons.

In the less simple model, which we are now beginning to develop, there can be real uncertainty about what has the best consequences. Ideas of what fairness or respect for persons demands, then, may play a larger role than in the simple model. We may throw up our hands and say, "We don't know what is for the best; let's see what looks fair (or satisfies the requirement of respect for persons)." Further, it may seem difficult to get any clear idea of whether some particular interpretation of fairness or of respect for persons has, on the whole, good or bad consequences.

The degree of confidence that an assessment of consequences reasonably can have varies from case to case. Here are a few examples of cases in which judgments of consequences—if we think we can make them—may intuitively seem highly relevant to a judgment of what should be done. The examples are chosen to illustrate both the variability of how much we are in the dark about the future, and also the variability of the confidence that we might reasonably have in a judgment of what is fair.

Discovering a Better Future?

Let us begin with an especially thorny case, the one presented earlier, of the denial to women of access to higher education 250 years ago, when hardly anyone thought of it as being unfair. The case is not thorny in the sense of being difficult to judge: it should be clear to everyone that the old arrangements were deeply unfair. What is thorny is the kind of estimate of consequences, of changing these arrangements, that would have been possible back then.

Imagine a dissenter 250 years ago from the consensus that women should not be allowed to attend universities. Such a dissenter might regard the portion of the moral order that encapsulated this consensus as not reasonably acceptable. The main reason for thinking that the moral order could be improved would have involved the likelihood that a sizable group of highly intelligent people (women) could have much more fulfilled lives if they had equal access to higher education.

This reason strikes me as entirely convincing, and surely will strike the great majority of readers in much the same way. But then, we have seen much of the playing out of the ideal of equal educational opportunity. Given hindsight, one might have an easier time seeing the strength of the reason than would have been the case when the conditions and assumptions of life were very different.

Here is one way of seeing the case. Sometimes our knowledge of the future is murky indeed, but some people can see clearly a negative in the present: something that involves negative value, or the deprivation of what we think would have positive value. Denial of educational opportunity to bright and capable people is a negative of this sort. We may lack a comprehensive vision of the competing values of possible futures; but there is one element that we can think we are clear about, namely the persistence in some possible futures of deprivation of educational opportunities.

Still, the general problem remains. How can one get a clear enough picture of alternative futures to be able to judge them? How could people 250 years ago have known what a society in which women could have higher education and a wide range of careers would be like? How do we know—to anticipate a case to be discussed shortly—that a society in which fighting to the death under specified circumstances is considered morally permissible will be generally more violent?

My answer will attempt to steer a middle course. My general view is that in such matters people typically are not clueless. On the other hand, they usually do not (and usually cannot) have anything like clear knowledge. Within this general view, there has to be recognition that cases vary. We may have a better idea of the short-run consequences of a specific change (e.g., treating extreme violence between consenting adults, under specified conditions, as acceptable) than of the long-run consequences of changes that have many ramifications, requiring modifications of established institutions and revised habits of social behavior.

Philosophical theorizing about the relevance of consequences to choice has often begun with the comparison of universes. X has better consequences than Y (with whatever moral implications one may judge this to have) if and only if X leads to a better universe than Y would. In one way, this makes sense: in assessing values to be associated with X and Y, there is no obvious reason to set any limit on the causal results of X and Y to be evaluated. If X somehow makes a difference in life in some remote galaxy, surely that matters? There is no a priori limit on what reasonably can be assessed short of the entire universe.

The actual process of weighing consequences (as part of judging what is preferable or permissible) looks quite different. To begin with the entire universe would be ludicrous. Instead, we begin (and sometimes also end) with immediate consequences of a familiar kind. We know for example that murder not only costs one or more lives, but also often inspires grief and a sense of loss among those close to the victim or victims, and a degree of fear among the surrounding population. Murders also of course have many other effects, possibly some of them good and very likely some of them bad. But usually judgments of what these will be, and of how good or bad they will be, are highly conjectural. Given the high degree of confidence in judgments of the familiar and usual immediate effects (which generally are quite bad), and the typically very low degree of confidence in judgments of other effects, we might reasonably concentrate on the familiar and usual immediate consequences. By and large, we approach the violation of central moral rules in this way.

Changes in basic social arrangements, on the other hand, may lack any set of familiar and usual consequences that we can judge confidently. Even after the change has occurred, we may have little confidence in our judgments, in part because it may be hard to decide whether some of the things that happened after the change are or are not consequences of the change. Here is a current example. Some years ago, the legal drinking age was raised from 18 to 21 in the United States. One motivation was the hope that there would be fewer alcohol-related automobile accidents. There is evidence (most of it anecdotal) that after the change, the amount of "binge" drinking among college students between 18 and 21 drastically increased. The illegality of drinking seemingly made it more attractive.

Let us assume for the sake of argument that this widespread impression is correct. Perhaps heavy drinking became linked (because of the prominent new age requirement) in some minds with being mature and free? Or perhaps there was the familiar appeal of what was forbidden, especially if the forbidding appeared irrational? Finally, there is the possibility—if indeed there was increased incidence of binge drinking—that it had little or no causal connection with the increased drinking age, but was the result of other changes in student-age culture.

In light of all of this, we might think that it would have been very difficult to judge in advance whether raising the drinking age would have on balance good or bad consequences. My guess is that the consequences have turned out, on the whole, to be bad. But this is far from the confident judgment that might anchor a claim to knowledge.

Our limitations in attempting to estimate in advance the consequences of a change in this simple case are a good indication of how very difficult it would have been 250 years ago to estimate the consequences of allowing equal access to higher education to women. Much of what has just been said applies to this case. In particular, someone who was trying at the time to estimate whether the proposed change in the moral order would create improvements in the quality of life of some people that would outweigh any negative results might well have a clear view only of the immediate future.

There is, however, one distinctive feature of this case. The long-term consequences of the proposed change in the moral order could have been anticipated to depend on other changes that would need to be progressively made. The contribution to quality of life of higher education for women would depend in part (although certainly not entirely) on access to professional careers. The degree to which such careers would be viable, in turn, might depend on further changes to the social infrastructure. In a way, then, what would have been at stake was not one change, but a whole series of changes. Estimating consequences in the long term would have been complicated by uncertainty as to whether the appropriate changes would take place and what forms they would take if they did.

It is hard to believe that many people could have had anything like a clear view of this. This suggests the following point. Even if consequences in quality of life matter greatly to the reasonableness of a change in the moral order, our advance knowledge of these consequences is typically limited; hence it helps to have another basis for a change in the moral order. Intuitive conceptions of fairness in fact have done most of the work in the major moral transformations of the last several hundred years.

The hope always is that the changes will lead to a higher quality of life for some, that will outweigh any negative consequences. We may well think, in the case of minority groups, members of unpopular religions, and women, that these hopes have been realized, although in each case more work on prevalent social attitudes or on the social infrastructure is needed. We can reasonably judge that the consequences have been, on the whole, positive. Does this reasonable judgment meet the standard of knowledge? I think that it does, but it has to be admitted that the relevant causal connections are tangled, and the relevant values cannot be assessed with any precision.

The next example can be understood in a particular context: the long-running debates about just what it is that justifies limitations of liberty for adults in an advanced liberal society. The classic liberal answer is that adults can be prevented from doing what they wish if it would harm others. Mill says this (1978, 9), and then both adds to this answer and qualifies it. He adds that there should not be the liberty to engage in public indecency (97) or to be a "nuisance" (53). The latter probably includes making very loud noise in dormitories in the middle of the night; the former includes doing things of an intimate nature in public that perfectly well could be done in private, and then might be unobjectionable.

One of Mill's qualifications to the claim that harm would justify limitation of liberty is that this does not (might not?) apply if those allegedly harmed consented. The major qualification is that the restriction is justified only if someone is harmed "directly" (11). Plainly, Mill does not want to justify social interference if the "harm" is that someone is deeply distressed by someone else's conduct, or has taken ruinous or expensive steps (which were unnecessary) in response to that conduct. We tend to assign the damage in such cases principally to how people choose to respond to a situation, and at most only slightly to what was inherent in the situation itself. Readers generally will have no difficulty in seeing that what Mill has in mind as direct harm is being murdered, raped, beaten up, or stolen from. Harm that is psychological, a product of how someone reacts, will normally count as indirect harm.

Even with its qualifications, Mill's account of liberty invites counterexamples. A persuasive one has been offered by the conservative commentator Irving Kristol (1971). He asks us to consider the possibility of gladiatorial contests in Yankee Stadium, before consenting adult audiences, between well-paid gladiators who are willing to risk their lives for high stakes. Kristol's point seems to be that there are certain things that cannot be permitted, even if they do not in any obvious way involve harm to people who are not consenting adults.

Joel Feinberg (1990, 128 ff.) has discussed this case in a way that is complex, and admits of more than one interpretation. My reading is that Feinberg thinks that the case Kristol presents does involve likely harm to people who are not consenting adults, because of a kind of cultural corruption that might well lead to further acts of violence (to innocent people) outside of Yankee Stadium. Feinberg at one point (132) uses the phrase "clear and present danger" for this likelihood of harm (which links his position with one of Mill's qualifications; see Mill 1978, 53). But elsewhere, Feinberg's position seems to be simply that indirect harm to innocent people, if it is likely enough and serious enough, justifies social interference and limitation of liberty. (See the discussion of coarsening effects on 128; also see 168–169, 323.)

This position seems highly reasonable to me. But what is relevant to our investigation is the sense that most of us have that fights to the death in Yankee Stadium (or on television), would lead to generally higher levels of violence in society. It certainly looks like a good bet. But do we know it to be true? Could it turn out that such publicly available extreme violence would provoke a backlash of sorts, causing very many people to examine their own tendencies to violence? Or might it become socially compartmentalized and have no significant wider effect?

These relatively benign scenarios seem unlikely. But one may be reminded of a fairly recent case in which reasonable forecasts were falsified. In the mid-1990s, highway speed limits in vast areas of the United States were increased by 10 miles an hour, which in practice meant that many of the drivers who already exceeded speed limits by 10 or 15 miles an hour (driving at 65 or 70 miles per hour on major highways), now could be expected to drive at 75 or 80 miles per hour. This was widely predicted and is generally agreed to have come about. It was also predicted that the increased speed limits would lead to a significantly increased number of highway fatalities. This stood to reason: crashes are more serious at higher speeds, and (other things being equal) are less easy to avoid. Reports in the months after the speed limits were increased, though, indicated that there had been no significant increase in highway fatalities (for data, see Stephen Moore 1999, 1). Might countervailing factors similarly limit the negative effects of public fighting to the death? It seems highly unlikely, but perhaps we do not really know.

It should be noted that some of the examples thus far are of cases in which, while consequences might well affect our view of whether a change should take place, there also will be intuitions related to morality that might well influence many people's views. Two hundred and fifty years ago, one might have had an intuitive sense that it was only fair that women have access to higher education. A much more common intuition at that time, though, almost certainly would have been that there was something unsavory about the non-traditional arrangement that this would represent. (If such an intuition now seems bizarrely faulty to us, we should bear in mind that there also were intuitions of fairness in the past—e.g., the fairness of eldest sons inheriting—that also now seem bizarrely faulty. Intuitions can be useful, but what seems obvious is nevertheless not the last word.)

In the case of fighting to the death in Yankee Stadium, many of us will have (above and beyond an estimate of likely consequences) an intuition that this would be unsavory, a blot on our social order. Like the other intuitions just mentioned, this one always can be criticized as faulty. But this will not, and should not, prevent it from having a role in our decision of what public policy should be, especially if we are in doubt about the consequences of the options open to us.

It is instructive, then, to realize that there are cases—unlike the ones just discussed—in which there is no plausible way of deciding what should be done that does not rely on an estimate of consequences. As remarked in earlier chapters, some public policy decisions in which issues of fairness or propriety do not figure prominently are like this. Many decisions of budgetary priorities are examples. It can be the case that none of the alternatives look unsavory or unfair, but a decision must be made. Alternatively, considerations involving fairness or propriety look evenly balanced, but (again) a decision must be made. In either sort of case, the judgment must be made on the basis of consequences: where the money probably would do the most good. Consequentialism of the simplest sort—the sort that urges that we simply choose, on a case-by-case basis, whatever seems likely to have the best consequences—is most at home in such public policy decisions.

Finally, there is the example of a normal murder. By a normal murder, I mean one that does not involve obviously extraordinary circumstances or unusual justifications (such as, say, an imaginary case in which the only way to prevent an epidemic is to murder a person carrying the plague). Even in the case of a normal murder, it would be foolish to claim to be entirely certain of all of the consequences unto the tenth generation. There is always room to imagine that, for example, someone might have murdered Hitler's great-grandfather before he had a chance to have children. Nevertheless, we are safe in saying that murders typically bring highly negative consequences, both directly to someone whose life is cut short and indirectly to those who mourn or who feel less safe. This justifies a high degree of confidence that, in any likely case, not committing a murder will have better consequences than committing one, and arguably a yet higher degree of confidence that the consequences of general respect for a rule of not committing murders will be good. A similar point can be made in relation to our knowledge of consequences of torture, rape, and theft.

Values to Be Compared

Thus far in this chapter, the emphasis has been on the difficulty of having anything remotely like knowledge of the future. One pair of difficulties that attend consequentialism are independent of this. They concern the values to be compared when one decides whether one state of affairs is, or is not, better than another.

One difficulty concerns the grounds for confidence of any judgment of how good or bad any possible outcome is, was, or will be. Even if we stipulate what the outcome would be like, how can we know what value to attribute to it? Consequentialists in the past have tended to finesse this difficulty by making broad assumptions about what value depends upon. One appealing simplification is the Benthamite one of equating value with the amount of pleasure minus pain. A moreup-to-date simplification is that of equating value with the sum of positive preferences (weighting each preference according to its intensity) minus negative preferences.

The second difficulty concerns comparison of values. Suppose, for the sake of argument, that our choice is between an action that we actually know will lead to outcome A (with value X), and one that we know will lead to outcome B (with value Z). Will we always be able to say which of the two outcomes is better (i.e., whether X is greater or less than Z, or whether perhaps there is a tie)? Will we be able to say how much better one is than the other?

In the dream life of consequentialists, neither of these is a difficulty (and we do know the future). In the real world, both present problems. It is not that we cannot make judgments of value. If someone is planning a murder, the likely future in which the victim has lost her or his life and the many survivors are grieving can be compared to the likely alternative future in which none of this is true. Usually we can judge that the second possible future is almost certainly considerably better than the first, even if we cannot be entirely certain either of the forms the two will take or of further consequences—and even if we cannot supply precise numbers or means of precise comparison for any two scenarios.

An honest vocabulary for our knowledge of the future would give a prominent role to words like "probably" and "very likely," "might well happen," and "real risk." Let me suggest that an honest vocabulary for our sense of values to be compared would give a prominent role to words like "pretty awful," "not so bad," "bearable," "with some bright spots," and "moderately appealing," along with "about as good/bad," "probably a bit worse," "marginally less attractive," and so on. In favorable circumstances, we could legitimately use such a vocabulary. In less favorable circumstances, we might have to concede our inability to grasp (or simply to evaluate) the ramifications of what is at stake, which leaves us in a very poor position to make estimates of value. It might be that the new world that we can dimly anticipate is so alien to us that we cannot begin to get a sense of whether it would be "sort of nice" or awful, or whether it would be liberating or constricting for many people. Imagine a medical breakthrough that would extend the normal lifespan to nearly 200 years. How good or bad would the consequences be?

The Epistemology of Non-Instrumental Value

Let us look more closely at our limitations in making judgments of value, by which I mean the value that something has in its context, apart from its causal contribution to other things. Here is a summary account, which I have developed elsewhere (Kupperman 2005a), of the grounds one might have for such judgments. A central claim is that one is sometimes in a good position to make a judgment of value, and sometimes not. In some circumstances, no one is in a position to make anything like an assured judgment of value.

What can put you in a good position to make a judgment of value? There is a loose analogy here with cases in which someone can claim to know what happened because she or he is an eyewitness. Any claim of what happened is corrigible—people do make mistakes—but by and large, we trust the reports of experienced people with good eyesight and an unobstructed view, and we think they have a right to be confident of their judgments of what happened. It is very likely that such judgments will turn out to be correct; and, if they are correct, we say that the eyewitnesses who made them know what happened.

To put forward this analogy is (among other things) to endorse Aristotle's idea that some people are especially good at making some kinds of ethical judgments, such as the people who see that the good life cannot be determined merely by pleasure or by honor and prestige. Experience of life plays a part in this. One factor can be a wide range of possible comparisons. David Hume suggests in "Of the Standard of Taste" (1742/1985, 226–249) that no one can judge how really good a poem is who has not appreciated some great poetry, and in much this way, very fine experiences can make someone a better judge of what might be wonderful in life.

All of this is to fill in the loose analogy between having good eyesight and being a good judge of the values in question. What is analogous to having a clear view of what happened? Surely the answer must include knowing what the thing to be evaluated is like, which includes knowing what it is like to someone experiencing it.

The great difficulty here is that experiences, even of what in broad outline is the same thing, do vary. Certainly when people talk about what such-and-such was like, or what it felt like, there usually are significant variations in what they say, which often point to different degrees of positive or negative evaluation. This suggests a considerable degree of indeterminacy in any value we might want to assign to a state of society or of the world. If we talk about common experiences (e.g., "being rejected in love," "achieving success in a long-term project you really cared about") it looks very much as if what people take in, and how they take things, can vary greatly. Being rejected in love can be awful, but maybe more awful for Bloggs than for Jones, and Smurf hardly seemed to notice it, going on to a new love.

Finally, if my account is correct, there are some important judgments of value that we simply are in no position to make. An example is the judgment of whether, apart from the instrumental values of promoting positive experiences, the existence of a beautiful unperceived world has more value than that of an ugly unperceived world. Do we have anything to go on here? It is tempting to think that such judgments can be made a priori; but when G. E. Moore (1903, 83–85) says that intuition tells him that the existence of the beautiful unperceived world has more non-instrumental value, in my view he is saying no more than that this is the answer he feels like giving.

The strong implication is that we are, by and large, in a better position to make judgments of values within our own life and experiences than within the life and experiences of others. Can we make value judgments in relation to other people's lives? It may be important to specify here that such judgments can well be tacit: it is often rude and intrusive to make such judgments out loud. But it also is, on the other hand, extremely artificial to eschew entirely such judgments. For one thing, other people's lives exhibit possibilities which (with some variation) conceivably could enter our lives, so that a sense of whether other people's lives are going well or badly in various respects can be integral to our thought about how our lives best would go. Also, value judgments are implicit when we feel sorry for other people, which involves a sense that aspects of their lives have not gone as well as they should have. Envy also suggests implicit value judgments, that someone else has something of value.

Let me suggest that we sometimes are in a fairly good position to make value judgments in relation to other people's lives, although very often our confidence in such judgments should be limited. Here are three ways in which we can be in a position to evaluate experiences or other elements of other people's lives. One is that if we know someone well, we have some degree of empathy. We can have a strong sense of the qualities of that person's life and of whether it is going well. There is always the possibility, of course, that there are hidden aspects, tensions, or joys even in the life of someone we know quite well. But surely all judgments of value are corrigible, both in the evaluation of what we think it is that we are judging, and also in our sense of what it is that we are judging. Even what is going on in our own life may be less clear to us than we think. Occasionally we may have at least as good a sense of another person's life as we have of our own.

There can be cases in which we do not know someone well, but have an account of that person's life that seems to us (perhaps correctly) to provide a good sense of that person's life. A good biography could do this. Novels, plays, films, and histories also can sometimes give us a sense of a life, or of aspects of a life. Novels, plays, and films in particular can suggest qualities (desirable or undesirable) of various sorts of lives. Indeed, much of the sense of life that people assemble when they are growing up is drawn from such sources.. It goes without saying that these can be seriously misleading, sometimes giving us a very truncated or distorted sense of how the world works and what it is like to have certain experiences. Even a source that is not deceptive in such a drastic way might be misleading in some respect.

Finally, there are some aspects of people's lives and experiences that almost anyone can take in, so that there can be some reasonable confidence in a judgment of value. These are chiefly the aspects of life that lend themselves to talk of our "common humanity." Most of these aspects are highly negative.

The thought here is that there is an asymmetry within value-laden experience. What gives joy or creates an ongoing feeling that life is going well can vary greatly from person to person. Some ongoing positive experiences (such as those of love, especially between parents and children) are widely enough shared that we often think we know the kind of value they have even in a stranger's life. But most of what excites or delights someone else might well not excite or delight us. We think, though, that what it is like to have sustained, unremitting severe pain or to have the people you most love killed before your eyes is likely to be much the same for other people as it would be for us. There appears to be considerable convergence in the ways in which most of the things we think would be worst in life enter various people's lives. The convergence is not complete: temperament does matter, and there are people (e.g., trained Buddhists) who do not suffer in the way most of us would. But usually we think we have no trouble in having a sense of other people's suffering and of the negative values that it involves.

The last several paragraphs are an outline of an area of values that is less dimly lit than most of what we think of as the possible values (positive or negative) in the world. Consequentialism requires judgments of the values of various possible sets of consequences. Even when we are in a moderately good position to arrive at such estimates, they are in general not very precise. It should be clear that we are very often in a poor position.

Why have the great philosophers who advocated consequentialism not worried more about these difficulties? Part of the answer is that the professional training of philosophers lends itself to construction of models—of how things might be in reality—rather than engagement with the available scraps of evidence of how things actually are. Models that are simple and elegant are especially appealing.

A very brief account of the most tempting (but faulty) models can round out this part of our exploration of the difficulties of consequentialism. (For a fuller account, see *Six Myths about the Good Life*, written concurrently with this book.) When we see how these models are inadequate, we can see that (in this area) there is no clear and simple way out of the difficulties for consequentialism.

One model that is perennially appealing is hedonism. There is no doubt that pleasure and pain play major roles in motivating us, including (as Aristotle noted) setting the pattern of our motivations in childhood. It is arguable also that everyone desires pleasure, or at least (where no pleasure is expected) things the thought of which is pleasant. Someone looking for a simple generalization might well gravitate to the view that pleasure is the good.

Pleasure, however, is not merely a feeling; it is a tentative (or not so tentative) evaluative response to an object, something in which we take pleasure. It is plausible to suppose, then, that what the pleasure is in matters to its value. Some pleasures might then seem fairly trivial (and perhaps of less value) in comparison with some others. What of the pleasure in something quite corrupt, such as the pleasure that a really accomplished torturer might take in a good day in the torture chamber? It is because of questions like these that Plato argued, in the *Philebus*, that different kinds of pleasure have different sorts of value. It is plausible to suppose that sadistic pleasures might have either negligible or negative values.

Recent psychological evidence also bolsters the case against hedonism and indicates that regarding pleasure as a major goal is often a very poor strategy. The discovery of what is termed the "hedonic treadmill" is that life-changing events, such as winning the lottery or (on the negative side) becoming paraplegic while still young, which might be thought to have a drastic effect on pleasure levels, do so only for a brief period. This is because of the phenomenon of "adaptation." After a little while, it simply takes more to please the lottery winner, and less to please the paraplegic (see Brickman, Coates, and Janoff-Bulman 1978).

There are exceptions to this pattern. They seem mainly to consist of pleasures closely related to sense of self. There seems to be continued pleasure for people who have mastered skills and exercise them. In a well-known study, Csikszentmihalyi (1990) found that people report that the experiences of being caught up in the flow of a skilled activity are the best that life can offer them. The pleasure in these cases looks valuable, but a natural question is why we should not conclude that the experience of the skilled activities themselves (and not merely the element of pleasure) has significant value.

Then there are cases in which highly skilled but challenging activities appear to involve some pain or frustration and not huge amounts of pleasure, but the people who have engaged in them nevertheless value them highly. One classic case is that of Wittgenstein, whose deep involvement in philosophical thought clearly involved much frustration and few signs of great pleasure, nevertheless saying before his death, "Tell them I've had a wonderful life" (Malcolm 1984, 81). Why can't we take this evaluation at face value, and think that it might well be correct? Only someone bent on keeping a theory simple, by keeping its value element simple, could disregard such testimony.

Another appealing simplification is that the end of life is happiness, period. Happiness though, like pleasure, is tied to features in the world. In particular, as noted in a previous chapter, a major element on which happiness depends is how one feels about oneself and one's life. Someone who is lucky in every endeavor, and has many pleasures, but who does not like herself or himself will never be happy.

The obvious thought is that if someone is happy, the kind of life that features in this happiness is surely relevant to its value. If someone reports being happy because of finally having visited all fifty state capitals, or having completed a collection of bottle caps, a normal response might be "Get a life." The happiness in this case does not look as desirable or enviable as the happiness that arises from genuine achievements and warm human relationships. Further, if someone as a result of an accident has a right-side frontal lobotomy and becomes as happy as a clam, we normally feel sorry for such a person instead of regarding her or him as now having a desirable kind of life.

It also can be argued that, even if we agree that a moderately high degree of happiness counts considerably toward the desirability of a life, it is possible to be too happy. An ideal of entire happiness is hard to separate from smugness and complacency. It also is hard to imagine how someone who is that thoroughly happy could be motivated to improve the world or various features of her or his life.

Finally, there is the appealing generalization—whose appeal in part rests on the convenience of questionnaires in getting the relevant data—that what is valuable is preference satisfaction. This simplification has familiar weaknesses. We should want to know what preferences are being satisfied. The satisfaction of those that are corrupt or trivial arguably can be assigned only negligible value, however intense they are. Also, a world in which everyone's preferences are entirely satisfied looks like a dystopia rather than a utopia.

When we compare values of possible outcomes, commonly what we compare features different forms of excellences or drawbacks, which might attract or repel one in different ways. The familiar analogy is with comparison of apples and oranges. There is a skeptical temptation to say that such comparisons of value cannot be made. But virtually anyone would value a firm, crisp apple over a moldy orange, and would value a world in which the arts and sciences were flourishing and most people were moderately happy over a backward world in which there was widespread misery (but in which, nevertheless, a few beautiful laments were being composed). Often we can reasonably say, "This outcome would be better than that outcome."

It may be much harder, though, to say how much better. Also, there often are cases in which each side of what is to be compared has some positive features and some negative ones, and it looks as if we are not in a position to say that one would be better than the other. Such comparisons can involve a "judgment call"; and when two people disagree, there often are no clear criteria for saying that one has better judgment than the other. This real-world quandary is very far from the idealized "calculus of values."

Conclusion

It perhaps should be no surprise that our general knowledge of consequences and of their likely value looks more secure in relation to the core elements of familiar morality—and then mainly in the short run—than, say, in relation to changes in basic social arrangements. Once we take this in, consequentialism (even of the indirect, qualified sort outlined in chapter 9) looks like a theory tailored for ideal or nearly ideal circumstances of judgment: either for dealing with familiar sorts of actions in familiar sorts of settings (when we have long experience of consequences) or for cases in which somehow we know almost everything there is to know about the future, and there is nothing of a deeply unfamiliar nature that needs to be judged. Most of the judgments of what we should do that we find most challenging do not fit in either of these categories.

We often are not in a good position to make the requisite judgments of values. Even when we are, the judgments that appear justified are typically imprecise. Available comparisons often look extremely imprecise. Sometimes, at most we can say that one outcome probably will be about as good as another (or is marginally worse, or perhaps much better).

Does all of this mean that consequentialism is a theory more fit for archangels (to borrow R.M. Hare's term) than for human beings? We should not be too quick to accept this conclusion. Consequentialist considerations are not entirely useless for us humans. The final chapter will develop this point.

11

The Evolution
of Ethical Theories

The preceding chapters have examined some of the appeal of leading ethical theories, and also their difficulties and some gaps in their possible justification. These lines of thought will be brought together in the final chapter, which argues for the place of consequentialist elements in any acceptable ethical theory but also makes clear how limited this place will be. The present chapter is an interlude. It will explore ways in which an ethical theory can develop through time, and in particular the variations in Kantian and consequentialist ethical theories.

One reason for this interlude has to do with the mind-sets of some very accomplished philosophers. Because much of philosophical training is ahistorical, even a sharp-witted philosopher can think of an ethical theory (say Kantian ethics or consequentialism) as if it is a single unchanging entity. Anyone who reads through the philosophical literature of the last few decades can be struck by, for example, how many bright and interesting philosophers simply assume that consequentialism is (for all intents and purposes) act consequentialism. This can allow some of them the pleasure of arguing against the least sophisticated and least plausible form of a theory not their own.

All of this goes along with another mind-set that is a block to understanding. The ethical theory monoliths are thought of as competitors in a contest in which there can be at most one winner. Partisans of Kantian ethics, contractualism, and consequentialism tout the claims of their favorite theory to be, in the end, the one correct one.

There are at least two ways in which one can dissent from this competition model. It can be claimed that the optimal forms of Kantian ethics, contractualism, and consequentialism actually converge. Derek Parfit elegantly argues for this in a book in preparation, *Climbing the Mountain*.

My own approach in these concluding chapters differs, because of a concern with ethical judgment in less than ideal conditions, in which knowledge of likely consequences is limited and key intuitions are unreliable. I already have argued that each of the theories thought to compete contains some important truth, and that none (in any present form) can claim to be the entire truth. The final chapter will continue and round out this argument.

A further complication should be mentioned. The number of ethical theories thought to be competing against one another sometimes can rise to four. Virtue ethics (exemplified in classical philosophy by Aristotle and Confucius, and in recent ethics by such figures as Philippa Foot, Alasdair Macintyre, Michael Slote, Rosalind Hursthouse, and Christine Swanton) is often on the list. This seems to me a mistake even more serious than the ones just mentioned. An ethical theory can be expected to fulfill (or attempt to fulfill) a number of functions. All the same: a major function shared by Kantian ethics, contractualism, and consequentialism is that of providing guidance in decision procedures. In the appendix, I will argue that this cannot plausibly be regarded as a major function of virtue ethics, which really does answer different questions from those primarily addressed by the other theories, and in this sense cannot be regarded as competing with them. This, it should be said, is not to denigrate virtue ethics, which in my view is useful in important ways. Its usefulness is chiefly in providing insights into matters that often are not sufficiently attended to by Kantians, contractualists, and consequentialists.

The Evolution of Kantian Ethics

Anyone who keeps up with the philosophical literature has to be impressed with the amount of serious probing of the structure and possibilities of Kantian ethics in recent books and articles. There has been major work by a number of philosopher-scholars, including Christine Korsgaard, Stephen Darwall, Onora O'Neill, J. B. Schneewind, and Thomas Hill, Jr. Any proper examination of this literature, and the comparable literature on contractualist ethics and on consequentialism, would amount to an entire book rather than a short chapter. What follows, accordingly, is a sketch rather than a comprehensive examination and refers chiefly to two recent Kantians whose ideas seem to me to be especially useful: Alan Donagan and Barbara Herman.

One can begin with some remarks on Kant and his intellectual world. Here are three features that stand out. First is that Kant was committed to a bedrock assumption (radical for his time) of the moral equality of all rational beings. This is connected with his admiration for Rousseau, which some commentators (e.g., Cassirer 1981, 86 ff.) have emphasized. A second, related feature was that Kant (unlike, say, Aristotle and Confucius) was not what could be termed a moral elitist. He assumed that virtually all rational beings had basic moral knowledge, in broad outline knowing right from wrong. Third, the primary vehicle of this moral knowledge was awareness of the validity of certain moral rules, including the familiar ones that forbid murder, theft, breaking promises, and so on.

The discussion of the previous chapters suggests that if we are to accept the second and third of these assumptions, they need to be qualified. They are more clearly true of the familiar core of morality than of the whole of morality. That is, they work extremely well for the ordinary case of murder, theft, rape, or torture. But besides these there can be complicated and unusual cases in which it is not entirely clear that one should follow familiar moral rules, and also there are moral decisions embedded in the fabric of personal relations. In relation to cases of both sorts, the established rules can look problematic and oversimple or irrelevant. Despite this need for qualification, Kant's assumptions have much to be said for them and do point toward something of importance.

Maxims are pivotal in Kant's account of the workings of the categorical imperative (especially in its first form), and it is clear that in Kant's view, moral knowledge will be keyed to application of the right moral rule, which can be expressed in a maxim that will pass the test of the categorical imperative. This subsumes the assumption that morality consists of general rules, which certainly accords with the common sense of most people. In his examples in the *Grundlagen*, Kant gives the impression that these valid moral general rules will be broad; although the second half of the *Metaphysics of Morals* could be interpreted as leaving room for the possibility of more complicated and less broad rules.

Could a generally valid rule have exceptions? An example most often proposed involves the innocent person hunted by a would-be murderer, who demands that you tell where the prospective victim is hidden. You could protectively lie. Kant famously denied that this was morally acceptable (although the option of saying nothing, neither lying nor telling the truth, was not ruled out). This view can be unpalatable to more modern sensibilities. An interesting example of an eminent Kant scholar interpreting Kant not really to be so unpalatable is found in a paper by H. J. Paton (1953–54). It is true that Kant did say the unpalatable thing, but he was old and thought he was defending German philosophy against aspersions made by a foreigner (Benjamin Constant). The suggestion is that what he said on that occasion cannot be considered part of, or to follow from, his philosophical outlook. A more recent Kantian ethicist, Barbara Herman, makes a point of eschewing "rule-fetishism" (1993, 27).

It would be instructive to have a clear sense of possible differences in attitudes toward general rules between Kant's day and ours. It certainly seems possible that, in the circles in which Kant would have moved, many people were more "principled" in their reluctance to allow exceptions to generally valid rules than might be the case now. There is a relevant anecdote of Kant's friend Green faulting him because Kant was late for a carriage ride (cf. Abbott 1898, xlvii). It would be interesting to know whether Kant thought that he was seriously at fault in being a couple of minutes late.

The logic of the case suggests this possibility. A world in which everyone is always late is incoherent and self-contradictory. If someone says, for example, "I'll be there at 2 o'clock," this would no longer be taken at face value, and there would be no expectation of a 2 o'clock arrival. Hence being late for an appointment clearly fails the test of the categorical imperative. It fails in much the way in which breaking a promise fails. (If everyone always broke promises, saying "I promise . . ." would no longer have the meaning it now has.) Indeed, being late could be argued to fall under the heading of promise-breaking. But it also can seem a special case, and in what follows I will treat it as one.

Few nowadays would share a firmly negative attitude toward being late for appointments, at least if someone was not very late and not much was at stake. To see clearly what is involved, one needs to separate two lines of thought that easily can be conflated. One is that virtually everyone, philosophers included, has moral blind spots. John Stuart Mill, who was so much in advance of his time in his discussion of the status of women, arguably had a blind spot in relation to imperialism. His remarks on the wrongness of the Chinese prohibition of importation of opium (1859/1978, 94–95) suggest a justification of the arrogant and brutal Opium War. Moral blind spots often can become more obvious after the fact. What one takes as dramatic moral progress in the last couple hundred years in widely accepted ideas about the treatment of women, ethnic minorities, religious minorities, and so on can often lead us to think of people in the past—those who in many respects seemed decent— and wonder "How could they?" The next thought is that there could be matters in which people a few hundred years from now might wonder, say, about me and most of my friends, "How could they?" Everyone can think of some possibilities.

A second line of thought is that an ethical philosophy can benefit from reinterpretation or reformulation, and that this can be more apparent at a later time than it was when the philosophy was first introduced. Problems or strains in the original formulation can become increasingly evident simply because of opportunities for further reflection, although it also may be that a changed sensibility (in matters pertaining to personal interactions, including those that raise moral questions) makes it easier to see the need for improvement.

The two lines of thought, it seems to me, can be quite separate. Mill's blind spot in relation to the Opium War had nothing to do with his utilitarianism. If Kant took seriously his lateness for the carriage ride with Green, on the other hand, this would seem not so much to involve a blind spot as to indicate a weakness in the original form of Kantian ethics, a weakness that became manifest in other areas.

The case for diagnosing something (a weakness in theory) that goes well beyond a mere blind spot is this. Being late for appointments can be serious sometimes, when a great deal clearly is at stake and the one who waits has depended on the other. In such cases, the lateness not only cannot be willed to be a universal law but also manifests (unless there is some valid excuse) a lack of respect for persons. Hence it seems correct (and not foolish or insensitive) to hold that lateness on some occasions can raise moral issues. But whether a specific case of lateness does raise such issues is a more complicated matter than Kant's ethics was equipped to recognize. If it seems to us that self-reproach in the case of Kant's lateness would have been unwarranted (or at least excessive), there are two reasons which bear on the interpretation of morality.

One is that we may well think that—in matters of being late, as well as lying and breaking promises—we should distinguish between cases that are essentially trivial or minor (so little is at stake) and those that are serious. The trivial ones could be brushed aside; the minor ones might justify criticism of a sort milder than that associated with moral censure. We might say things like "Couldn't you be more careful?" or "It would be nice if we always could take you at your word." The word "inconsiderate" can be used. Such language is at home in judgments that lack the power of those that use phrases such as "violations of trust" or "our right to assume that you will do (or mean) what you say."

Here is a money-related example of how most of us do make the distinction between trivial and serious matters. Suppose that a man realizes, after a few minutes, that he has been given a penny too much in change. Would we think that he should run back to return the penny?

The other reason why we might think that seriously faulting someone for being slightly late is excessive is this. Under the influence of thinkers like Mill, many of us are inclined to narrow the territory of morality, leaving more territory outside the boundary between morality and those other areas in which a poor choice will not be regarded as "morally wrong." Mill remarks that we can disapprove of foolish or tasteless behavior without believing that it should be subject to the kind of negative pressure that is appropriate for immorality (Mill 1859/1978, 75–82). His basic position is that only direct harm to others qualifies for this pressure (9 and 11). A result of this broad shift is that a great deal of behavior that is irritating, and does in a way indicate some lack of respect for persons, but does not rise to the level of real harm would now be termed "inconsiderate," placing it outside of the boundaries of morality.

Let us return to trivial or minor lies and promise breaking. It is possible to treat many cases of these along lines like those of our treatment of inconsiderateness. Depending on the case (and the available justifying reasons), we might censor a lie or instance of promise breaking, but if very little was at stake, we would not consider them immoral. There are some lies or instances of promise breaking, of course, that we do not censor at all, because we regard them as having a good reason. As Barbara Herman observes, the difficulty with tying moral judgment to rules is that "it ignores details" (1993, 74). The strength of Herman's version of Kantian ethics is that rules of moral salience can be understood as "defeasible interpretations of a more fundamental moral conception" (90).

Why could not a distinction between trivial lies or promise breaking and serious cases have been evident at the start (say, to Kant and his contemporaries)? Everyone can have her or his theory about this. Some may think that a fear of "slippery slopes" (of, e.g., trivial lies gradually being followed by less trivial ones) played a part. My own view is that the pioneers of Kantian and consequentialist ethics (i.e., Kant and Bentham) were also influenced by Newton envy. There was a sense that real knowledge of importance should be precise and take the form of entirely valid generalizations. There is a poignant expression of Newton envy at the very beginning of Mill's *Utilitarianism* when he states that he hopes that there can be progress in ethics in the way that there has been in the sciences.

My suggestion thus far has been that one can generally respect what is taken to be a moral rule (e.g., "Promises should be kept"), while on some occasions thinking that violations of the rule are not serious enough to qualify as morally wrong, and perhaps also holding that some violations are justified. How can we meaningfully combine these views? Couldn't someone challenge the combination and say, "Either you believe that promises should be kept or you don't"?

A path to an answer can be found in a joking story of Wittgenstein's (1953, 33e). He imagines a man asking him to teach some children a game. He teaches them how to gamble with dice. When the man expostulates that that was not what he meant, Wittgenstein wonders whether that exclusion had been in the man's mind. The likely answer, of course, is "no." The story is meant to free us from the illusion that meanings are somehow (always) in the mind of a speaker or writer.

Alan Donagan makes a very similar move in his discussion of implicit exceptions to rules (1977, 93). Someone can say, "Promises ought to be kept," but if we keep a promise to meet a friend for coffee with the foreseeable cost of someone's life or of our own best chance at happiness, that person also can credibly say, "I didn't mean that you should keep a promise in a case like that." This is generally understood, but that does not mean that any of us will be able to spell out exactly what the tacit built-in exceptions to the rule will be.

Donagan holds a form of Kantian ethics and does an excellent job of defending central Kantian insights. But a late-twentieth-century understanding of what can be meant by accepting a moral rule will differ from the more straightforward interpretation embraced by Kant. Donagan can advance a Kantian ethics that avoids "rigorism."

Other recent commentators (including philosopher-scholars already mentioned in this chapter) have worked to present Kantian ethics in a way that might seem more congenial to contemporary audiences than it has often seemed. The humane and humanistic side of Kant has been emphasized. Most such presentations are largely correct. The less appealing view had centered on the architecture of Kantian ethics, especially as it is represented in the *Grundlagen*; and there is little doubt that a wider reading of Kant reveals a picture that is both more complex and more humanistic.

Would Kant recognize his ethics if he were to read such accounts? We cannot be certain, of course. But then the question is "Does it matter?" Theories, both in the sciences and in philosophy, have a life of their own. They are not required to retain the form, in all its details, that they were originally given.

Before we examine the evolution of consequentialist theories, a word should be said to establish that there are variations among contractualist theories also. Any contractualist ethics will represent a moral order that, it is contended, anyone reasonably should accept. A natural question is "reasonably accept, instead of what alternative?" In the contractualist ethics implicit in Hobbes's *Leviathan*, the choice is between a state of nature (with all of its obvious disadvantages) and the sort of morality that is well established in our society. Hobbes is quite convincing that the latter reasonably should be preferred. But what if the choice is among a number of moralities, some of them variations of the one we are used to, along with the state of nature? There is no clear room in Hobbes's philosophy for this consideration.

The contrast between this and the best-known late-twentieth-century contractualist ethics, that of John Rawls, is striking. It is not merely that Hobbes's choice is one that might actually have happened (although there is no reason to think it actually did), whereas Rawls focuses on an imagined choice made by minimally informed agents in an "original position." It is also that Rawls's choice is among a very wide range of options, so that the question is no longer so much what would be a good choice as what would be an optimal choice.

Rawls's version of a contractualist choice also has a somewhat Platonic flavor. We should imagine choosing once, for all time. The correct choice will eternally govern us. If we look at actual moral orders (and not merely at abstract principles that might govern them), it becomes entirely clear that social contracts evolve, in part because of growing sensitivity in some areas, and sometimes also because of changing conditions. The reader probably does not need reminding of the ways in which prohibitions of racism and sexism now are prominent parts of the social contracts that almost all of us recognize. A contractualism that takes account of such developments, and that is not timeless, would be very different from the more familiar forms.

Let us turn to consequentialism, and first to its deliberately simple early formulation as act consequentialism (the view usually attributed to Jeremy Bentham). This version of consequentialism has a certain immediate, pre-reflective plausibility. Why not always try directly to make the world a better place?

One of Bentham's claims concerned values: the good we should promote was pleasure minus pain. This, too, has considerable appeal. All or almost all of us want pleasure, and most of us would like to avoid pain. Further, the formula for value seems precise as well as simple. One might think that eventually pleasure and pain, and the values attached to them, could be measured precisely. Nevertheless, the value system cannot stand up under reflection, as I have explored elsewhere (Kupperman 2006). John Stuart Mill half-saw this, as he made clear in an essay on Bentham, although his remarks in *Utilitarianism* fall short of a total rejection of the view.

There is a terminological point related to this. "Consequentialism" and "utilitarianism" have connected meanings, although the differences are treated differently by different philosophers. In what follows, I will treat utilitarianism as a species of consequentialism. The idea is that utilitarianism is a conjunction of consequentialism with a value system that bases ideas of the good entirely on subjective preferences (what people like, want, or would prefer). Non-utilitarian forms of consequentialism (e.g., Marxist consequentialism) can have different sorts of values. Given this terminology, I will use the wider term "consequentialism" in what follows even in some places in which others might simply speak of the narrower category of utilitarianism.

It should be remarked that the proper fates of consequentialism and of utilitarianism arguably are different. The final chapter will argue that consequentialist considerations in some areas should have an important role, and sometimes should be directly decisive, in any acceptable ethical theory. Utilitarianism, on the other hand, ought to be regarded as dead. The simplistic value system, especially when values are regarded as precise and measurable, renders it unacceptable.

Let us agree with Bentham's most basic intuition, that the point of ethics is to make the world a better place. Act consequentialism (as already noted) then can seem a natural expression of this intuition. But there are two obvious sorts of problems. One is this: What if what will (or will likely) have the best consequences involves doing something that we normally would consider morally wrong? This challenge can be sharpened. Suppose that the superiority in consequences for the normally immoral sort of deed looks very slight. Suppose also that what seems likely to have the best consequences is not merely something that normally would seem wrong, but indeed is something that normally would seem monstrously wrong. If we put these two suppositions together, we see that act consequentialism can recommend choices that are strongly counterintuitive. Further, some of the arguments developed in chapter 9 strongly suggest that to recommend such choices can have very poor consequences and that if they are not to be recommended, they count as wrong.

The other obvious problem is that a philosopher who lives in the real world, as Mill clearly did, will realize that often we cannot know the consequences of an action that looks promising but is of a sort normally judged immoral. Mill probably would have been willing to say that in some of these cases, we are not even in a good position to estimate the chances of the consequences turning out to be good, very good, bad, or very bad.

Because of this, Mill recommends that in cases of this general sort we simply follow established moral rules (1861/1979, 24). G. E. Moore made a similar recommendation (1903, 155 ff.). Given such considerations, we might think that rule consequentialism, which holds that we should follow rules whose general acceptance has optimal consequences, is superior to act consequentialism. There has been considerable controversy among consequentialists, for several decades, over whether act or rule consequentialism is superior (and sometimes over which one represents Mill's position). My own view is that moral rules do have very definite uses, but that in the end both act and rule consequentialism are unacceptable. Both of these conclusions emerge if we look at two points about rule consequentialism.

The first point relates to a book that cleverly undermined the competition between act and rule consequentialism, David Lyons's *Forms and Limits of Utilitarianism* (1965). Lyons pointed out that in any case in which an established moral rule recommended something other than the optimific act (the one that would produce the best consequences), we could modify the moral rule by introducing clauses that would make it recommend the optimific act in the case at hand. The modified rule would be more complicated than the original one had been, but it would be superior by an obvious standard (what makes the world a better place). This leads to the conclusion that the best set of moral rules would lead to the same decisions as act consequentialism. Hence the idea that act and rule consequentialism are competing views rests on an illusion. Thoroughly improved rule consequentialism collapses into act consequentialism.

Taken on his own terms, Lyons was clearly right. From my point of view, though, something had gone terribly wrong. At issue is whether ethical philosophy should be viewed as a search for formulas that in the abstract will ground the best set of decisions (thus mimicking the precision and abstraction of Newtonian physics), or whether it should be concerned with what will work best under real-world conditions (thus, in a way, looking more like engineering than physics).

From the latter perspective, there is a problem with Lyons's line of argument. General moral rules are extremely useful in preparing large populations (of varying degrees of intelligence, retentiveness, and conscientiousness) to deal with ethical problems. The most familiar of such rules are simple enough to be taught to small children and retained by adults. Even when they are not the last word in deciding what should be done, they can provide a useful orientation. Further, given the general tendency of those of us who are not angels to try to rationalize (possibly immoral) things that we would like to do, the early inculcation of these general rules provides counterbalancing inhibitions.

Extremely complicated general rules, with clauses for special kinds of cases, would not have these advantages. Lawyers, and lawyerlike philosophers, could use them in interesting ways. But for the general population, they would be virtually useless. We need to bear in mind the central insight of contractualism, that a major contribution of morality to our lives is in the formation of a moral order in a society, that coordinates our actions and enables us to be relatively secure. The moral order requires rules that can be easily remembered, widely understood, appreciated, and followed.

In short, a rule consequentialism that is built around very complicated rules (so that it is equivalent to act consequentialism in its recommendations) would be extremely deficient in practice. A difficulty here should be noted and met. The estimation of the consequences of widespread adoption of any particular moral strategy may look even further beyond our reach than does calculation of the consequences (to the end of time) of a particular action (see Griffin 1997, 46–48). In this case, however, likely bad consequences are so evident (even though we cannot say exactly how bad they would be) that we can safely reject a rule consequentialism that is built around rules of unlimited complexity.

We also can reject a rule consequentialism that is built around simple moral rules. Even if we allow for cases in which such rules turn out to have implicit exceptions (generally understood, but hard to specify in advance), there are other cases that are more clearly damaging to traditional rule consequentialism. These involve no general understanding of implicit exceptions but, rather, unusual circumstances in which we are justified in doing something that normally would be considered morally wrong. The most dramatic such cases are those in which catastrophic consequences are likely if the familiar (and generally useful) rule is followed. In the final chapter, I will argue that we can be justified in violating familiar moral rules in circumstances of that sort.

To summarize the discussion thus far: if offered a choice between (a) the case-by-case approach of act consequentialism, and (b) unswerving loyalty to what is (by some consequentialist standards) an optimal set of rules, we should reject both. It is not difficult to think of a form of consequentialism that has most of the advantages of rule consequentialism and is on the whole superior. We can call it policy consequentialism. We could agree generally to follow familiar moral rules that seem to have proved their usefulness, and not to violate them lightly (i.e., without significant justification—what is requisite depends on the case). To say this, though, is to scratch the surface. We need to look more closely at some of the difficulties of consequentialism.

A very general problem for consequentialism, at least in our world, is that it will be employed by human beings. Some of the ramifications already have been touched upon. Our knowledge of the future is limited. We are inclined to rationalize things that we are tempted to do, even if a more dispassionate analysis would lead to rejecting them. Here are two other products of our humanity that create problems for consequentialism of the simplest sort. One is that we cannot constantly ask ourselves, "What is the best thing to do now?" We lack the energy and attentiveness to do this incessantly, and it turns out that even the effort to do it would typically have negative consequences. The other product is that we are to a large degree governed, even at moments when we do pause and ask, "What is the best thing to do now?," by habits of mind and, often, by the momentum of what we have been doing.

One way to move beyond act consequentialism and at the same time emphasize the power of the underlying consequentialist intuition is this. We can look at the most plausible kinds of case in which it seems wrong to choose the act that we think would have the best consequences. These include many of the cases in which the seemingly optimific act runs counter to morality, loyalty to friends and family members, professional ethics, or habits of decency. The thought, then, is that all of these kinds of exception are connected with practices, policies, habits of mind, or character traits that, on the whole, have good consequences (cf. Kupperman 1981 and chap. 9 of this book). All of this leads naturally to the thought that being guided by practices, policies, habits of mind, or character traits that on the whole have good consequences is a more reliable route to making the world a better place than act consequentialism is. To see this is to see that we should jettison act consequentialism in order to fulfill (rather than reject) the imperative to make the world a better place. It leads to what Pettit and Brennan (1986) have called restrictive consequentialism.

The reason we have to make this move is, as R. M. Hare (1981) put it, we are human beings and not archangels. The vulnerability to temptation and rationalization is part of this contrast. But a major part is this: we cannot, computer-like, make methodical decisions every minute of our lives.

Indeed, even if we could, we should not want to. Much of the joy and interest of life comes from spontaneity, especially improvisation, at moments when rules, methods, and established policies are far from our thought. As suggested earlier, if something alerts us that a great deal hangs on a choice that we are about to make, we probably should for the moment eschew spontaneity and think seriously about what we should choose. But to abandon or drastically curtail spontaneity throughout a life would normally be a bad strategy, even if our rejection of the strategy leads on some occasions to less than optimific acts being chosen.

Further, it looks psychologically impossible to come at all close to some requirement that we incessantly judge cases on, as it were, their own merits. Even very intelligent human beings will rely on habits of mind, precedents, or rules most of the time. Indeed, most of life, for almost all of us, is a matter of carrying on. There can be breaks in this, at "existential moments." But the breaks cannot be constant.

An easy way for a reader to get a sense of the two poles of choice-making is this. Think about what it is like to drive a car. It is very important in emergencies to be alert to all sorts of possibilities, and the best alternative may turn out to be something one would not have anticipated. But to maintain this level of conscious alertness for every moment of a drive would be exceedingly wearing, and usually unnecessary.

One of the differences between life and driving a car of course is this: in life, when a great deal is at stake, one more often has a good deal of time to decide. Even in emergencies, drivers often have to rely on habits of mind. This difference, however, should not be overstated. Even given time, many of us can find it difficult to get beyond our habits of mind, or to do the sort of thing we would not normally do. Further, some moral decisions, or ones about the direction of our life, may have to be made in very little time. The speed of the Milgram experiments was commented on earlier. Some subjects must have been guided mainly by their habits of mind, including perhaps a habit of cooperating with authorities who seemed to know what they were doing. A habit of sometimes thinking twice, and varying one's behavior accordingly, might have helped.

We are not all entirely the same in these matters; but it remains the case that consequentialism needs to give an important place to practices, policies, habits of mind, and character traits that appear generally to have good consequences. Part of the importance of not lightly violating familiar moral rules or, for that matter lightly deviating from familiar patterns of behavior in matters of importance, can be understood in relation to this. We need policies in these areas, and to feel ready to deviate from a policy has a psychological force that verges on not really having a policy. In much the same way, to feel very ready to take someone else's property in an unusual case verges on not really having a character trait of being honest in such matters. This is not to say that deviations from our normal policies could never possibly be justified by the circumstances of a case, but it strongly suggests that any deviations should be reluctant and probably not the first thing that comes to mind.

At this point, a possible criticism of my story of the evolution of consequentialism should be dealt with. It is that, as the image presented of consequentialism progressively comes to include elements associated with other theories, my account of what consequentialism is becomes too inclusive. Is the form that has just presented really consequentialism? Of course, one can use the label as one likes, but let me suggest that the criticism smacks of the view (which I have been arguing should be discredited) of ethical theories as sharply discrete and competing monoliths. There are other angles from which we can see that this view should be discredited. Consequences do play a role in Kantian ethics, even in Kant's original version—as Mill pointed out (1861/1979, 4). The very short official line was that consequences do not matter ("Do right though the heavens fall"). All the same, an important imperfect duty is to make others happy; and this implies the importance of likely (if perhaps not actual) consequences. We should get used to the idea of theories including elements of one another.

Is there a further step in the progressive complication of consequentialism? The previous chapter points to a direction. Consequentialism has to be tempered by the realization of our partial ignorance (greater in some areas than in others) of what the consequences of something will be or are likely to be. This problem for consequentialists has been pointed out by Alan Donagan (1977, 199ff., and in correspondence) and, more recently, by James Griffin. The fact that it took me so very many years to take in the implications of this is my tribute to the power of entrenched patterns of thought.

The next chapter will be designed to show, among other things, what kinds of claims consequentialists can make. It will chart the roles of consequentialist considerations within an acceptable ethical theory.

12

A Modulated Case for
the Primacy of Value

A case was outlined in chapters 5 and 8 that contractualism is, to a degree, right. It argued that a general basis for any moral judgment consists of its ability to play a part in an acceptable moral order. A moral judgment is acceptable if and only if any moral agent can reasonably accept it.

There are parts of the story that need further explanation. What do we mean by speaking of what an agent can "reasonably" accept? Also, there are many imaginable moral orders, and historically there have been many actual moral orders in various societies. What could be meant by speaking of an "acceptable" moral order?

Further, as we have seen in chapter 9, if contractualism gives a true account of morality, there is considerable truth also in consequentialism—at least in the abstract, as a general logical account of ethics (and not merely morality). Can we reconcile these truths?

The argument of this chapter is that considerations of quality of life (in the sense of what is rewarding, having non-instrumental value) play a crucial role in grounding contractual moral systems, and also in supplying their central rules. Does this mean that quality of life is the most fundamental base of ethics, even more fundamental than the base of being able to be included in an acceptable moral order? Is the theory that will emerge from this book a multi-level version of consequentialism?

The answer to the last two questions is "Yes and no." As earlier remarked, we need to be mindful, in ethics as much as in the sciences, of the distinction between the logic of discovery and the logic of justification. It would be abnormal, I think, for an acceptable moral order to be arrived at on purely consequentialist grounds. There are strong arguments that some elements of an acceptable moral order, including the requirement (with exceptions) to keep promises, conceptually could not be arrived at on the basis of how much they contributed to quality of life (see Rawls 1955). Any plausible story of how an acceptable moral order is arrived at will be complicated, with a large role for evolved intuitions of reasonableness and fairness, and probably not a huge role for direct appeals to what does or does not contribute to values in life.

On the other hand, once a set of moral judgments has been meaningfully developed as a putative moral order, it can be justified or criticized in a variety of ways. Some of these forms of argument, again, will appeal to evolved intuitions of reasonableness or fairness. Others may appeal directly to quality-of-life considerations, such as the ways in which the moral order makes (or would make) segments of the population miserable.

Part of the argument of this chapter is specifically that quality-of-life (in the sense of what is valuable) considerations are decisive in the justification or criticism of a moral order. In this sense, the theory to emerge from this book claims a limited primacy in ethics for quality-of-life judgments. The primacy is limited in two respects. One is that it extends to justification and criticism of a putative moral order, but not to its discovery. The other is that there are other kinds of good reasons that typically play a role in justification or criticism of a putative moral order. But I will argue that whatever force these have depends largely on how well they seem to point toward quality-of-life considerations.

"Reasonable" Acceptance of a Moral Order

What do we require of an acceptable moral order? Certainly, it has to afford protection, so that ordinary life can be reasonably peaceful and secure. This involves some specific coverage: a moral order that does not include prohibitions against murder, rape, torture, and theft cannot be doing its job in any thorough way.

There also is a requirement of fairness. This seems obvious, and internal to the nature of justice. Given entrenched intuitions, most of us think we have a fairly good idea of what fairness means. We saw in chapter 6, though, that what fairness consists of is a complicated subject.

Anyone who believes that it should be easy for a clear-minded person to arrive at an entirely acceptable morality might think, "Why not treat everyone in the same way?" This could be held to be the key to a valid morality. It even can be suggested that a luminously clear sense of fairness involved in this is "hardwired" into humans and other higher primates.

A recent experimental datum was that a capuchin monkey appeared to be making a complaint (appealing to fairness?) when another monkey was given a grape whereas the complaining monkey had been given something much less appealing. On one interpretation, the monkey knew that all monkeys should be treated the same. If we could just wipe from our minds the obfuscating by-products of class, status, gender, and ethnicity (it might seem), we could see quite clearly that everyone should be treated the same. This imperative might look like a natural outcome of the developments of the previous centuries, in which the rights of women, minority groups, representatives of unpopular religions, and others have increasingly been respected.

There are two major difficulties, though. One is that is not easy to decide who is to be included in "everyone." Controversies over the moral status of the human fetus highlight this difficulty. The other is that some might be plausibly included for some purposes, but not for others. The discussion in chapter 6 examined how this might be the case for animals and for mentally incapacitated humans. Here, again, there is ample room for controversy concerning the rights of the insane, the severely retarded, and those suffering from Alzheimer's disease. The fact that the tendency of recent centuries has been toward equality of moral consideration (at least among human beings) does not carry any implications that would resolve all of these controversies and difficulties.

All of this is consistent with the following picture. An acceptable moral order not only must be effective in providing basic protections (largely discouraging people from committing murder, rape, torture, theft, etc.), but also must be fair and must be seen as fair. Fairness is, as we have seen, a changing and somewhat contestable concept. But it includes the imperative that everyone be given the same moral treatment, unless there are relevant differences. The tendency of recent centuries has been to construe "everyone" increasingly broadly and "relevant differences" increasingly narrowly, so that (for almost all purposes) it is far less plausible than it used to be to regard gender, race, religion, or social class as relevant to how someone is morally entitled to be treated.

The breadth of appeal within a society of a moral order matters to much of this. A moral order that does not inspire widespread allegiance cannot be very effective in providing basic protections. Any group that, in effect, feels itself excluded may well be less influenced in its conduct by the contents of the prevailing moral order. Further, the felt exclusion could be viewed in terms of unfairness.

How much inclusion does there need to be for a moral order to be acceptable? At one extreme there could be a Quaker-like ideal of everyone in the society accepting the moral order and regarding it as entirely fair. This is surely not feasible, though, in part because inevitably there will be people who have irrational prejudices and are very insistent about how these should be respected within the society. This is part of the problem of people whose tastes and interests are not readily reconcilable with those of most people in the society.

Take, for example, someone who has a taste for violence. We could imagine her or him to be morally scrupulous, not engaging in or encouraging violence against anyone who is not a consenting adult. This person's violence then might take the form of street fights in which all of the participants want to fight. Even if consent is stipulated, many of us might regard all of the brawls this would lead to as unacceptable in a civilized society. The person with a taste for violence, on the other hand, might regard a society without many brawls as unacceptably tame. Similarly, someone with extremely conservative views about relations between the sexes might find a society unacceptable if its women go about without veils and abundant clothing.

Disaffection of such kinds must be regarded as normal, especially within a pluralistic society. Further, such disaffection is not subversive of a moral order in the way in which rejection of, say, central prohibitions of murder, rape, torture, and theft would be. Unless it is very widespread, it represents a strain rather than a major challenge.

The picture thus far is that to be acceptable, a moral order must be capable of widespread acceptance. We have noted that meeting this requirement is consistent with there being elements (that are not central) of the order that a significant number of people regard as unacceptable. A further point is that continuing widespread acceptance requires a widespread perception that the moral order is, by and large, fair (even though intuitions of fairness are always contestable).

How might a moral order be seen as unfair? One way is if the quality of life of a segment of the population falls below what it might be expected to be. Might a moral order be seen as unacceptable even if it is not seen as unfair? One might imagine a case in which (perhaps because of excessive moral demands of various sorts) people's quality of life generally falls below what it might be expected to be. The falling short of value in life might be shared fairly but still experienced as a falling short.

Criticizing/Justifying a Moral Order

This leads us back to the earlier suggestion that judgments of value often provide a better basis for justifying or criticizing an existing moral order than they do for supporting a new moral order. This suggestion may look highly questionable, on the face of it. If we find a moral order or some of its elements faulty, is that not to find a new moral order (or new elements) desirable? Also, can we really justify an existing moral order without implicitly or explicitly comparing it to alternatives (which we might have supported but choose not to)?

Part of the answer to these doubts rests on what we expect of the consequences of an option that we are to recommend. Do we expect them to be the very best that are possible? Or can we recommend an option if the relevant consequences merely seem likely to be better than those of the most obvious alternatives, and we judge that they are likely to be good enough?

The name for this kind of strategy is "satisficing" (see Slote 1984; Pettit 1984). The idea of settling for what is "good enough" looks counterintuitive if one thinks in terms of ideal conditions of judgment (say, the judgments made by archangels who know the future and are immune to mistakes or moral lapses). If all of this were true, why not choose what has the best consequences?

If there is limited knowledge of the future, and real chances of mistakes, matters look quite different. What seems fairly safe and likely to be beneficial then can be recommended even if there is nothing like thorough knowledge of the alternatives. (To delay decisions until there is more knowledge might well be futile and would itself have bad consequences.) In much this spirit, we also can judge that an element of an existing moral order is simply not good enough, even if we lack a grasp of the consequences of the major alternatives (and may need to know a lot more if we are to determine which is likely to be beneficial).

The judgment that some Northerners made, in the decades leading up to the Civil War, that slavery was unacceptable is a good example of this. Clearly, there were alternatives to slavery—including various ways in which former slaves could be treated and perhaps helped—but not a clear awareness of how these might play out, or of which might draw the sustained public support that it would require. Political arrangements, including the degree to which voting rights would be protected, were one of the variables. There were some who favored a program of "repatriation" to Africa. The alternatives that involved considerable remedial assistance to former slaves may have seemed desirable to a caring person. But such a person might well have doubted whether necessary resources would have been made available; because of this, there would be room for a judgment that alternatives that seemed less ideal would have better chances of sustained support. The one thing that surely could have been clear—that one could know—was that it was better that slavery be abolished.

A similar point applies to someone who decided, at some point in the eighteenth century, that it was unacceptable that women were kept out of universities. Such a judgment would leave room for a range of options: universities or colleges for women only, integration of women into existing universities, or programs for non-resident women involving what would amount to university extensions, and doubtless others still. Given hindsight, we can see that the best choice was probably "all of the above." But at the time, it might not have been so clear how any one of these alternatives would work out. Arguably the one clear thing, to someone who was sensitive to the values of women (as well as men) having opportunities to fulfill themselves in a variety of ways, would have been that it was desirable that women have access to higher education.

Hence we have two judgments, unspecific in key details, that I contend would have been highly reasonable at the time: that slavery should be abolished, and that women should not be excluded from higher education. Could something more positive and specific have been justified on the basis of likely consequences? Could someone at the time, given the general lack of knowledge of how the future would play out, have justified on the basis of consequences our present moral order (as opposed to the various barely imaginable alternatives)? It is hard to claim that in either case there would have been a high level of justification of such a specific option. (Indeed, in both cases what actually has happened can be criticized as "too little, too slowly," but it remains unclear whether anything better was, in that climate of opinion, genuinely possible.)

The conclusion thus far has been that we can have considerable confidence in a specific judgment that a moral order is faulty in some respect. If the fault is serious, it supports an imperative that that element of the moral order be removed or seriously modified. But, on the positive side, it supports what may be only a non-specific judgment that there should be a better alternative.

This is an attempt to disarm objections to a feature (namely that judgments of consequences can play a role in criticism that they generally do not play in discovery of a moral order) of the account of the primacy of value that will follow. Are there other elements in this account that might seem counterintuitive? Here are two. It might be thought that how great a role the value of some consequences plays in ethics should depend only on how good (or bad) the consequences are likely to be. Certainly (as was true in the two cases just discussed), harm that is primarily deprivation of opportunities for self-fulfillment can count in criticism of a moral order. But I will argue that likely physical or financial harm has an especially important role—greater than that of corresponding positive consequences—both in criticism of elements of a morality, and also in formation of central moral rules. I will argue also that short-term harm of this sort tends to have a larger role than long-term forms of harm.

The main reason in both cases is this: Most of what a moral order accomplishes requires a near consensus within a society, which in turn requires a common vision of what the morality emphasizes as objects of concern. Hence short-term physical or financial harm plays a major role in part because it can be more apparent to virtually everyone than are long-term or more subtle forms of harm. In the world of archangels, this presumably would be different, but this is how morality works for humans.

Why the emphasis on obvious harm rather than on positive consequences? Part of the answer lies in a feature of human psychology and experience of values: a greater emphasis on what can go wrong than on what can go right. I will expand on this, and on other reasons, later in the chapter.

The Primacy of Value

It may be helpful for us, in beginning this account, to look more closely at the functions of normative ethics. These are multiple. Propositions or entire systems about what is desirable in life and about how people should behave are designed to accomplish many things. They help to structure our perceptions of the world, placing things or events of certain sorts in the foreground of what we notice. They are designed to make us fit for society and to promote harmonious, smoothly running societies. Most fundamentally, they are designed to make the world better than it otherwise might be. It would be hard to defend an ethics that did not make that claim. "What's the point?" one might say.

As chapter 7 pointed out, to think that something is very important is not necessarily to think that one should constantly and consciously aim for it. An indirect and less calculating approach can be more effective. This is often observed in relation to personal happiness. Happiness may be more likely if one becomes engrossed in various activities and relationships without constantly thinking, "How will this contribute to my happiness?" Similarly, it may be that our chance of making the world a better place than it might be would improve if we did not incessantly ask ourselves whether this or that will make the world a better place.

In this respect, there is a contrast between thoughts (on occasion, and normally not incessantly) about whether such and such an element of an ethics really does make the world a better place and, on the other hand, an ongoing reflective preoccupation with such questions. The former is reasonable; the latter can verge on neurosis and be counterproductive. Compare the pair of cases in which someone incessantly calculates strategies for personal happiness, or someone does not but finds that something keeps making her or him unhappy (or feels missing in life), and asks whether life could be adjusted to become happier. In both instances, there is a fundamental desideratum (to be happy, to make the world the better place), which — if things are going reasonably well — is best not dwelt upon. But if things are not going well, one can revisit the fundamental desideratum and ask hard questions.

The argument of chapters 8–10 supports the view that it is implausible to regard immediate judgments about the consequences of particular actions as in general determining their rightness. The world is made better than it might have been if much of what we do is determined by considerations—such as traditional moral obligations, love, loyalty to friends, dedication to central personal projects, and so on—that do not themselves require reckoning of consequences. In this pattern of thought, any concern about the state of the world hovers outside the borders of what we consider and becomes relevant only in unusual and serious cases in which what normally is acceptable risks being quite damaging.

A simple view of the place of value in normative ethics, then, would be this. Considerations of value should not play a part in the general run of decisions as to what we should do. There is room, of course, for some reflective thought about what is really desirable in life, and works like the *Nicomachean Ethics* do supply this need. Further, considerations of value can function as a constraint on an ethical system or a moral order. If it is felt that life generally would be less desirable in a world that generally adhered to the ethical system, or that life is less desirable within the moral order than it should be, that is a very serious difficulty. Value in short, in this simple view, comes into ethics either in matters of personal orientation and pursuit of happiness or as a constraint.

I will argue for a view that is somewhat like this, but is less simple. It is that there is a concern for value, and especially to avoid negative values, that occurs at all levels of normative ethics. At the most fundamental level, judgments of value assume a dominant role when it looks as though elements of a moral order are doing (or general adherence to an ethical system would do) serious damage to quality of life. But judgments of value also play an important role in everyday moral decisions of many ordinary sorts. Many of the rules at the heart of traditional morality can be explained only by reference to judgments of value, conjoined with the difficulties of making certain kinds of judgments of value and of predicting the future. Also, there are public policy decisions in which consideration of consequences will normally play a major role.

Here are five claims that together comprise the modulated view of the primacy of value within ethics.

1. Even everyday moral decisions that are explicitly made in terms of traditional moral rules implicitly rely on judgments of the values typically at stake in following these rules. We have seen that one cannot judge the total consequences of any action, even a callous murder, through time with anything like entire confidence. As J. S. Mill pointed out, when we lack sufficient confidence in judgments of the consequences of an action, we have "secondary principles" (i.e., traditional moral rules) to fall back on (1861/1979, 24–25). There is considerable experience over time that observing the rules against dramatic forms of immediate physical and financial harm (e.g., murder, rape, torture, theft, etc.) has better short-term consequences than violating them would. Hence our willingness, in the general run of cases, to judge that one simply should not murder, rape, torture, steal, and so on rests on a general sense that the short-term consequences of such actions typically (in what falls within our purview) have negative values.

2. It is no accident that the rules at the core of traditional morality (and in current moral orders) are mostly prohibitions, like the ones just mentioned. This answers to an emphasis in most people's thoughts on the importance of avoiding highly negative experiences. There are reasons why the values that play a central role in an acceptable moral order will be mainly negative values, things that the moral order is designed to protect against.

3. Mill's suggestion is in effect that, even if we have some degree of confidence that violating a central traditional moral rule might have good consequences, this is (normally) outweighed by our confidence that following such rules has better consequences than violating them. However, there can be extreme cases, in which (on a present occasion) it is unusually clear that there is a strong risk of catastrophic consequences if the traditional moral rule is followed. In that event, estimation of short-run consequences can assume a prominent role that would be out of place in ordinary cases to which traditional moral rules apply.

4. There are cases in which estimation of short-term consequences normally will be directly decisive, even though the immediate calculation of consequences does not seem very secure. In these, none of the traditional moral rules can determine our decision, and none of the other possibly overriding considerations (professional obligations, demands of friendship, etc.) examined in chapter 9 apply. Public policy decisions, such as choices of how public money is to be allocated or of what tax policy should be, typically have this character. In such cases, it may well be that an estimate of the values of the likely short-term consequences of various alternatives is all one has to go on. Because of this, estimated values will play a crucial role.

5. Finally, any attempt to enable an ethics to make the world better than it might be should include criticism, and possible revision, of elements of a moral order. A major difficulty in this is that of getting a sense of what the future would be if the moral order remained unchanged, and of what it would be if the moral order were changed along certain lines. Because of this, we rarely can have complete assurance that one future would be better than another.

Much of this difficulty remains under any circumstances. However, we are in a somewhat better position to make a judgment if we have had enough experience of one of the alternatives to know that it is working badly. There still can be a worry that any cure would be worse than the disease: reforms do sometimes seem to make the world worse. But, when it is clear that an element of a moral order introduces negative values (or the deprivation of certain positive values) into the lives of a number of people, and when the heart of a proposed change is that this effect be erased, it can look as if there is a reasonable degree of confidence that the change will make the world better.

Creating a new element of a moral order, not clearly linked (or directly opposed) to any existing element, is a risky business. Simply negating an existing element (even though inevitably further new elements will develop around this change, and there will be unintended consequences) can look less risky. It makes a difference also if the undesirable element in the existing moral order is sharply negative in such a way that the sense of it could become widely shared.

Recent examples that have been given are the abolition of slavery, and the insistence on not denying to women opportunities that are open to men. It makes a difference that the undesirable element in the existing moral orders, in both of these cases, was sharply negative in a way that most people came to see. As in relation to the general prohibitions of murder, rape, torture, and theft, the clear likelihood of eliminating highly negative values counts for a great deal, against the background of our generally unclear sense of the future.

These five claims add up to a highly qualified consequentialism. Judgments of value have a primacy in ethics, but this is compatible with their having in many cases only a negligible explicit role. Each of these claims carries with it complications that need to be examined. In what remains, I will argue for the five claims and also explore the complications.

Arguments, Complications

(1) The argument for the first claim starts from the fact that moralities around the world have tended to consist of broad general rules for governing actions likely to have immediate consequences for people who are taken to matter that are generally (in the case of prohibitions) obviously negative or (in the case of positive requirements) obviously positive. An example of this is the weight placed on what have been standard interpretations of "Thou shalt not kill." Theft also has been widely stigmatized. A common positive rule is the one that requires saving a life when one is especially well positioned to do so. In all of these cases, the immediate consequences of what is prohibited or required are usually both significant and obvious.

A complication in this generalization about actual moralities in various societies in the past or present should be noted. I am certainly not suggesting that all actions that most of us now would agree generally have immediate and significant (negative or positive) consequences have been, or now are, always included among what actual moral orders prohibit or require. There is no genuine congruence of that sort. There has been, however, a growing convergence.

The attentive reader will have noticed two implicit concessions above of lack of congruence. One is in the phrase "people who are taken to matter," which opens the door to the thought that in many places and times there have been people who simply were not taken to matter, or who were taken to matter far less than others. The other is in the omission of rape and torture, when sharply negative deeds were mentioned that generally have been treated as central objects of moral condemnation.

In all of this, a crucial factor has been limited sympathy. There is a case for holding that benevolence or sympathy is an element of normal human psychology (along with selfishness and a great deal else). David Hume and (two thousand years before him) Mencius both made such a case, along remarkably similar lines, although Mencius seemed much more alive to the possibility that benevolence might turn out to be selective, coming to the surface on some occasions and not on a great many others.

A great many early or primitive societies did not regard harm to strangers as being even remotely comparable to harm befalling members of the group. Further, harm to slaves, social inferiors, or women often is taken far less seriously than harm to male members of a privileged group. We get a small taste of this in the episode in

Shakespeare's *Henry V*, act 4, scene 8, following the battle of Agincourt when a report of English casualties itemizes dead aristocrats, followed by "and none other of name."

It is striking (and from our point of view, disgusting) that when rape was taken seriously in early societies, it was often in light of its having violated somebody's property rights. People who have been tortured have often been those regarded as in some way disqualified from normal treatment. Such attitudes have become less common, but they persist in some societies today.

Further, there can be a joy in cruelty that most of us would rather not think about (and that Hume and Mencius, to their credit, probably found unimaginable except in the case, which both discuss, in which someone loses his or her humanity). Some of the more disturbing passages in Nietzsche, and in the work of Bertolt Brecht, deal with this. The joy may be more widespread than one might first think, and could be linked to something seemingly innocuous that is still very evident: the curious pleasure that some take in detailed stories of atrocities, or (when someone has been killed) in close-up news photos of the faces of grieving family members. Might some of the satisfaction stem from a reduction of anxiety, with the sense of a great evil alighting on someone else (and thus passing you by)?

Be that as it may, the direction of what most of us would regard as moral progress has been marked by the extension of sympathy to strangers and to people of different gender, sexual orientation, or social status, and to animals. Because of this, there is convergence toward the idea that the "people who matter" consist of everybody, along with growing support for the idea that some or all animals also matter. One mark of this convergence is that it now seems obvious that the kinds of immediate harm that most require moral sanction include torture and rape as well as murder and theft.

The argument for Claim 1 is mainly this. Murder, torture, rape, and theft, and saving lives share an important feature. It is that they typically involve immediate consequences which would be generally agreed to have significant disvalue or value. There may be some odd exceptions, such as the secret murder of an entirely isolated person who is terminally ill and very much wants to die. But such cases are unusual.

The simplest explanation of why general rules involving murder, torture, rape, theft, and saving lives have an important role in morality is that we do care about the immediate consequences of such actions. If we were some very different sort of life form, for whom being murdered, raped, tortured, or stolen from (or having one's life saved) was normally not very important, these actions would hardly be sanctioned or recommended at the heart of morality. As it is, given our general uncertainty about the future and lack of consensus in most judgments of value, these represent the clearest cases in which we can design a morality to lessen the incidence of some bad consequences and increase the incidence of some good ones.

(2) The argument for the second claim relies on features (a) of typical human experience of values, (b) of the ways in which positive and negative values can be created, and (c) of the ways in which a moral order can be effective. All of these factors are such that protection against negative values will be most emphasized in any acceptable and effective moral order.

(a) It is striking that negative experiences are often evaluated as more negative than seemingly comparable positive experiences are evaluated as positive. In some cases, which have been analyzed by psychologists as revealing "negativity bias," it looks as if this verges on the irrational (see Rozin and Royzman 2001). An example is when people are more upset by losing an item than they are pleased by acquiring it.

However, it is arguable that some highly negative experiences really are more negative in their values than highly positive experiences are positive. Here is one way to see the plausibility of this. Imagine a choice between two ordinary weeks on one hand, and on the other a week of the best you can imagine combined with—in any order you prefer—a week of the worst you can imagine. Which would you choose?

Whether this tilt toward emphasizing the negative is analyzed as a quirk of human psychology or is viewed as sometimes revelatory of an asymmetry in available values, it is understandable that it would be reflected in the construction of an ethics. It is striking that John Stuart Mill, attempting to characterize the promotion of happiness, emphasizes elimination of "the grand sources of suffering" (1861/1979, 20). Prevention of suffering, and more generally protection, are important human needs.

(b) There appear to be more reliable ways of creating negative values than of creating positive values. Certainly there are things that can be done to a person that are virtually certain to create an awful life for them. (There may be a few people for whom this is not true, such as trained Buddhists; but these are rare.) Are there comparable things that would virtually guarantee that someone have a wonderful life? Psychological variables, and the unpredictability of human responses, become more prominent in the answer to this question. It is because of this that positive social programs, when they are not simply designed to remove causes of misery and suffering, usually are framed in terms of providing opportunities rather than certainties. Because of this, there is a much clearer role for morality in blocking causes of misery and suffering than in the chancy business of producing positive values.

(c) It also is the case that other people's highly negative experiences often are easier to relate to, and to appreciate the (negative) value of, than are other people's positive experiences. There do appear to be strongly shared patterns of negative value attached to certain kinds of experiences, ranging from migraine headaches to being tortured for days in a dank, windowless prison. Certainly there is a widespread sense that our common humanity emerges strongly in most kinds of negative experiences. Many positive experiences seem more individualized. What makes one person euphoric or very happy may well do little for another. Further, what seems wonderful to one person may seem humdrum to another.

Some forms of other people's happiness, however, are experiences we can readily identify with, such as happiness in love or in family life; conversely, there are instances of misery that are highly idiosyncratic. That said, it must be added that most of the striking forms of human suffering cluster around what Mill called the "grand sources of suffering," which include disease and poverty, or around wounds and privations inflicted by other people. As already noted, there are no comparable "grand sources" of happiness.

This greater ability to identify with and appreciate the highly negative value of certain experiences matters to inclusion in a moral order. A moral order gains its power from widely shared responses that in aggregate can have the effect of sanctioning behavior that is forbidden and of promoting what is recommended. Actions that cause a markedly negative value in a highly visible way (i.e., such that both the causation and the negativity of the result are evident to almost everyone) are especially suitable for emphasis in a moral order.

(3) The argument for the third claim has to walk on both sides of the line between dogged compliance with traditional moral rules and their violation. The first part of the argument (the part that supports dogged compliance in the vast majority of circumstances) starts from an examination of what it is to accept a moral rule. Really to accept it, so that you are reliably someone who wouldn't do such-and-such, requires internalizing the rule. This includes seeing the world in such a way that violations of the rule become salient. It also includes inhibitions about violating the rule. It is not merely that you think that you should not; it is also that you would find it difficult, or perhaps impossible, to violate the rule even if you became convinced that (in an extraordinary case) it somehow was necessary. This kind of attitude counterbalances our tendencies to look for exceptions in our favor. A moral order works well if large numbers of people have this inhibited mind-set in relation to central moral rules. If we assume that general respect for the rules has good consequences, then such widespread internalization will heighten good consequences.

In the argument that immediately follows, one needs to separate theft (and also promise breaking) from murder, rape, torture. The latter typically are much more serious forms of harm, and the argument to follow will be that it takes a strong risk of something that involves a very large number of people and is catastrophic to justify any violation of the rules governing them. We are prepared to excuse promise breaking and theft, however, on grounds that are less exacting. A textbook case is the one in which the only way to save a life is to commandeer someone's car without the owner's permission. (Even then, though, the person who took the car has a residual obligation to provide restitution and recompense.)

Let us return to murder, rape, and torture. It is easy to imagine that there might be cases in which one of these would have good consequences (because of unusual circumstances) that seem somewhat to outweigh the bad ones. If we think that we are confronted with such a case, should we violate the rule? Mill's suggestion (already noted) is that our limited knowledge of the future entitles us to little confidence in such a judgment, which will be outweighed by our greater confidence in the general pattern, in which violations of central rules tend to have serious negative short-term consequences. The argument is that, all of this considered, it is better to play safe and follow the relevant central rule. Such a policy may turn out to work better in some cases than in others, but in the general run of cases (which is what we do know something about), it will have good consequences.

There is another factor to be considered, as counting against our agreeing that a weighty central rule in the kind of case just described should be violated. The costs, in terms of loosening our adherence to highly useful moral rules, could well be considerable. They also would be difficult to assess. If we were to agree in one case, and then in another, that the prospect of somewhat better consequences justified violation of a central rule, at what point can it be said that we no longer have firm allegiance to these rules? At which point in the process (of what some would consider to be our corruption) would most of the damage have been done?

If we take seriously the social costs of undermining such allegiance, then very remarkably good consequences affecting large numbers of people would be required to outweigh these costs. Absent a clear view of these, it would seem deeply risky to agree that violation of the central moral rule was justified. It was argued previously that a characteristic of morality is that something can be morally acceptable only if its recommendation can be included in an acceptable moral order. If, in the cases under discussion, that is not possible, then violating the central moral rule in those cases is morally unacceptable.

Highly likely short-term catastrophic consequences of following the familiar rule can be a different matter. The clearest cases would involve the strong risk of devastating damage (e.g., millions of people killed) and would constitute emergencies. There are two reasons why it seems reasonable to treat such cases as exceptions to rules. One is simply the stipulated great weight of the risks to be avoided. The good consequences of avoiding the risks would have a greater margin over the likely costs, which makes worries about our uncertain knowledge of the future (and unintended consequences down the road) less bothersome. The other reason is that the spectacular and extraordinary risks represent a highly distinctive kind of case, one that may be unlikely often to recur. This will diminish any illocutionary costs of our agreeing that the violation is justified.

To violate a central moral rule because of the prospect of somewhat good consequences is to enter a region of slippery slopes, in which a variety of semi-plausible cases for further violations will present themselves. Really it is to undermine morality, for the sake of possible gains that are both uncertain and not huge. To violate a central moral rule because of a strong risk of a catastrophe has much stronger justification, and the exposure to slippery slopes will be less because of the dramatic distinctiveness of the case.

In the end, one cannot prove that a weighty central moral rule should be violated if it is the only way to avoid a likely catastrophe. But there is a strong argument that it cannot be ruled out. It has been argued at various points in this book that the function of ethics is to make the world better than it might be. If a catastrophe that would make things much worse is imminent, then it might seem irrational to refuse to deviate from following rules that generally make the world better when, this time, following them would bring disaster.

Very likely, none of us will ever have to make a choice of the sort under discussion. Someone who did have to make such a choice could be convinced by the arguments just given that a weighty central rule of morality should (this time) be violated, but still be unable to bring herself or himself to do it. The useful inhibitions that morality promotes can be like that. Let me point out, though, that there can be moments in which a generally useful inhibition should be overcome, and that there are known cases (less fantastic and extreme than those involving likely catastrophes) that illustrate this.

By and large, the known cases involve emergencies of familiar sorts, especially those in wartime. We have strong inhibitions against allowing innocent people to die when there is a chance that they could be saved. Normally, someone who does allow an innocent person to die in such circumstances would be considered to have some moral responsibility for the death. Recall, however, R. M. Hare's case (described in chap. 6) in which some sailors on a ship have gone overboard, but the ship is about to come under enemy fire unless it quickly steams away. We would normally think (given this very strong risk) that the ship's captain should quickly steam away, leaving the sailors to drown, although we also think that a decent person in that position would feel terrible. The inhibition (about allowing an innocent person to die) probably could not be, and certainly should not be, eliminated. But someone who is not rigid and who is mindful that the basic function of morality is to make the world better than it otherwise would be should be prepared to override the inhibition. Similarly, it seems very plausible to hold that a case in which there is a strong risk that millions will die if one does not violate a central moral rule can be one in which inhibitions should be overriden.

(4) The fourth claim may well seem not very radical. It often has been noted that forms of direct consequentialism (such as classical utilitarianism) are more at home in public policy decisions than they are in moral decisions in everyday life. The argument is straightforward. A decision in which one looks for the option that would likely have the best consequences is claimed to be appropriate when (in effect) there is no special factor of weight (e.g., morality, professional requirements) that bears on the choice. If no special factor of that sort is relevant, then why not make things (on the whole) better than they otherwise would be? The question looks unanswerable.

This seems at least approximately right in relation to a large number of public policy decisions. It often is generally agreed that in these cases we have very little to go on apart from informed estimates of likely consequences. The informed estimates often are provided by economists and political commentators.

Three complications should be noted. One is that even if morality or professional requirements or other mitigating factors do not have a clear bearing on the cases under discussion, this need not mean that there is nothing to go on apart from a reasoned estimate of consequences. Many people may have an intuitive sense (but not all of them the same intuitive sense) of which possible consequences are most likely or most important. It was remarked in chapter 3 that chess masters sometimes make their moves on the basis of something that is somewhat comparable (a positional sense) rather than relying entirely on a direct calculation.

The second complication is connected with the fact that experts (not to mention politicians and bureaucrats) often disagree. Often, this is in cases in which it looks as if no one is really in a position to know, even for the short run, which of the options will have the best possible consequences. Some opinions will appear better based than others, but that may be all that one can say.

Our lack of real knowledge can create a case for polemical stances that are more guarded than those that are appropriate when central elements of traditional morality are in play. If, lacking a really secure sense of the future, we make a moral decision by appeal to traditional moral rules, at least we are appealing to a generally shared (and seemingly secure) basis for moral judgment. If, lacking a really secure sense of the future, we formulate a public policy decision on the basis of our best estimate of the values of likely short-run consequences—one that differs from the estimate that others arrive at—we are in a much poorer position to consider those who differ from us immoral, or morally at fault. Cromwell's words to the general assembly of the Church of Scotland, "I beseech you, in the bowels of Christ, think it possible that you may be mistaken," can be addressed to all parties—at least if any mistakes are honest mistakes. We may consider our opponents to be unreasonable, but the tone of discourse appropriately will be lower key than in the first case. In a nutshell: most political arguments should lack the heat of moral arguments.

A third complication, which deserves an entire book in its own right, is this. Public policy decisions generally are political decisions. A part of politics involves alliances in which person X trades support for measure A (which does not seem to X to be desirable) in return for Y's support for measure B (which does seem to X, but not to Y, to be highly desirable). Someone who is very good at this could conceivably accomplish much that is useful (as well as being complicit in some things that are not). The ethics of politics is a rich and complex special subject. Let us merely assume here that there are some cases in which political exigencies reasonably could overrule someone's estimate that a certain option is likely to have optimal consequences. If so, then political exigencies would join morality, professional requirements, and so on among the factors, absent which it makes sense to support what looks likely to have optimal consequences.

(5) The strength of the argument for the fifth claim can be appreciated only if one abandons the static, ahistorical models of so much recent ethical or social philosophy and looks at the ways in which societies and their moral orders have developed through time. Examples from the last few hundred years, involving norms for treatment of racial minorities and women, already have been cited. One could add to the list the changes that eliminated demands for religious conformity, and that substituted legal bankruptcy for the imprisonment of debtors. In all of these cases, there was a strong sense that the traditional norms were counterproductive and that they prevented some values of human life from flourishing. Hume was very aware of processes of this sort, as in his discussion (noted in chap. 9) of the rejection of the "monkish virtues" (1751/1975, no. 219, 270).

There is no suggestion in this that the direction of change in moral norms is always positive. Nevertheless, my guess is that the great majority of readers will agree that the examples above are positive, that they reflect dim but growing realizations that things could be better. The argument for claim 5 is simply that (a) it makes sense to effect a change in the moral order that consists of removing something thought to have a negative effect on values in life, and (b) any doubts that it is reasonable to focus on removing the negative element without a clear vision of the future that will result can be allayed by pointing to cases in which this is actually what occurred. When debtors were no longer judged to be deserving of imprisonment, and when it was finally considered unreasonable to prevent adherents of religions deemed incorrect from attending English universities, it was highly plausible to think that the future would be better in relevant respects as a result, even if there was no clear view of what that future would be like. This is even clearer in the abolition of slavery and the establishment of higher education for women.

The argument needs to be a little more complicated, for this reason. I have already remarked that, in some (perhaps all) of the transitions just instanced, evolved intuitive ideas of fairness did most of the work. So it is possible for someone to argue that the justification for such transitions is simply fairness, and that values (more broadly, making the world better than it otherwise might be) can be left out of the picture.

My reply to this line of thought has been that ideas of fairness are contestable, and consequently a reasonable test of any idea of fairness is its consequences: whether it makes things better or worse. A running example of an idea of fairness that in the end failed this test is the fairness (which for a long time seemed intuitively obvious) of having the eldest son inherit an entire estate. It may help to have a more contemporary example of the point that ideas of fairness are contestable, and consequently require such justification. As I write these lines (Oct. 13, 2004), there is an op-ed piece by Charles Murray in the *New York Times* that opens with "Five percent of Americans pay 54 percent of all personal income taxes. They do not use more government services than other Americans; they use fewer. Why is this fair?"

Any reader who puts temporarily to the side her or his political leanings can see that there is a degree of plausibility, as intuitions go, in what Murray says. How do we evaluate this conception of fairness? No doubt there can be a casuistry of fairness, as there is a casuistry of so many things, and an opponent of Murray can present a different intuition of fairness that also has a degree of plausibility. But it seems hard to deny that our evaluation of the likely consequences attached to opposing intuitions has—and should have—a great deal to do with our evaluation of the intuitions. A lot depends on whether one thinks that, on the whole, progressive income tax has good consequences or has bad consequences.

One way of looking at all of these cases is this. Intuitions of fairness and reasonableness are very suggestible. They are heavily influenced by what has been the norm and could be taken for granted. (Only in this way can we understand those in the past, who seemed in some respects decent people yet saw no problem in slavery or the disenfranchisement of women.) Very often—as when a rich person pays more tax than a poor person, usually at a higher ("progressive") rate—intuitions can be heavily influenced by how the case is presented, especially in the connections that are made. This is where casuistry, which is the philosophical counterpart of good lawyering, can play a part.

Plainly, it would be good to have some justification of a change in a moral order that is more solid than intuitions or casuistry. Nothing in these chapters promises a rock-solid justification: the defects in our knowledge of the future have repeatedly been emphasized. But there are cases in which we have present experience of negative values attached to elements of a moral order, and it then becomes highly plausible to suppose that removing these elements would lead to a significantly better future (even if we are unable to be clear about its outlines and details). All of this provides a basis for evaluating and perhaps revising our intuitions of fairness and reasonableness: they can become, as Hume said about the "monkish virtues," no longer acceptable once we understand what they do for human life.

Conclusion

My running assumption has been that much of the point or function of ethics is to make the world better than it might otherwise be. There certainly is a burden of argument on anyone who wants to claim that there is some other major function (say a religious or formalistic one) that points in a different direction. It can be asked why God would not want the world to be better than it might otherwise be, or (along the lines of the running argument in chapter 9) why we should be guided by whatever formalistic considerations are nominated if their guidance makes things worse rather than better.

If the point of an ethics is to make the world better than it might be, how could we connect this to everyday moral decisions? We have seen that systematic calculation of consequences of actions, on a case-by-case basis, is far from being a secure route to making the world a better place. So many values in the future look conjectural. On the other hand, there are real, highly predictable values immediately consequent on certain kinds of action.

The cases in which we are most likely to be clear about immediate consequences of significant value (or disvalue) involve physical or financial harm or its prevention. Effects of this sort are usually easier to predict than are effects in making people happy. So the least one might do, one thinks, in using ethics to make the world better than it might be is to systematize rules governing these cases. This is especially plausible when we bear in mind the special weight that often is assigned to negative events and experiences in life.

Further, in constructing a moral order, which relies on social pressure in controlling transgressors, it is highly desirable that there be a widely shared common vision of the cases to which rules apply. This is most likely when the relevant processes and effects are physical or financial. A process of depressing or demoralizing someone usually cannot be evident to almost everyone in the way in which the infliction of physical or financial damage typically is. Any prolonged process also is less liable to grab people's attention than a single dramatic event will. Hence the values that look clearest, sharpest, and easiest to predict in the immediate future are those attending certain major forms of physical or financial harm: murder, rape, torture, and theft. These traditional moral rules would not have the weight they do in morality if we did not (given relevant information) usually agree on the nature of what happened and generally agree on the relevant judgments of value.

It has been emphasized throughout this book that there is more to morality than the rules at its core, and that there is more to ethics than morality. It should have been made clear also, especially in this chapter and the chapters preceding it, that the roles of judgments of consequences in ethics vary considerably from case to case. A degree of ignorance is always a factor, and in relation to the core of morality, what we can get most people to see in roughly the same way and to agree on is also a major factor. The core of morality emerges, in this view, as a compromise between something ideal (for beings far superior to us) and the requirements imposed by morality's place within the design of a cohesive society.

Appendix

Virtue Ethics

In recent years, virtue ethics has been promoted as a viable ethical theory, seemingly competitive with Kantian ethics and with consequentialism. Its roots go back as far as Aristotle and Plato (and, I would add, even further back to Confucius), and its exponents in more recent times include such prominent philosophers as Philippa Foot, Alasdair Macintyre, and Rosalind Hursthouse. But like its apparent rivals, it may have some weak points as well as merits. Both will be considered here.

Two serious criticisms of virtue ethics will be considered here. One is that it is less adequate than are its rivals in providing decision procedures for moral choices. The other is that the idea of "virtue" in virtue ethics is untenable. Virtue ethics is usually formulated in terms of durable character traits ("virtues") concerned with various kinds of choice. But recent work in psychology shows that the notion of such durable character traits — each trait keyed to a special kind of choice, but going across behavior in a wide variety of situations — is faulty. Hence, virtue ethics, if it is to have any use, has to be reframed without reference to what traditionally have been considered virtues. It should rather be concerned more directly with good or bad choices.

Let us consider the first criticism first. It needs to be put in perspective. Can a virtue ethics provide serious and useful guidance in life? It is hard to deny that Aristotle does this, and Confucius impressively lays out a path in life (a *dao*) that we can follow.

The critics, though, have in mind decisions in particular cases, rather than about a general and persisting orientation. An obvious way of getting guidance about decisions in particular cases from a virtue ethics is to say that the right choice in any situation is the one that a virtuous person would make. Aristotle (1984, 1745–1746, 1104b–1105b) makes remarks along these lines. But such a maneuver smacks of something close to circularity. To know what counts as a virtuous person, we have to know a good deal about what choices are virtuous, and this is supposed to tell us what the virtuous choice is in a situation at hand. It looks like knowing the answer is part of what is needed to know the answer.

Perhaps the appeal to what we know about virtues is not useless, and the circularity is not complete. First, we do have a good general idea of the kinds of choices, some of them requiring unusual fair-mindedness and ability to resist temptations and pressures, that are characteristic of a virtuous person. This can be useful. In many situations in which we might be tempted to violate established norms, to ask what a virtuous person would do is an effective reminder that will help us in our choice.

It may turn out that nothing in our general idea of what virtuous choices are like will include the solution to a tricky moral case. Lacking confidence in our own ability to see our way clear in this instance, we might well be influenced by the views of people who are identifiably (in general terms) highly virtuous. This presumably was part of what Aristotle had in mind.

Jerome Schneewind (1997), though, has pointed out that two people who are by normal standards virtuous can differ in their solutions to a moral problem. Perhaps one of them is more virtuous (in general, or in some specific relevant respect) than the other, and should be listened to? But how can we determine this with any great confidence without presupposing the correctness of one of the answers to the moral problem? We are back to something like circularity.

Rosalind Hursthouse contests this charge of circularity, and she defends the claim that "an action is right if it is what a virtuous agent would characteristically (i.e., acting in character) do in the circumstances" (2003, 187). She makes a good case for holding both (a) that sometimes a process that includes identifying virtuous people and then asking what they would do can be helpful in making a decision in a particular case, and (b) that both utilitarianism and deontology do not give us the entirely definite guidance that some people imagine. The latter point can be illustrated in the case of utilitarianism by the many cases in which there is considerable uncertainty about consequences, and in that of deontology by all of the cases that, as Kant says in the second half of the *Metaphysics of Morals*, require the exercise of casuistry.

All the same, virtuous agents do sometimes arrive at different solutions to moral problems. Sometimes it is very plausible to say that two agents who arrive at different solutions can both be right. Hursthouse says this in relation to abortion (1997, 219n). Abortion, though, is a special case in a number of ways. The deeply personal nature of a decision is linked to other factors, including (arguably) the fact that important relevant features can differ so markedly from one case to another. If two people who are virtuous by normal standards differ about whether it is justified to kill an innocent person in order to avoid the likely death of thousands—or differ about capital punishment—it would seem far less plausible to hold that both are right.

Schneewind has a point. When two consequentialists or two Kantians disagree about what is right, there are resources within the theories that could help to point us in the direction of a solution, although, it should be added, the most reasonable decision (especially in the case of the consequentialists) may turn out to be that we really do not know what is right. It is far from clear that virtue ethics has resources within it that can help to point us in the direction of a solution to a case in which (a) two virtuous people disagree about what is right, and (b) it seems extremely implausible to suppose that both could be right.

The general point is that in many moral decisions—just the ones we most need advice about—it seems heavy-handed and circuitous to begin deliberation by asking what a virtuous person would do in this case. As Robert Louden (1997) says, "virtue theory is not a problem-oriented or quandary approach to ethics." In problem cases, we should look elsewhere for help. Often, a simpler and clearer line of thought involves saying such things as "X is required by a moral code that any reasonable person would will to be everyone's moral code" or "To do Y would cause large numbers of people to suffer."

Let me suggest, all the same, that it does not count heavily against virtue ethics that what the virtues are can be an inadequate guide to particular moral decisions. It would count heavily if every theoretical approach to ethics were assumed to have the same goals and to be concerned with the same functions. In my view, virtue ethics is largely concerned with questions different from those central to Kantian ethics, consequentialism, or contractualist ethics.

There is some overlap. Annette Baier (1987) has pointed out that ethical theories have a variety of concerns and functions. Any theory will provide us with a view of what ethics is and of the forms that moral decisions take. Virtue ethics fulfills this function, although what it brings more clearly into view can be somewhat different from what Kantian ethics and consequentialism bring into view.

Certainly, Kantian ethics, consequentialist theories, and some forms of contractualism do offer guidance, which often can be very helpful, in making moral decisions. It would be a mistake to view this guidance very simply, by assuming that theories provide algorithms that enable you to determine what the Kantian, consequentialist, or contractualist solution for a particular case is. For one thing, as Kant pointed out, one needs judgment to connect principles of a case.

A good example is determination of whether capital punishment is ever justified. As had been earlier remarked, Kant contended that, if society were ever to dissolve, its members ought first to execute the last murderer. It would be too quick and glib to hold that Kant did not understand his own theory. Let me (as someone who has no brief for capital punishment) suggest that respect for persons could be interpreted as, among other things, not treating adults like children, and that it could be thought that this in turn requires holding people strongly responsible (in a way that can involve the death penalty) for terrible crimes. Respect for persons can, of course, be interpreted in very different ways. The point is that intelligent Kantians need not agree. There also are plenty of cases in which the judgments of intelligent consequentialists or contractualists can differ among themselves. Different sets of possible consequences can weigh heavily with different consequentialists, and there is almost always room for disagreement about probabilities. The inherently vague contractualist idea that a choice is permissible if and only if it is not forbidden in a moral code that a reasonable person could accept allows differences in what counts as "reasonable."

All of this said, it has to be conceded that the theories just referred to often can be useful in helping us to organize our thinking about moral decisions. There certainly are cases, also, in which we can say what the moral choice is that most Kantians, most consequentialists, or most contractualists would recommend, given their seemingly different slants on moral decision-making. Virtue ethicists would certainly recommend that one behave virtuously, but that is not to say much. They also might recommend that the state of ones likely future virtues be given weight in making a choice; but it is open to Kantians, consequentialists, and contractualists to concur with this.

What, then, does virtue ethics offer that is distinctive? One thing is this. Although it is true that representatives of other theoretical approaches sometimes have given serious attention to how someone can acquire virtues, and even to what it is like to be virtuous, major virtue ethicists such as Confucius and Aristotle have provided extended accounts of the stages of virtue acquisition and of the psychology of genuine virtue. Kant and Mill have said some useful things relevant to these topics. But any Kantian or consequentialist who devoted the elaborate and probing attention comparable to that of Confucius or Aristotle would be thought of as very like a virtue ethicist.

One reason that virtue acquisition and the psychology of genuine virtue are treated as important is the contention by philosophers such as Confucius and Aristotle that whether a person is truly virtuous determines how much value he or she will experience in life. Confucius suggests that only a truly virtuous person can abide long in happiness or long cope with misfortune (*Analects*, bk. 4.2, 102), and that to be truly virtuous is to be relatively secure in (and serene about) major satisfactions, whereas people who are not truly virtuous worry more about luck and are more prone to being anxious. Aristotle's treatment of the relation between virtue and eudaemonia is well-known. Because of these and kindred considerations, "What kind of person should one want to be?" is much more commonly treated as the central question of ethics in classical Greek, Chinese, and Indian philosophies (despite differences and oppositions within all of these families of philosophy) than in recent Western philosophy.

In short, even if virtue ethics does not offer all that much useful guidance in the process of moral decision making in specific cases, it can offer a great deal in relation to other major questions of life. The focus and functions of virtue ethics are strongly connected to the development and values of personhood. They simply are not entirely the same as those of the other theories mentioned.

This leads to a question that should be obvious. Why should virtue ethics be viewed as in some sense a competitor of these theories? One can be generally suspicious of the competition model for the relations among ethical theories, a model that seems more at home in sports than in philosophy. Hare (1993) has pointed out that there are many consequentialist elements in Kantian ethics. But the competition model seems especially inadequate when virtue ethics is brought into relation with other theoretical approaches. Its results are not going to be the same. Nor will there necessarily be opposition, because the questions are so different.

All of this is to defend virtue ethics against the charge of being useless. Indeed, virtue ethicists can make their own charges. These include the accusation that a Kantian or contractualist ethics or consequentialism provides an excessively abstracted and depersonalized view of ethics *if* attention is not paid to (a) the importance in life of being a certain kind of person, and (b) the role of this in ethical decision. These theories also can lend themselves to (as was argued in the first part of this book) studies that ignore the roles of interpretation and of judgments of value in particular cases. (It should be emphasized here that if a theory lends itself to an oversimplification, that certainly does not mean that every single practitioner of the theory succumbs to the appeal of oversimplification.)

Why would someone be drawn to what is arguably an excessively abstracted and depersonalized view of ethics? Part of the answer, I have suggested, is Newton envy: a strong desire among many ethical philosophers of the last 250 years to arrive at an ethics that would rest on a small number of general principles (with some smoothing out of vagueness and problems of interpretation in the statement of these principles). One gets a strong sense of this motivation from the introductory remarks of, say, Mill's *Utilitarianism*.

There is also this appeal. Any account of an ethical decision that does not embed it, even implicitly, within the arc of a person's life can be an attractively short story. Its lessons also can seem especially suitable for general consumption.

This brings us to the second criticism of virtue ethics, at least as it normally has been pursued. It can begin with the thought that personhood, if one wants to speak of it, is not as simple as used to be widely thought. Situationist psychology, especially, has introduced complications. Indeed, one can look at the elements of one's self and say, as the spirits possessing some unlucky swine in the New Testament did, "Our name is legion." The moral of all of this is: "Forget personhood. Just look at what the appropriate solution, for anyone, is of any specific moral problem."

This line of thought has been developed most prominently by Gilbert Harman (see Harman 1999/2001). He is one of a number of philosophers who have been impressed by the Milgram experiment and other results cited by situationist psychologists. John Doris offers a more complex version of a similar view, although he makes some concessions (2002, chap. 4).

The situationist evidence that Harman and others rely upon show that most people (a) will behave very differently in some unusual circumstances from the way they behave in familiar circumstances, and (b) indeed will behave very badly (even though one might assume that most of those who behave badly are moderately virtuous in ordinary life). Further, there is situationist evidence that even in ordinary life, most people will exhibit virtues (such as honesty or courage) more reliably in some kinds of circumstance than in others.

Harman appears to read into this that the idea (so prominent in the thought of Plato, Aristotle, and Confucius) of genuine, reliable virtue is at best an abstract ideal rather than something to be found in the real world. He also concludes that traditional notions here are highly misleading: there is nothing that fits their description of character traits. Finally he suggests that virtue ethics should be pursued without any assumption or claim that there are actually virtues. We can simply ask what the virtuous thing to do on this or that occasion is. If Harman is right in this, then a "corrected" virtue ethics would have very little to add to what is offered by a theory or theories of how particular moral decisions are to be approached.

All of this lies in an area of controversy, both in philosophy and in psychology. There certainly is strong evidence (some of which Harman cites) for some conclusions about what *usually* or *most often* is true. The temptation then, especially among philosophers who are eager for generalizations about what is *always* true, is to leap from the evidence to a strong generalization. Let us pause, and ask what we know and also what seems likely.

There is considerable evidence for two conclusions, from the Milgram experiment and the nearly contemporary Stanford Prison Experiment, and also from experience in Europe during the Nazi occupation and in China during the cultural revolution. One is that in difficult, dangerous, or disorienting circumstances, a great many people (perhaps in some cases most people) will make choices that most of us would judge morally wrong. This further suggests that many (perhaps most) people who seem morally virtuous really are not. This is a conclusion, as chapter 4 pointed out, that is also indicated in Mark Twain's "The Man That Corrupted Hadleyburg." Plato and Confucius would also accept this conclusion. It is not that they think that most people are evil; rather, the view is that the great majority of people are in some zone intermediate between genuinely good and definitely evil, with their behavior very much depending on circumstance.

The other conclusion that seems justified (especially in the light of data like those provided by the Milgram experiment) is that it is highly doubtful that most people have character traits relevant to virtue that remain the same over a broad range of circumstances. Let us define a broad character trait as one that manifests itself in a fairly consistent way whatever the circumstances. Then the evidence points toward the conclusion that character traits, if there be such, by and large are not broad.

It should be pointed out, before we press forward, that the conclusion just stated is consistent with a claim that there may be instances of broad character traits here and there. Perhaps a few people who have strong self-discipline (or are extremely simple) have them? Further, to say that broad character traits are somewhat uncommon is not to say that character traits are uncommon. A character trait could be narrow rather than broad: for example, Bloggs may be reliably honest in money matters, but not in matters connected with his love life. Even more narrowly, Bloggs may be reliably honest in money matters if friends and associates are involved, but not if insurance companies are involved.

Thus the two conclusions above (that seem to follow from available evidence) need not be as extreme as they first might look. All the same, they go against much common sense about what people are like. But common sense varies from one time and place to another, and sometimes can be simple-minded. Let me say that I accept these conclusions. My guess is that many people who have witnessed social behavior in a society under extreme pressure also would accept them. They are most likely to startle someone who has grown up in fairly comfortable circumstances in a stable liberal society.

The temptation is to move from these conclusions to a smoother, even stronger version. This could include the dictum that there are no genuinely virtuous people, period. Another tempting dictum might be that if most or nearly all people do not in fact have broad character traits, then there are no character traits. The idea of genuine virtue will be taken then as an abstract ideal, and the idea of character traits as a psychological oversimplification.

But do we *know* any of this? What we do know is that it appears that there are some circumstances in which we could probably expect most people to behave immorally (Plato's ring of invisibility is a good thought experiment along these lines). We also know (or may well think we know) that there are no perfect people: that for anyone, there will be some circumstances in which he or she is liable to behave badly. This leaves a further question, though: Can we assume that to be imperfect is not to be genuinely virtuous? I have argued elsewhere (Kupperman 2006, chap. 6) against such an assumption.

A reply that often is made to the evidence that sometimes most people behave badly is this. Even if it is widely thought (at least in societies that are relatively stable, peaceful, and prosperous) that most people are virtuous, virtue ethics is not committed to such a view. It is very clear that the view of some classical virtue ethicists, including Plato and Confucius, is that true virtue is possessed only by a fairly small minority of the population. It should be emphasized (again) that this is not to suggest that most people are evil. Confucius's view is explicitly that most people can be led to follow the way but not to understand it. Situationist psychology will govern all or almost all of their actions. The fourth-century B.C.E. Confucian philosopher Mencius puts this in down-to-earth terms: in good years (i.e., times of good harvests), the young men are mostly lazy, and in bad years, they are mostly violent. Plato's view appears to be that most people are morally inadequate, but this need not amount to being evil.

To assess the role of virtues in virtue ethics, we can assume that a virtue is roughly equivalent to a character trait having to do with a particular area of conduct (e.g., courage or generosity). We then can ask whether, given whatever truth there is in situationist psychology, we can maintain that there actually are character traits. If the answer is "no," then Harman's challenge is successful.

Bear in mind the distinction between broad and narrow character traits. There is no situationist evidence that no one has any broad character traits. There is considerable evidence that such traits are much less common than most people might suppose. There is no situationist evidence that most people do not have narrow character traits.

There is an ongoing debate in psychology between situationists and personologists (cf. Funder 1999) which, like many long-standing debates, seems increasingly to center on matters of emphasis. Even if one entirely takes the situationist side, the available evidence does not suggest either that there is no such thing as genuine virtue or that there are no character traits. Philosophers who have accepted situationist insights, however, have sometimes gone well beyond both the evidence and what situationist psychologists would say.

Genuine virtue arguably is more uncommon and more difficult than most people think. Confucius especially emphasizes the role of self-criticism in becoming virtuous (*Analects*, bk. 5.26, 114; bk. 7.1–3, 123). Aristotle also suggests that awareness of one's characteristic mistakes should be factored into some decisions, leading to compensatory adjustments. (See Aristotle 1984, 1109b, p. 1751.) The best virtue ethics does something important in focusing our attention on the difficulties of being virtuous and also on the values it makes possible.

Conclusion

It seems highly misleading to regard virtue ethics as competitive with theories such as consequentialism, contractualism, and Kantian ethics. Virtue ethics focuses on questions different from those usually addressed by practitioners of those theories. Virtue ethics especially can provide insight into the sense of self that many virtuous people have, which can play a major role in the values in their lives. It also can examine the processes in which someone becomes virtuous, and the role that virtues can play in providing connections within a meaningful life.

At the root of this is the sense that, as Christine Swanton (2003, 26) puts it, virtues express inner states that are fine. The phrase "inner states" clearly is open to interpretation; that understood, I think she clearly is right. A virtue ethics such as the one that Harman favors simply leaves that out. Why would we shift to such a virtue ethics? Part of the impetus is that genuine virtue can come to look much rarer than most people suppose and that broad character traits also turn out to be much more uncommon than most assume. All of this is important. But to suggest that there never is genuine virtue and never are broad character traits would be to go beyond the evidence. To regard the concept of "character trait" as entirely useless is to go even further beyond the evidence, all of which is consistent with the view that many people have narrow character traits.

Bibliography

Abbott, Thomas Kingsmill. 1898. Memoir of Kant. In *Kant's Critique of Practical Reason and Other Works on the Theory of Ethics*. London: Longmans, Green, xiii–lxiv.

Argyle, Michael. 1987. *The Psychology of Happiness*. London: Methuen.

Aristotle. 1984. *Nicomachean Ethics*. In *Complete Works of Aristotle*, Vol. 2, ed. Jonathan Barnes. Princeton, N.J.: Princeton University Press.

Arpaly, Nomy. 2003. *Unprincipled Virtue*. New York: Oxford University Press.

Baier, Annette. 1987. Hume, the Women's Moral Theorist? In *Women and Moral Theory*, ed. Eva Kittay and Diana Meyers. Totowa, N.J.: Rowman and Littlefield, 37–55.

Bales, R. Eugene. 1971. Act Utilitarianism: Account of Right-Making Characteristics or Decision-Making Procedure? *American Philosophical Quarterly* 8: 257–265.

Bennett, Jonathan. 1974. The Conscience of Huckleberry Finn. *Philosophy* 49: 123–134.

Blass, Thomas, ed. 2000. *Obedience to Authority: Current Perspectives on the Milgram Paradigm*. Mahweh, N.J.: Lawrence Erlbaum.

Brandt, Richard. 1965. Toward a Credible Utilitarianism. In *Morality and the Language of Conduct*, ed. Hector-Neri Castaneda and George Nakhnikian. Detroit, Mich.: Wayne State University Press, 107–143.

Brickman, P., D. Coates, and R. Janoff-Bulman. 1978. Lottery Winners and Accident Victims: Is Happiness Relative? *Journal of Personality and Social Psychology* 37: 917–927.

Brooks, Roy L. 1996. *Integration or Separation?* Cambridge, Mass.: Harvard University Press.

Card, Robert. 2004. Consequentialism, Teleology, and the New Friendship Critique. *Pacific Philosophical Quarterly* 85: 149–172.

Cassirer, Ernst. 1981. *Kant's Life and Thought*. Translated by James Haden. New Haven, Conn.: Yale University Press.

Confucius. 1938. *Analects*. Translated by Arthur Waley. New York: Vintage Books.

Crisp, Roger, and Michael Slote. 1997. *Virtue Ethics*. Oxford: Oxford University Press.

Csikszentmihalyi, Mihaly. 1990. *Flow. The Psychology of Optimal Experience*. New York: Harper and Row.

Donagan, Alan. 1977. *The Theory of Morality*. Chicago: University of Chicago Press.

Doris, John. 2002. *Lack of Character*. Cambridge: Cambridge University Press.

Driver, Julia. 2002. *Uneasy Virtue*. Cambridge: Cambridge University Press.

Feinberg, Joel. 1990. *Harmless Wrongdoing*. New York: Oxford University Press.

Foot, Philippa. 1978a. Moral Arguments. In *Virtues and Vices*. Berkeley: University of California Press, 96–109.

——.1978b. Moral Beliefs. In *Virtues and Vices*. Berkeley: University of California Press, 110–131.

——.1978c. Virtues and Vices. In *Virtues and Vices*. Berkeley: University of California Press, 1–18.

Funder, David C. 1999. *Personality Judgment: A Realistic Approach to Person Perception*. San Diego, Calif.: Academic Press.

Gallie, William B. 1964. *Philosophy and the Historical Understanding*. London: Chatto and Windus.

Gilligan, Carol. 1982. *In a Different Voice*. Cambridge, Mass.: Harvard University Press.

Griffin, James. 1997. Incommensurability: What's the Problem? In *Incommensurability, Incomparability, and Practical Reason*, ed. Ruth Chang. Cambridge, Mass.: Harvard University Press, 35–51.

Hamilton, V. L. 1992. Thoughts on Obedience: A Social Structural View. *Contemporary Psychology* 37: 1313.

Hare, R. M. 1963. *Freedom and Reason*. Oxford: Clarendon Press.

——. 1981. *Moral Thinking*. Oxford: Clarendon Press.

——. 1993. Could Kant Have Been a Utilitarian? *Utilitas* 5: 1–16.

Harman, Gilbert. 1999. Moral Philosophy Meets Social Psychology. *Proceedings of the Aristotelian Society* 99: 315–331.

——. 1999/2001 Virtue Ethics Without Character Traits, Gilbert Harman Web site, 1999. Also in *Fact and Value*, ed. Alex Byrne, Robert Stalnaker, and Ralph Wedgewood. Cambridge: MIT Press, 2001, 117–27.

Hartshorne, Hugh, M. A. May, and Frank Shuttleworth. 1930. *Studies in the Organization of Character*. New York: Macmillan.

Herman, Barbara. 1993. *The Practice of Moral Judgment*. Cambridge, Mass.: Harvard University Press.

Hume, David. 1739/1978. *Treatise of Human Nature*, 2nd ed. Edited by L. A. Selby-Bigge, revised by P. H. Nidditch. Oxford: Clarendon Press.

——. 1742/1985. Of The Standard of Taste. In *Essays Moral, Political, and Literary* ed. Eugene Miller. Indianapolis: Liberty Classics, 226–249.

——. 1751/1975. *Enquiry Concerning the Principles of Morals*. In *Enquiries*, ed. L. A. Selby-Bigge, revised by P. H. Nidditch. Oxford: Clarendon Press.

Hursthouse, Rosalind. 1997. Virtue Ethics and Abortion. In *Virtue Ethics*, ed. Roger Crisp and Michael Slote. Oxford: Oxford University Press, 217–238.

——. 2003. Normative Virtue Ethics. In *Virtue Ethics*, ed. Stephen Darwall. Malden, England: Basil Blackwell, 184–202.

Jackson, Frank. 1991. Decision-Theoretic Consequentialism and the Nearest and Dearest Objection. *Ethics* 101: 461–482.

Kant, Immanuel. 1785/1981. *Grounding of the Metaphysics of Morals*. Translated by James Ellington. Indianapolis: Hackett.

——. 1788/1898. *Critique of Practical Reason*. Translated by Thomas Abbott. London: Longmans Green.

——. 1797/1996. *The Metaphysics of Morals*. Translated by Mary Gregor. Cambridge: Cambridge University Press.

Keats, John. 1970. *Letters*. Edited by Robert Gittings. London: Oxford University Press.

Kohlberg, Lawrence. 1981. *The Philosophy of Moral Development: Moral Stages and the Idea of Justice*. San Francisco: Harper and Row.

Kovesi, Julius. 1967. *Moral Notions*. London: Routledge and Kegan Paul.

Kristol, Irving. 1971. Pornography, Obscenity, and the Case for Censorship. *New York Times Magazine*, March 28.

Kumar, Rahul. 2003. Reasonable Reasons in Contractualist Moral Argument. *Ethics* 114: 6–37.

Kupperman, Joel J. 1968. Confucius and the Problem of Naturalness. *Philosophy East and West* 18: 175–185.

——. 1981. A Case for Consequentialism. *American Philosophical Quarterly* 18: 305–314.

——. 2002. A Messy Derivation of the Categorical Imperative. *Philosophy* 77: 485–502.

——. 2005a. The Epistemology of Non-Instrumental Value. *Philosophy and Phenomenological Research* 65: 659–680.

——. 2005b. A New Look at the Logic of the 'Is'-'Ought' Relation. *Philosophy* 80: 343–359.

——. 2006. *Six Myths about the Good Life*. Indianapolis: Hackett.

Langer, Ellen. 1989. *Mindfulness*. Reading, Mass.: Addison Wesley.

La Rochefoucauld, Duc de la. 1665/1959. *Maxims*. Translated by L. W. Tancock. Baltimore: Penguin.

Lomasky, Loren. 1983. A Refutation of Utilitarianism. *Journal of Value Inquiry* 17: 259–279.

Louden, Robert. 1997. On Some Vices of Virtue Ethics. In *Virtue Ethics*, ed. Roger Crisp and Michael Slote. Oxford: Oxford University Press, 201–216.

Lyons, David. 1965. *Forms and Limits of Utilitarianism*. Oxford: Clarendon Press.

Malcolm, Norman. 1984. *Ludwig Wittgenstein. A Memoir*, 2nd ed. London: Oxford University Press.

Mencius. 1970. Trans. D. C. Lau. London: Penguin Books.

Meyers, Diana. 1987. Personal Autonomy and the Paradox of Feminine Socialization. *Journal of Philosophy* 84: 619–628.

Milgram, Stanley. 1974. *Obedience to Authority*. London: Tavistock.

Mill, J. S. 1859/1978. *On Liberty*. Edited by Elizabeth Rappaport. Indianapolis: Hackett.

——. 1861/1979. *Utilitarianism*. Edited by George Sher. Indianapolis: Hackett.

Moore, G. E. 1903. *Principia Ethica*. Cambridge: Cambridge University Press.

Moore, Stephen. 1999. Policy Analysis. Speed Doesn't Kill. The Repeal of the 55 MPH Speed Limit. Cato Institute, http://www.cato.org, May 31, 1999.

Paton, H. J. 1953–1954. An Alleged Right to Lie, A Problem in Kantian Ethics. *Kant Studien* 45: 190–203.

Pettit, Philip. 1984. Satisficing Consequentialism. *Supplementary Proceedings of the Aristotelian Society*, 165–176.

——. 1997. The Consequentialist Perspective. In Marcia Baron, Philip Pettit, and Michael Slote, *Three Methods of Ethics: A Debate*. London: Blackwell.

Pettit, Philip, and Geoffrey Brennan. 1986. Restrictive Consequentialism. *Australasian Journal of Philosophy* 64: 438–455.

Plato. 1997. *Complete Works*. Edited by John M. Cooper. Indianapolis: Hackett.

Rawls, John. 1955. Two Concepts of Rules. *Philosophical Review* 64: 3–32.

——. 1958. Justice as Fairness. *Philosophical Review* 67: 164–194.

——. 1971. *A Theory of Justice*. Cambridge, Mass.: Harvard University Press.

Rochat, Francois, Olivier Maggiani, and Andre Modigliani. 2000. The Dynamics of Obeying and Opposing Authority: A Mathematical Model. In *Obedience to Authority: Current Perspectives on the Milgram Paradigm*, ed. Thomas Blass. Mahweh, N.J.: Lawrence Erlbaum, 161–192.

Rozin, Paul, and Ed Royzman. 2001. Negativity Bias, Negativity Dominance, and Contagion. *Personality and Social Psychology Review* 5: 296–300.

Salzman, Ann L. 2000. The Role of the Obedience Experiments in Holocaust Studies: The Case for Renewed Visibility. In *Obedience to Authority. Current Perspectives on the Milgram Paradigm*. Mahweh, N.J.: Lawrence Erlbaum, 125–143.

Scanlon, T. M. 1998. *What We Owe to Each Other*. Cambridge, Mass.: Harvard University Press.

Scheffler, Samuel. 1993. *The Rejection of Consequentialism*, 2nd ed. Oxford: Clarendon Press.

Schneewind, Jerome. 1997. The Misfortunes of Virtue. In *Virtue Ethics*, ed. Roger Crisp and Michael Slote. Oxford: Oxford University Press, 178–200.

Sherman, Nancy. 1988. Common Sense and Uncommon Virtue. *Midwest Studies in Philosophy* 13: 97–114.

Sidgwick, Henry. 1907. *The Methods of Ethics*, 7th ed. London: Macmillan.

Singer, Peter. 1993. *Practical Ethics*, 2nd ed. Cambridge: Cambridge University Press.

Slote, Michael. 1984. Satisficing Consequentialism. *Supplementary Proceedings of the Aristotelian Society*, 139–163.

Smart, J. J. C. 1977. Benevolence as an Over-riding Attitude. *Australasian Journal of Philosophy* 55: 127–135.

Stocker, Michael. 1976. The Schizophrenia of Modern Ethical Theories. *Journal of Philosophy* 73: 453–466.

Strawson, P. F. 1961. Social Morality and Individual Ideals. *Philosophy* 36: 1–17.

Swanton, Christine. 2003. *Virtue Ethics. A Pluralistic View*. Oxford: Oxford University Press.

Thomson, Judith Jarvis. 1997. The Right and the Good. *Journal of Philosophy* 94: 273–298.

Tversky, Amos, and Daniel Kahneman. 1984. Choices, Values, and Frames. *American Psychologist* 39: 341–350.

Williams, B. A. O. 1973. Critique of Utilitarianism. In J. J. C. Smart and B. A. O. Williams, *Utilitarianism: For and Against*. Cambridge: Cambridge University Press.

Wilson, Timothy. 2002. *Strangers to Ourselves*. Cambridge, Mass.: Harvard University Press.

Wittgenstein, Ludwig. 1953. *Philosophical Investigations*. Translated by G. E. M Anscombe. London: Macmillan.

Index